COMPUTER NETWORK PERFORMANCE SYMPOSIUM

Sponsored By SIGCOMM, SIGMETRICS & SIGOPS And The University Of Maryland

College Park, Maryland
April 13-14, 1982

A Publication of the ACM
Special Interest Group on
Measurement and Evaluation

Volume 11 Number 1
Spring 1982

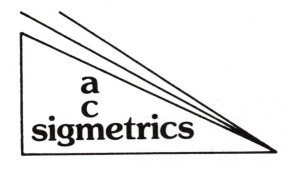

PERFORMANCE EVALUATION REVIEW

ACM Order No. 536820

The Association for Computing Machinery
11 West 42nd Street
New York, New York 10036

Additional copies of these Proceedings may be ordered prepaid from:

ACM Order Department
P.O. Box 64145
Baltimore, MD 21264

Please state the ACM Order Number:

Prices: ACM Members: $12.00 prepaid
         All others: $16.00 prepaid

ACM Order No. 536820

ISBN 0-89791-069-9

Message From The General Chairman

Computer networks are rapidly evolving from unique products to the commercial marketplace. Public packet switching networks are in operation in many countries; large organizations are acquiring private packet networks. Local area networks, scarcely considered just a few years ago, have leapt to prominence in the marketplace. Computer vendors have their own network architectures for interconnecting their systems.

What performance can the end user of these networks expect? What metrics should be used to compare products? How can performance claims be verified? How will protocol standards impact performance?

This is the first symposium to focus exclusively on computer network performance. The subject of the symposium intersects the areas of interest of the three sponsoring ACM Special Interest Groups: SIGCOMM (Data Communication), SIGMETRICS (Measurement and Evaluation), and SIGOPS (Operating Systems). The goal is to bring together experts in both analytical and experimental aspects of network performance to provide a total picture of the current state-of-the-art. The symposium program was selected so as to reflect this balance, with five sessions of refereed papers (less than half of the number of papers submitted), and two panel sessions.

We are fortunate to have Dr. Leonard Kleinrock as the Keynote Speaker. He is the author of the seminal reference, "Queueing Systems, Volume II: Computer Applications," and mentor of many contributors to the field. Dr. Kleinrock will address "The Challenge of Local Networks."

We are grateful to the Department of Computer Science at the University of Maryland for their cooperation and for arranging the use of the facilities of the Center of Adult Education. I wish to thank the members of the symposium committee, the program committee, authors, panelists, and referees for their efforts in making the symposium successful.

David C. Wood
General Chairman
ACM Computer Network Performance Symposium

Symposium Committee

Chairman

David C. Wood
The MITRE Corporation
1820 Dolley Madison Blvd.
McLean, VA 22102

Program Co-Chairmen

Ashok K. Agrawala
Department of Computer Science
University of Maryland
College Park, MD 20742

David A. Ault
The MITRE Corporation
1820 Dolley Madison Blvd.
McLean, VA 22102

Arrangements

Satish Tripathi
Department of Computer Science
University of Maryland
College Park, MD 20742

Exhibits

D. Bruce McIndoe
Computer Sciences Corporation
8728 Colesville Road
Silver Spring, MD 20910

Publications

Harold Highland
Hofstra University
562 Croydon Road
Elmont, NY 11003

Publicity

Rebecca Hutchings
Honeywell Information Systems Inc.
7900 Westpark Drive
McLean, VA 22102

Registration

Diana L. Ricci
GTE Subscriber Network Products
8301 Greensboro Drive
McLean, VA 22102

Treasurer

William H. Blankertz
The MITRE Corporation
1820 Dolley Madison Blvd.
McLean, VA 22102

Tutorial

Carl A. Sunshine
USC Information Sciences Institute
4676 Admiralty Way
Marina Del Rey, CA 90291

SIGMETRICS Liaison

Dennis Conti
Digital Communications Corporation
11717 Exploration Lane
Germantown, MD 20767

SIGOPS Liaison

David Redell
247 Horizon Avenue
Mountain View, CA 94043

Artist

William R. Succolosky
Honeywell Information Systems Inc.
7900 Westpark Drive
McLean, VA 22102

Program Committee

Vinton Cerf
Defense Advanced Research Projects Agency
Information Processing Techniques Office
1400 Wilson Boulevard
Arlington, VA 22209

Raj Kanodia
GTE Telenet Communications Corporation
8229 Boone Boulevard
Vienna, VA 22180

Jeffrey Mayersohn
Bolt Beranek and Newman
50 Moulton Street
Cambridge, MA 02138

David L. Mills
COMSAT Corporation
Transmission Systems Laboratory
950 L'Enfant Plaza, S.W.
Washington, D.C. 20024

Robert S. Printis
Xerox SDD
3333 Coyote Hill Road
Palo Alto, CA 94304

Walter C. Roehr
CONTEL Information Systems, Inc.
1850 Samuel Morse Drive
Reston, VA 22090

Mitchell G. Spiegel
CONTEL Information Systems, Inc.
301 West Maple Avenue
Vienna, VA 22180

Fouad A. Tobagi
Department of Electrical Engineering
ERL 230
Stanford University
Stanford, CA 94305

Stuart Wecker
Technology Concepts Incorporated
115 Austin Road
Sudbury, MA 01776

List of Referees

E. Arthurs
Steven C. Bruell
Larry Dowdy
Dominico Ferrari
Harvey A. Freeman
Karen Gordon
G. Scott Graham
Bruce L. Hitson
John B. Holmblad
Greg T. Hopkins
Albert Jeng
Simon S. Lam
Ron Larsen

Ed D. Lazowska
Kuang Shin Lin
Madhav Marathe
Anneliese Von Moyrhauser
N. B. Meisner
Jeff Mohr
C. W. Nelson
Jerry D. Noe
Holger Opderbeck
T. F. Piatkowsky
Jonathan B. Postel
K. K. Ramakrishnan
Joy Reed

Glenn Ricart
Mischa Schwartz
John Silvester
B. W. Stuck
J. S. Su
Ashok Thareja
Satish K. Tripathi
Graeme J. Williams
Nam Woo
Jeffrey W. Yeh
Yechiam Yemini
John Zahorjan

Table of Contents

SESSION 1: KEYNOTE ADDRESS

Chair: David C. Wood
The MITRE Corporation
McLean, VA

KEYNOTE SPEAKER
Leonard Kleinrock
University of California at Los Angeles
Los Angeles, CA

The Challenge of Local Networks

SESSION 2: ANALYTICAL MODELS

Chair: Ashok K. Agrawala
*University of Maryland
College Park, MD*

Modeling a New Technique for Accessing Shared Buses

P. V. Afshari, S. C. Bruell & R. Y. Kain
University of Minnesota
Minneapolis, Minnesota

1. Introduction

Consider a queueing system in which customers (or jobs) arrive to one of Q separate queues to await service from one of S identical servers (Figure 1). Once a job enters a queue it does not leave that queue until it has been selected for service. Any server can serve any job from any queue. A job selected for service cannot be preempted. In this paper we consider jobs to be in a single class; for the multiple class result see [AFSH81a]. We assume once a queue has been selected, job scheduling from that queue is fair. In particular, our results hold for first come first serve as well as random selection [SPIR79] and, for that matter, any fair nonpreemptive scheduling policy within a queue. We assume that arrivals to each queue follow a Poisson process with the mean arrival rate to queue q being λ_q. The S identical exponential servers are each processing work at a mean rate of μ.

This system is general enough to be adaptable for modeling many different applications. By choosing the policy employed for queue selection by the servers, we can model multiplexers, channels, remote job entry stations, certain types of communication processors embedded in communication networks, and sets of shared buses. In this paper we will use the latter application to discuss a realistic situation. The elements ("jobs") in the queues are messages to be sent from modules connected to the shared bus of the system. The servers are the buses; their service times are equal to the message transmission times. The queues are in the interface modules connected to and sharing the buses.

Many communication systems fit the model depicted in Figure 1. For example, a channel multiplexer may be viewed as a server that removes requests from one or more queues formed in the device(s). The multiplexer selects one of the queued requests and the channel (the server) is then allocated for the entire time required to perform that request. A shared bus with a centralized controller is similar to the channel multiplexer.

A distinguishing characteristic of these types of servers is the method used to select a queue. Selection schemes include priority [KLEI75], round robin [SMIT79], random [SMIT79], and load balancing (as described in this paper). The performance of the system depends upon which selection policy is used [BAIN81]. For example, as is shown in a subsequent section, the load balancing selection policy evenly distributes mean waiting times among the queues (even when there is a different arrival rate to each queue).

Now consider a shared bus with a distributed access control. The commonly used selection schemes can also be used in a distributed system. Round robin scheduling can be implemented using a form of token passing. Random selection can be achieved by variations of CSMA/CD; specifically, let the devices wait for a random delay selected from an exponential distribution before accessing the bus and assume that the bus accessing time is negligible with respect to bus use time.

2. Load balancing scheduling

In this paper we will study the system under a queue selection policy which is sensitive to the length of the (device) queues and which therefore dynamically changes the share of service which each queue receives. The scheduling policy is as follows: when a server becomes free it selects the next message from the qth queue with probability p_q given by:

$$p_q = \frac{n_q}{\sum_{j=1}^{Q} n_j} \quad (q = 1, 2, \ldots, Q)$$

where n_q denotes the number of queued messages in queue q and Q is the number of queues. Hence, the queue with the most messages will have the highest probability of receiving service next. This scheduling scheme will tend to even up the waiting times of unserviced messages in the different queues. (Other papers have analyzed different multiple queue systems; see for example [CHU81, LEIB61, CHOW77].)

Once again consider a shared bus with a distributed access control. Our load balancing selection policy can be achieved by modifying the random selection technique (described previously) by having each device make an exponentially distributed random delay with its mean delay time proportional to the inverse of the number of queued messages [AFSH81b].

The objectives of this paper are:

(1) To show a complete mathematical analysis of the system depicted in Figure 1 (with the above queue selection policy);

(2) To show that this type of service station and queueing discipline gives rise to a product form solution and hence is yet another type of server which can be incorporated into a BCMP network of queues [BASK75,BRUE80,SPIR79]; and

(3) To show several interesting applications of this type of service center.

3. The M => M Property

Muntz [MUNT72,MUNT73] has shown that any network of queues has a 'simple' solution if each service station has a Poisson departure process whenever it has a Poisson input process. He refers to this as the M => M property (Markov implies Markov). Attempting to embed a service center without this property into a queueing network makes the derivation of a closed form solution a formidable task at best. Another important aspect of Muntz' work is that it helps us find a solution for a system if it does have the M => M property.

We will briefly review Muntz' technique here; further details can be found in [MUNT73]. Consider an arbitrary queueing system with the set of all feasible states denoted by S. Assume that jobs (messages) arrive to the system according to a Poisson arrival process with rate λ. Let $s_i \varepsilon S$ and let $|s_i|$ denote the number of jobs in the system in state s_i. Also, let S_i+ be the set of states with one more job in the system than when the system is in state s_i; i.e.,

$$S_i^+ = \{ s_i^+ \mid s_i^+ \varepsilon S \text{ and } |s_i^+| = |s_i| + 1 \}$$

Let the state transition rate from state s_i+ to state s_i be denoted by $R(s_i+ \to s_i)$. A system has the M => M property if it satisfies the following condition:

$$\text{For all } s_i \varepsilon S \quad \sum_{s_i^+ \varepsilon S_i^+} \frac{P(s_i^+) \; R(s_i^+ \to s_i)}{P(s_i)} = \lambda$$

4. The General Assumptions

Assume that the stochastic process which describes the behavior of this system is an irreducible Markov chain and that the system will reach a steady state in which there is a nonzero probability of being in any logically possible state. We also assume that arrivals to the individual queues are Poisson, each with parameter λ_q, $q = 1,\ldots,Q$.

Service times are identical and follow an exponential distribution function with parameter μ.

A system state can be represented by a Q+1-tuple $(n_0, n_1, n_2, \ldots, n_Q)$ in which n_q is the number of messages in queue q and n_0 is the number of messages being processed by servers; the equilibrium probability of being in this state is denoted by $P(n_0, n_1, n_2, \ldots, n_Q)$.

5. A Two Queue One Server System with Different Arrival Rates

We now consider the two queue case in which the arrival rates to the individual queues are denoted by λ_1 and λ_2. We write the flow balance equations for this system as

$$(\lambda_1 + \lambda_2 + \mu)P(1,n_1,n_2) = \lambda_1 P(1,n_1-1,n_2) + \lambda_2 P(1,n_1,n_2-1) +$$

$$\mu \frac{n_1+1}{n_1+n_2+1} P(1,n_1+1,n_2) + \mu \frac{n_2+1}{n_1+n_2+1} P(1,n_1,n_2+1)$$

with the boundary condition

$$P(1,0,0) = \frac{(\lambda_1+\lambda_2)}{\mu} P(0,0,0)$$

where $P(0,0,0) = 1 - \frac{\lambda_1+\lambda_2}{\mu}$

Using Muntz' technique to solve the above system of equations we come up with the following equations for the equilibrium state probabilities of feasible states:

$$P(n_0,n_1,n_2) = \rho^{n_0} \rho_1^{n_1} \rho_2^{n_2} \frac{n!}{n_1! \, n_2!} P(0,0,0)$$

where $\rho_q = \lambda_q/\mu$, $\rho = \rho_1 + \rho_2$, and $n = n_1 + n_2$.

6. The General Q Queue S Service System

We are now prepared to solve the problem in a general form. We start as usual, by writing the flow balance equations:

$$(S\mu + \sum_{q=1}^{Q} \lambda_q)P(n_0,n_1,\ldots,n_Q) = S\mu \sum_{i=1}^{Q} \frac{n_i+1}{n+1} P(n_0,\ldots,n_i+1,\ldots,n_Q) +$$

$$\sum_{m=1}^{Q} P(n_0,\ldots,n_m-1,\ldots,n_Q) \lambda_m \quad (n_0=S) \quad \text{where} \quad n = \sum_{q=1}^{Q} n_q$$

7

with the boundary condition

$$P(n_0,0,\ldots,0) = \frac{(\sum_{q=1}^{Q} \lambda_q)^{n_0}}{\mu^{n_0} \cdot n_0!} P(0,0,\ldots,0) \qquad (n_0 \leq S)$$

where $P(0,0,\ldots,0)$ is given by

$$P(0,0,\ldots,0) = \left[\sum_{n=0}^{S-1} \frac{(S\rho)^n}{n!} + \frac{(S\rho)^S}{s!(1-\rho)} \right]^{-1} \quad \text{where } \rho = \sum_{q=1}^{Q} \rho_q \text{ and } \rho_q = \frac{\lambda_q}{S\mu} .$$

The following equations give the equilibrium probability for feasible sates for the Q queue S server system:

$$P(n_0,n_1,\ldots,n_Q) = \frac{(\rho S)^{n_0}}{n_0!} \prod_{q=1}^{Q} \rho_q^{n_q} \frac{n!}{\prod_{m=1}^{Q} n_m!} P(0,0,\ldots,0)$$

7. Performance Measures

From the equilibrium state probabilities we can compute many interesting performance measures; for example, mean queue lengths and mean waiting times in the system. For the sake of clarity, we derive these performance measures for a simple system with two queues, one server, and different arrival rates to each queue. Then we proceed to the multiple queue, multiple server case.

The first case we consider is shown in Figure 2. From Section 5 we know that the equilibrium state probabilities are given by

$$P(n_0,n_1,n_2) = \rho^{n_0} \rho_1^{n_1} \rho_2^{n_2} \frac{n!}{n_1! \, n_2!} (1-\rho)$$

We want the marginal probability distribution, $P_q(n_q)$[1]. The standard approach is to sum over all other variables (except n_q) in the above equation, but performing such a summation is difficult. Instead, if one starts from

$$\mu P(1,n_1,n_2) = \lambda_1 P(1,n_1-1,n_2) + \lambda_2 P(1,n_1,n_2-1)$$

which is an intermediate step in the derivation of the above equation, one can find the marginal distribution more efficiently. Accordingly, we start by summing over n_2:

$$\sum_{n_2=0}^{\infty} P(1,n_1,n_2) = \rho_1 \sum_{n_2=0}^{\infty} P(1,n_1-1,n_2) + \rho_2 \sum_{n_2=0}^{\infty} P(1,n_1,n_2-1)$$

---

[1] From now on our notation for marginal probabilities will omit the subscript since it is always clear from context what marginal probability we are interested in.

8

Eventually we arrive at

$$P(n_1) = (1 - \rho) \; \phi(n_1) + \rho \; (1 - \frac{\rho_1}{1-\rho_2})(\frac{\rho_1}{1-\rho_2})^{n_1}$$

where $\quad \phi(n_1) = \begin{cases} 1, & n_1 = 0 \\ 0, & \text{otherwise} \end{cases}$

Let $\bar{n}_1$ denote the mean queue length for queue 1. It can be determined in the standard way:

$$\bar{n}_1 = E[n_1] = \sum_{n_1=0}^{\infty} n_1 \; P(n_1)$$

$$= \rho \; (1 - \frac{\rho_1}{1-\rho_2}) \sum_{n_1=1}^{\infty} (\frac{\rho_1}{1-\rho_2})^{n_1} \cdot n_1$$

$$= \rho_1 \; \frac{\rho}{1-\rho}$$

By symmetry we can also write:

$$\bar{n}_2 = \rho_2 \; \frac{\rho}{1-\rho}$$

Let $\bar{n}_0$ be the average number of messages occupying servers: it can be determined from:

$$\bar{n}_0 = E[n_0] = 1 \cdot P(1) = \rho$$

If we view this system as a birth and death queueing system, we know that the mean queue length is $\bar{n} = \rho/(1-\rho)$. It is easy to verify that $\bar{n} = \bar{n}_0 + \bar{n}_1 + \bar{n}_2$.

If we let q_1 denote a message's mean queueing time in queue 1, we can easily derive from Little's formula [LITT61] that:

$$q_1 = \frac{\bar{n}_1}{\lambda_1} = \rho_1 \; \frac{\rho}{1-\rho} \; \frac{1}{\lambda_1} = \frac{\rho}{\mu(1-\rho)}$$

And by symmetry,

$$q_2 = \frac{\rho}{\mu(1-\rho)}$$

As we can see, though the arrival rates to the queues are different, the mean queueing times are the same. If the system had only one queue with an arrival rate equal to the total arrival rate to our two queue system, we would still have the same mean queueing time.

The mean waiting time that a message encounters as a result of entering one of the queues is $w_i = q_i + s$ where $s \; (= 1/\mu)$ is the mean service time of the station. We see that

$$w_1 = q_1 + s = \frac{\rho}{\mu(1-\rho)} + \frac{1}{\mu} = \frac{1}{\mu(1-\rho)}$$

and by symmetry

$$w_2 = \frac{1}{\mu(1-\rho)}$$

Again we observe that $w=w_1=w_2$, where w is the mean waiting time in a single queue system with the same total arrival rate.

Now consider the marginal probability distribution for the multiple queue, multiple server system depicted in Figure 1. As before, it is difficult to obtain the marginal probabilities from the equilibrium state probabilities. Instead we start from

$$S\mu \ P(n_0, n_1, \ldots, n_Q) = \sum_{q=1}^{Q} P(n_0, \ldots, n_q-1, \ldots n_Q) \ \lambda_q \quad (n_0 = S)$$

which is an intermediate step in the derivation of the equilibrium probabilities. By summing and manipulating this expression, we obtain

$$P(S, n_q) = P(S) \ (1 - \frac{\rho_q}{1-\rho+\rho_q})(\frac{\rho_q}{1-\rho+\rho_q})^{n_q}$$

and

$$P(n_q) = (\phi(n_q) \sum_{n_0=0}^{S-1} \frac{(\rho S)^{n_0}}{n_0!} + \frac{(\rho S)^S}{(1-S)S!} \ (1 - \frac{\rho_q}{1-\rho+\rho_q})(\frac{\rho_q}{1-\rho+\rho_q})^{n_q}) \cdot$$

$$\cdot \ P(0,0,\ldots,0)$$

It is also easy to show that

$$P(n_0) = (\frac{(\rho S)^{n_0}}{n_0!} + \frac{\rho}{1-\rho} \ \frac{(\rho S)^S}{S!} \ \phi(n_0-S)) \cdot P(0,0,\ldots,0) \qquad (n_0 <= S)$$

The mean queue length is derived in the standard way:

$$\bar{n}_q = E[n_q] = \sum_{n_q=0}^{\infty} n_q \ P(n_q)$$

$$= P(C)(1 - \frac{\rho_q}{1-\rho+\rho_q}) \sum_{n_i=0}^{\infty} n_i \ (\frac{\rho_i}{1-\rho+\rho_i})^{n_i}$$

Hence,

$$\bar{n}_q = P(S) \ \frac{\rho_q}{1-\rho}$$

The case $q=0$ must be treated separately:

$$\bar{n}_0 = \sum_{n_0=0}^{\infty} n_0 P(n_0) = \rho \ S$$

10

The mean queueing time can be derived by using Little's formula [LITT61]:

$$q_i = \frac{\overline{n}_i}{\lambda_i} = P(S) \frac{\rho_i}{1-\rho} \cdot \frac{1}{\lambda_i} = P(S) \frac{1}{S\mu(1-\rho)}$$

The mean waiting time for a message that joins queue i consists of a mean queueing time and a mean service time. It is given by:

$$w_i = P(S) \frac{1}{S\mu(1-\rho)} + \frac{1}{\mu}$$

8. Summary

We have determined, for a multiple queue, multiple server queueing system with a load balancing scheduling policy, the equilibrium state probabilities, the marginal probabilities, the mean queue length, the mean queueing time, and the mean waiting time, (which is the same for all queues).

We have also shown [AFSH81c] that, since our service center type has Muntz' $M => M^1$ property [MUNT72, MUNT73], it can, in fact, be incorporated into a network of queues and that the statistics for this network can be determined using the simple computational techniques described in [BUZE73, BRUE78, BRUE80, REIS80].

We have shown in [AFSH81b] that a load balancing station behaves with respect to average values similar to a multiple class FCFS station [BASK75]. But we also showed that the variance of the waiting time distribution was different, for example, for that FCFS station and a load balancing station.

---

[1] If the arrival process is Poisson then the output process is also Poisson.

References

[AFSH81a] Afshari, P.V., Bruell, S.C., and Kain, R.Y., "On a Multiple Class, Multiple Queue, Multiple Server System," in preparation.

[AFSH81b] Afshari, P.V., Bruell, S.C., and Kain, R.Y., "On the Load Balancing Bus Accessing Scheme," submitted to IEEE Transaction on Computers.

[AFSH81c] Afshari, P.V., Bruell, S.C., and Kain, R.Y., "A Dynamic Load Balancing Scheduler in a Multiple Queue, Multiple Server System," University of Minnesota, Computer Science Technical Report 81-23, July 1981.

[BAIN81] Bain, W.L., and Ahuja, S.R., "Performance Analysis of High-Speed Digital Buses for Multiprocessing Systems," Proc. 8th Annual Symposium on Computer Architecture, 107-133, May 1981.

[BASK75] Baskett, F., Chandy, K.M., Muntz, R.R., and Palacios, F.G., "Open, Closed and Mixed Networks of Queues with Different Classes of Customers," JACM 22, 2, 248-260.

[BRUE78] Bruell, S.C., "On Single and Multiple Job Class Queueing Network Models of Computing Systems," Ph.D. Thesis, Computer Sciences Department, Purdue University, December 1978.

[BRUE80] Bruell, S.C. and Balbo, G., Computational Algorithms for Closed Queueing Networks, Operating and Programming Systems Series, Peter J. Denning ed., Elsevier North-Holland, New York.

[BUZE73] Buzen, J.P. "Computational Algorithms for Closed Queueing Networks with Exponential Servers," CACM 16, 9, 527-531, Sept. 1973.

[CHOW77] Chow, Y.C. and Kohler, W.H., "Dynamic Load Balancing in Homogeneous Two-Processor Distributed Systems," Computer Performance, North Holland Publishing Company, K.M. Chandy and M. Reiser (Eds.), 1977.

[CHU81] Chu, W.W., Fayolle, G., and Hibbits, D., "An Analysis of a Tandem Queueing System for Flow Control in Computer Networks," IEEE Transactions on Computers 30, 5, 318-324.

[KLEI75] Kleinrock, L., Queueing Systems, Vol. I: Theory, John Wiley and Sons, New York.

[LEIB61] Leibowitz, M.A., "An Approximate Method for Treating a Class of Multiqueue Problems," IBM Journal, 204-209, July 1961.

[LITT61] Little, J.D.C., "A Proof of the Queueing Formula L=λW," Operations Research 9, 1961, 383-387.

[MUNT72] Muntz, R.R., "Poisson Departure Processes and Queueing Networks," IBM Research Report RC4145, IBM Thomas J. Watson Research Center, Yorktown Heights, New York.

[MUNT73] Muntz, R.R., "Poisson Departure Processes and Queueing Networks," Proc. Seventh Annual Princeton Conference on Information Science and Systems, 435-440.

[SMIT79] Smith, A.J., "An Analytic and Experimental Study of Multiple Channel Controllers," IEEE Transactions on Computers 27, 1, 38-49.

[SPIR79] Spirn, J.R., "Queueing Networks with Random Selection for Service," IEEE Transactions on Software Engineering 5, 3, 287-289, May 1979.

[REIS80] Reiser, M. and Lavenberg, S.S., "Mean Value Analysis of Closed Multichain Queueing Networks," JACM 27, 313-322, April 1980.

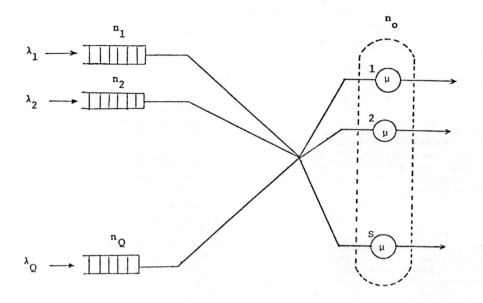

Fig. 1

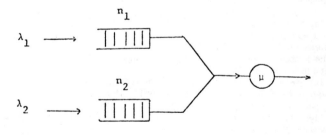

Fig. 2

Optimal Control of a M/M/m Queue

Aurel A. Lazar

Department of Electrical Engineering
Columbia University

Abstract

The problem of optimal control of a M/M/m queueing system is investigated. As in the M/M/1 case the optimum control is shown to be a window type mechanism. The window size L depends on the maximum allowable time delay T and can be explicitly computed. The throughput time delay function of the M/M/m system is briefly discussed.

I. Introduction

The problem of optimal control of simple queueing systems has received considerable attention in the recent literature. Kleinrock [3] and Barath-Kummar [1] have investigated the throughput time delay trade-off by employing the "power" as an optimization criterion. Schwartz [7] analyzed various control schemes and compared them by using both the power and the throughput as performance measures. Lazar [5] in investigating the optimal control of a M/M/1 queueing system has shown that a window type mechanism satisfies a maximum throughput under a bounded time delay criterion. In this paper an extention of the latter result to the more complex M/M/m case is given.

The optimal control of the M/M/1 queueing system was easily obtained (see [5]) since maximizing the throughput has been shown to be equivalent with minimizing the probability that the system is empty. Consequently, to find the optimal control one has to maximize a linear function under linear constraints. In the M/M/m case the function to be maximized turns out to be nonlinear. This is because the probability that the system is underutilized is a linear combination of the probabilities that at least one server is unused (see *Lemma* 2., section IV). In order to find the optimal control, therefore, a more involved method of proof has to be employed. The method of proof used here, although straightforward, is computationally very lengthly. Our efforts are rewarded, however, by the simplicity of the final results.

This paper is organized as follows. In section II the optimization criterion is presented. The class of optimum controls investigated maximize the throughput under a bounded average time delay criterion. In section III the optimal control of the M/M/∞ queueing system is presented. The results obtained for the M/M/∞ queue together with those for the M/M/1 queue give us a good intuitive feeling about the solution one might expect for the general M/M/m case treated in section IV. The main result in section IV is contained in *Theorem* 1. It is shown that

the optimum control is a window flow control type mechanism. The dependence of the maximum throughput on the window size L is explicitly stated. Finally, the throughput time delay function is shown to be continuous nondecreasing and piecewise convex.

II. The Optimization Criterion

Let us consider the queueing system depicted in Fig. 1. The upper queue which has an exponential server (μ_k), $1 \leq k \leq N$ has to be controlled corresponding to a suitable optimality criterion. The lower or "feedback queue" has an exponential server (λ_k), $1 \leq k \leq N$. Since there are a maximum of N packets in the above system, the upper queue can be seen as being a M/M/m queueing system with a finite buffer size N. Without any loss of generality, therefore, the feedback queue models the input stream to the a M/M/m system with a finite buffer size. A virtual circuit in a computer communication network toghether with its acknowlegdement path (feedback channel) can be modeled in this manner.

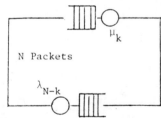

Fig.1   Model for the state dependent control of a M/M/m queue.

The average throughput and the average time delay are given by [2], [6]:

$$E\gamma^{(N)} = \sum_{k=1}^{N} \mu_k P_k$$

and

$$E\tau^{(N)} = \frac{\sum_{k=1}^{N} k P_k}{\sum_{k=1}^{N} \mu_k P_k} \quad ,$$

respectively, where

$$P_k = \prod_{l=0}^{k-1} \frac{\lambda_{N-l}}{\mu_{l+1}} P_0$$

and

$$P_0 = \frac{1}{1 + \sum_{k=1}^{N} \prod_{l=0}^{k-1} \frac{\lambda_{N-l}}{\mu_{l+1}}}$$

denote the probabilities that the upper queue contains k packets ($1 \leq k \leq N$).

Definition 1. $\lambda = (\lambda_k)$, $1 \leq k \leq N$, will hereafter denote the control.

In our model the available capacity of the access line to the upper queue is bounded by a maximum value. This is formally described in the following [4]:

Definition 2. The class of controls $\lambda = (\lambda_k)$, $1 \leq k \leq N$, satisfying the peak constraint

$$0 \leq \lambda_k \leq c \quad ,$$

for all k, $1 \leq k \leq N$, where c, $c \in R_+$, is a constant is called admissible.

Definition 3. The control $\lambda = (\lambda_k)$, $1 \leq k \leq N$, is said to be optimum over the class of admissible controls for a given T, $T \in R_+$, if the maximum

$$\max_{E_T^{(N)} \leq T} E_T^{(N)}$$

is achieved.

Let x_k denote the expression

$$x_k = \prod_{l=0}^{k-1} \frac{\lambda_{N-l}}{\mu_{l+1}} \quad (= \frac{p_k}{p_0})$$

for all k, $1 \leq k \leq N$. Thus

$$\sum_{k=1}^{N} x_k = \sum_{k=1}^{N} \frac{p_k}{p_0} = \frac{1 - p_0}{p_0} = \frac{1}{p_0} - 1$$

and

$$p_0 = \frac{1}{1 + \sum_{k=1}^{N} x_k}.$$

III. Optimal Control of the M/M/∞ Queue

In the case where the upper queue is a M/M/∞ system the server is specified by

$$\mu_k = k\mu \quad ,$$

for all k, $1 \leq k \leq N$.

In light of Definition 3 the optimal control of the M/M/∞ queueing system appears to be very simple. This is because the average time delay is given by:

$$E_T^{(N)} = \frac{\sum_{k=1}^{N} k p_k}{\mu \sum_{k=1}^{N} k p_k} = \frac{1}{\mu} \quad ,$$

and hence in minimizing the average throughput, the time delay does not appear as an explicit parameter.

Proposition 1. The optimal control $\lambda = (\lambda_k)$, $1 \leq k \leq N$, of a M/M/∞ queueing system with a maximum of N packets is given by $\lambda_k = c$ for all k, $1 \leq k \leq N$. The corresponding maximum throughput amounts to:

$$(E_\gamma^{(N)})_{max} = c \cdot \frac{\sum_{k=0}^{N-1} \frac{\rho^k}{k!}}{\sum_{k=0}^{N} \frac{\rho^k}{k!}} \quad ,$$

where $\rho = \frac{c}{\mu}$.

Proof: It is sufficient to show that

$$\frac{\sum_{k=1}^{N} k x_k}{1 + \sum_{k=1}^{N} x_k} \leq \frac{\sum_{k=1}^{N} k \frac{\rho^k}{k!}}{1 + \sum_{k=1}^{N} \frac{\rho^k}{k!}} \quad ,$$

or

$$\sum_{k=1}^{N} k(x_k - \frac{\rho^k}{k!}) + \sum_{k=1}^{N} \sum_{l=1}^{N} x_k \frac{\rho^l}{l!}(k-l) \leq 0 \quad .$$

The first term on the left hand side is negative since $x_k \leq \frac{\rho^k}{k!}$ for all k, $1 \leq k \leq N$. The second term is also negative since the expression is symmetric in k, l and

$$\frac{x_k}{x_l} \leq \frac{l!}{k!} \rho^{k-l} \quad ,$$

for all $k > l$. □

Lemma 1. The maximum throughput is strictly increasing with the number of packets N in the system, i.e.,

$$(E_\gamma^{(N)})_{max} < (E_\gamma^{(N+1)})_{max} \quad ,$$

for all $N \in N$.

Proof: We have to show that:

$$(\sum_{k=0}^{N-1} \frac{\rho^k}{k!})(\sum_{k=0}^{N+1} \frac{\rho^k}{k!}) < (\sum_{k=0}^{N} \frac{\rho^k}{k!})^2 \quad ,$$

or

$$1 + \sum_{k=0}^{N-1} \frac{\rho^{k+1}}{k!}(\frac{1}{k+1} - \frac{1}{N+1}) > 0 \quad ,$$

which is obvious since $k \leq N$. □

IV. Optimal Control of a M/M/m Queue

The server of a M/M/m queueing system is specified by [2]:

$$\mu_k = \begin{cases} k\mu & k \leq m \\ m\mu & k \geq m \end{cases} \quad ,$$

and let

$$\rho = \frac{c}{m\mu} \quad .$$

In order to simplify the proof of our main result (*Theorem 1*) a series of lemmas will be first given. In what follows we will assume that the number of packets in the closed system (see Fig. 1) is larger than the number of servers, i.e., $N > m$.

Intuitively, maximizing the throughput of a M/M/m system under a bounded time delay criterion appears to be the same as minimizing the probability that the system has at least one unused server. The exact statement is given in the following:

Lemma 2. The control $\lambda = (\lambda_k)$, $1 \leq k \leq N$ is optimal for a given T, $T \in R_+$, if it achieves the minimum

$$\min \left\{ \frac{m + \sum\limits_{k=1}^{m-1}(m-k)x_k}{1 + \sum\limits_{k=1}^{N} x_k} = \sum\limits_{k=0}^{m-1}(m-k)p_k \right\}$$

$$(1-\mu T) \sum\limits_{k=1}^{m} kx_k + \sum\limits_{k=m+1}^{N} (k-m\mu T)x_k \leq 0 \qquad (1)$$

where $0 \leq x_k \leq \frac{(m\rho)^k}{k!}$ for all k, $1 \leq k \leq m$, and $0 \leq x_k \leq \frac{m^m}{m!}\rho^k$ for all k, $m+1 \leq k \leq N$.

Proof: Since $E\,\tau^{(N)} \leq T$ is equivalent with

$$(1-\mu T) \sum\limits_{k=1}^{m} kx_k + \sum\limits_{k=m+1}^{N} (k-m\mu T)x_k \leq 0$$

and

$$E\,\frac{\tau^{(N)}}{\mu} = \sum\limits_{k=1}^{m-1} kp_k + m \sum\limits_{k=m}^{N} p_k = m - \sum\limits_{k=0}^{m-1}(m-k)p_k$$

$$= m - \frac{m + \sum\limits_{k=1}^{m-1}(m-k)x_k}{1 + \sum\limits_{k=1}^{N} x_k},$$

the optimum control $\lambda = (\lambda_k)$, $1 \leq k \leq N$, (if it exists) achieves (1). □

Remark. The control $\lambda = (\lambda_k)$, $1 \leq k \leq N$, is optimal for a given T, $T \in R_+$, if it achieves the maximum:

$$\max_{(1-\mu T)\sum\limits_{k=1}^{m} kx_k + \sum\limits_{k=m+1}^{N}(k-m\mu T)x_k \leq 0} \frac{\sum\limits_{k=1}^{m} kx_k + m \sum\limits_{k=m+1}^{N} x_k}{1 + \sum\limits_{k=1}^{N} x_k},$$

where (x_k), $1 \leq k \leq N$, verifies the conditions given in *Lemma 2* above.

Definition 4. The mapping $F : R_+ \to R_+$ given by

$$F(T) = \max_{E\tau^{(N)} \leq T} E\,\tau^{(N)}$$

is called the throughput time delay function.

Remark. The existence of F is left to the reader as a simple exercise.

The following is a technical result needed in the proof of *Theorem 1*.

Lemma 3. *Let us assume that* $\sum\limits_{k=m+1}^{N} x_k \leq \delta$. *Then:*

$$E\,\tau^{(N)} \leq \mu \frac{\sum\limits_{k=1}^{m} kx_k + m\delta}{1 + \sum\limits_{k=1}^{N} x_k + \delta},$$

and equality can be achieved iff

$$\sum\limits_{k=m+1}^{N} x_k = \delta .$$

Proof: We have to show that

$$\frac{\sum\limits_{k=1}^{m} kx_k + m\sum\limits_{k=m+1}^{N} x_k}{1 + \sum\limits_{k=1}^{m} x_k + \sum\limits_{k=m+1}^{N} x_k} \leq \frac{\sum\limits_{k=1}^{m} kx_k + m\delta}{1 + \sum\limits_{k=1}^{m} x_k + \delta},$$

which is equivalent with

$$\left[\sum\limits_{k=1}^{m} kx_k - m(1 + \sum\limits_{k=1}^{m} x_k) \right]\left(\delta - \sum\limits_{k=m+1}^{N} x_k\right) \leq 0 . \qquad □$$

Lemma 4. *The maximum average time delay* $T_{max}^{(L)}$ *achieved with* L *packets in a M/M/m system* $(m < L)$ *is given by*

$$T_{max}^{(L)} = \frac{1}{\mu}\left[1 + \frac{\frac{m^m}{m!} \sum\limits_{k=m+1}^{L} (k-m)\rho^k}{\sum\limits_{k=1}^{m} \frac{(m\rho)^k}{(k-1)!} + \frac{m^m}{(m-1)!} \sum\limits_{k=m+1}^{L} \rho^k} \right] \leq \frac{L}{m\mu} . \qquad (2)$$

Proof: We have to show that:

$$\left\{ \sum\limits_{k=m+1}^{L}(k-m)x_k \right\}\left\{ \sum\limits_{k=1}^{m} kx_k + m\sum\limits_{k=m+1}^{L} x_k \right\}^{-1}$$

$$\leq \left\{ \frac{m^m}{m!}\sum\limits_{k=m+1}^{L}(k-m)\rho^k \right\}\left\{ \sum\limits_{k=1}^{m} k\frac{(m\rho)^k}{k!} + \frac{m^{m+1}}{m!}\sum\limits_{k=m+1}^{L} \rho^k \right\}^{-1} ,$$

or

$$\sum\limits_{k=1}^{m}\sum\limits_{l=m+1}^{L} k(l-m)(x_l\frac{(m\rho)^k}{k!} - x_k\frac{m^m}{m!}\rho^l)$$

$$+ \frac{m^{m+1}}{m!}\sum\limits_{k=m+1}^{L}\sum\limits_{l=m+1}^{L} x_k\rho^l(k-l) \leq 0 .$$

Both expressions on the left hand side of the above inequality are negative since

$$x_l\frac{(m\rho)^k}{k!} - x_k\frac{m^m}{m!}\rho^l \leq 0 ,$$

for all k,l, $1 \leq k \leq m$, $m+1 \leq l \leq L$, and

$$\frac{x_l}{x_k} \leq \rho^{l-k} ,$$

for all l,k, $m+1 \leq l \leq L$, $m+1 \leq k \leq L$

Note also that

$$T_{max}^{(L)} < \frac{L}{m\mu} ,$$

since

$$\frac{1}{\mu}\frac{\sum\limits_{k=1}^{m} kx_k + \sum\limits_{k=m+1}^{L} kx_k}{\sum\limits_{k=1}^{m} kx_k + m\sum\limits_{k=m+1}^{L} x_k} \leq \frac{L}{m\mu}$$

is equivalent with

$$(L-m)\sum\limits_{k=1}^{m} kx_k + m\sum\limits_{k=m+1}^{L}(L-k)x_k \geq 0 . \qquad □$$

Remark. As in the M/M/1 case the right hand side of inequality (2) can be achieved assymptotically as $\rho \to \infty$. This situation arises when the served packets are fead back and rejoin instenteneously the queueing buffer. $L/m\mu$ is then the average time delay of the M/M/m queueing system having constantly L packets in the buffer.

Lemma 5. *The maximum average time delay is strictly increasing with the number of packets, i.e.,*

$$T_{max}^{(L)} < T_{max}^{(L+1)} \quad ,$$

for all L, $L > m$.

Proof: We have to show that

$$\{ \sum_{k=m+1}^{L} (k-m)\rho^k \}\{ \sum_{k=1}^{m} \frac{(m\rho)^k}{(k-1)!} + \frac{m^m}{(m-1)!} \sum_{k=m+1}^{L} \rho^k \}^{-1}$$

$$< \{ \sum_{k=m+1}^{L+1} (k-m)\rho^k \}\{ \sum_{k=1}^{m} \frac{(m\rho)^k}{(k-1)!} + \frac{m^m}{(m-1)!} \sum_{k=m+1}^{L+1} \rho^k \}^{-1}$$

After some simple algebraic manipulations this inequality can be reduced to

$$(L+1-m) \sum_{k=1}^{m} \frac{(m\rho)^k}{(k-1)!} + \frac{m^m}{(m-1)!} \sum_{k=m+1}^{L} (L+1-k)\rho^k > 0 \quad ,$$

which is true since both expressions on the left hand side are strictly positive. □

Theorem 1. *Given that $T_{max}^{(L-1)} < T \leq T_{max}^{(L)}$, $m < L \leq N$, the optimum control of a M/M/m queue with a maximum of N packets in the system is given by*

$$\lambda_k = \begin{cases} c & N-L+2 \leq k \leq N \\ \lambda_{N-L+1} & k = N-L+1 \\ 0 & 1 \leq k \leq N-L \end{cases} \quad ,$$

where

$$\lambda_{N-L+1} = \frac{1}{L/m\mu - T}[\frac{m!}{m^m}(\mu T - 1) \sum_{k=1}^{m} \frac{(m\rho)^{k+1-L}}{(k-1)!}$$

$$+ \sum_{k=m+1}^{L-1} (m\mu T - k)\rho^{k+1-L}] \quad . \tag{3}$$

Finally the maximum throughput is

$$F(T) = \mu \cdot \{(L-m) \sum_{k=1}^{m} k\frac{(m\rho)^k}{k!} + \frac{m^{m+1}}{m!} \sum_{k=m+1}^{L-1} (L-k)\rho^k \}$$

$$\cdot \{L - m\mu T + \sum_{k=1}^{m} [L-k-(m-k)\mu T]\frac{(m\rho)^k}{k!} + \frac{m^m}{m!} \sum_{k=m+1}^{L-1} (L-k)\rho^k \}^{-1} \tag{4}$$

Proof: Let us assume that $T_{max}^{(L-1)} < T \leq T_{max}^{(L)}$ with $m < L \leq N$. From $E_{\tau}^{(N)} \leq T$ we obtain:

$$x_L \leq -\frac{N-m\mu T}{L-m\mu T}x_N - \cdots - \frac{L+1-m\mu T}{L-m\mu T}x_{L+1} - \frac{L-1-m\mu T}{L-m\mu T}x_{L-1} - \cdots$$

$$- \frac{m+1-m\mu T}{L-m\mu T}x_{m+1} - \frac{m-m\mu T}{L-m\mu T}x_m - \cdots - \frac{2-2\mu T}{L-m\mu T}x_2 - \frac{1-\mu T}{L-m\mu T}x_1 \quad .$$

Therefore

$$\sum_{k=m+1}^{N} x_k \leq -\frac{N-L}{L-m\mu T}x_N - \cdots - \frac{1}{L-m\mu T}x_{L+1} + \frac{1}{L-m\mu T}x_{L-1}$$

$$+ \cdots + \frac{L-(m+1)}{L-m\mu T}x_{m+1} + \frac{\mu T-1}{L-m\mu T}[mx_m + \cdots + 2x_2 + x_1]$$

$$\leq \frac{1}{L-m\mu T} \sum_{k=m+1}^{L-1} (L-k)x_k + \frac{\mu T-1}{L-m\mu T} \sum_{k=1}^{m} kx_k \quad .$$

Hence by applying *Lemma 3* we get:

$$E_{\gamma}^{(N)} \leq \mu \{ \sum_{k=1}^{m} kx_k + \frac{m}{L-m\mu T} \sum_{k=m+1}^{L-1} (L-k)x_k + m\frac{\mu T-1}{L-m\mu T} \sum_{k=1}^{m} kx_k \}$$

$$\cdot \{1 + \sum_{k=1}^{m} x_k + \frac{1}{L-m\mu T} \sum_{k=m+1}^{L-1} (L-k)x_k + \frac{\mu T-1}{L-m\mu T} \sum_{k=1}^{m} kx_k \}^{-1} \quad ,$$

or

$$E_{\gamma}^{(N)} \leq \mu \{(L-m) \sum_{k=1}^{m} kx_k + m \sum_{k=m+1}^{L-1} (L-k)x_k \}$$

$$\{L - m\mu T + \sum_{k=1}^{m} [L-k-(m-k)\mu T]x_k + \sum_{k=m+1}^{L-1} (L-k)x_k \}^{-1} \quad . \tag{5}$$

In what follows we will show that the right hand side of the inequality above can be in turn bounded, i.e.,

$$\{(L-m) \sum_{k=1}^{m} kx_k + m \sum_{k=m+1}^{L-1} (L-k)x_k \}$$

$$\cdot \{L-m\mu T + \sum_{k=1}^{m} [L-k-(m-k)\mu T]x_k + \sum_{k=m+1}^{L-1} (L-k)x_k \}^{-1}$$

$$\leq \{(L-m) \sum_{k=1}^{m} k\frac{(m\rho)^k}{k!} + \frac{m^{m+1}}{m!} \sum_{k=m+1}^{L-1} (L-k)\rho^k \}$$

$$\cdot \{L-m\mu T + \sum_{k=1}^{m} [L-k-(m-k)\mu T]\frac{(m\rho)^k}{k!} + \frac{m^m}{m!} \sum_{k=m+1}^{L-1} (L-k)\rho^k \}^{-1} \tag{6}$$

and equality can be achieved if:

$$x_k = \begin{cases} \frac{(m\rho)^k}{k!} & k \leq m \\ \frac{m^m}{m!}\rho^k & k \geq m \end{cases} \quad . \tag{7}$$

The careful reader might have observed that the right hand side in the (in-) equalities (4) and (6) differ only by a constant factor. After some algebraic manipulations, inequality (6) can be reduced to

$$(L-m)[\sum_{k=1}^{m} k(x_k - \frac{(m\rho)^k}{k!}) + m \sum_{k=m+1}^{L-1} (L-k)(x_k - \frac{m^m}{m!}\rho^k)]$$

$$+ (L-m) \sum_{k=1}^{m} \sum_{l=1}^{m} (k-l)x_k \frac{(m\rho)^l}{l!}$$

$$+ \sum_{k=1}^{m} \sum_{l=m+1}^{L-1} (L-l)(m-k)[x_l \frac{(m\rho)^k}{k!} - x_k \frac{m^m}{m!}\rho^l] \leq 0 \quad .$$

All three terms on the left hand side of the inequality above are negative since:

$$x_k \leq \begin{cases} \dfrac{(m\rho)^k}{k!} & k \leq m \\[2mm] \dfrac{\rho^k m^m}{m!} & k \geq m \end{cases} ,$$

$$x_k \frac{(m\rho)^l}{l!} - x_l \frac{(m\rho)^k}{k!} \leq 0 ,$$

for all $k > l$, $1 \leq k \leq m$, $1 \leq l \leq m$, and

$$x_l \frac{(m\rho)^k}{k!} - x_k \frac{m^m}{m!}\rho^l \leq 0 ,$$

for all l, k, $1 \leq k \leq m$, $m+1 \leq l \leq L-1$.

One can easily see now that

$$x_L = \frac{1}{L-m\mu T}\left[(\mu T-1) \sum_{k=1}^{m} k\frac{(m\rho)^k}{k!} + \frac{m^m}{m!} \sum_{k=m+1}^{-1} (m\mu T-k)\rho^k\right] .$$

It remains only to show that

$$0 \leq x_L \leq \frac{m^m}{m!}\rho^L ,$$

or

$$0 \leq (\mu T-1) \sum_{k=1}^{m} k\frac{(m\rho)^k}{k!} + \frac{m^m}{m!} \sum_{k=m+1}^{L-1} (m\mu T-k)\rho^k \leq (L-m\mu T)\frac{m^m}{m!}\rho^L ,$$

which can easily be reduced to

$$\frac{1}{\mu}\left\{ \sum_{k=1}^{m} k\frac{(m\rho)^k}{k!} + \frac{m^m}{m!} \sum_{k=m+1}^{L-1} k\rho^k\right\}\left\{ \sum_{k=1}^{m} k\frac{(m\rho)^k}{k!} + \frac{m^{m+1}}{m!} \sum_{k=1}^{L-1} \rho^k\right\}^{-1}$$

$$\leq T \leq$$

$$\frac{1}{\mu}\left\{ \sum_{k=1}^{m} k\frac{(m\rho)^k}{k!} + \frac{m^m}{m!} \sum_{k=m+1}^{L} k\rho^k\right\}\left\{ \sum_{k=1}^{m} k\frac{(m\rho)^k}{k!} + \frac{m^{m+1}}{m!} \sum_{k=1}^{L} \rho^k\right\}^{-1} ,$$

or

$$T_{\max}^{(L-1)} \leq T \leq T_{\max}^{(L)} .$$

Thus the maximum throughput given by (4) is achieved if the equalities in (7) are satisfied. □

Remark. As in the M/M/1 case, since the lower queue will contain at all times at least $N-L$ packets, the optimum control can also be achieved by a control scheme using a total of $N=L$ packets. We require that

$$\lambda_k = \begin{cases} c & 2 \leq k \leq L \\ \lambda_1 & k = 1 \end{cases} ,$$

where λ_1 is exactly the right hand side of (3). Therefore the optimal control is a window type mechanism. The window size L can be easily derived from the maximum time delay of the system. Naturally the number of packets will depend on the maximum offered load (or line capacity into the M/M/m system).

Corollary. If $T = T_{\max}^{(L)}$ then

$$F(T_{\max}^{(L)}) = \mu \left\{ \sum_{k=1}^{m} \frac{(m\rho)^k}{(k-1)!} + \frac{m^{m+1}}{m!} \sum_{k=m+1}^{L} \rho^k\right\}$$

$$\cdot \left\{ 1 + \sum_{k=1}^{m} \frac{(m\rho)^k}{k!} + \frac{m^m}{m!} \sum_{k=m+1}^{L} \rho^k\right\}^{-1} . \tag{8}$$

Proof: From $T = T_{\max}^{(L)}$ we have

$$(\mu T-1) \sum_{k=1}^{m} k\frac{(m\rho)^k}{k!} + \frac{m^m}{m!} \sum_{k=m+1}^{L-1} (m\mu T-k)\rho^k = \frac{m^m}{m!}(L-m\mu T)\rho^L$$

and therefore

$$\lambda_1 = c .$$

The corresponding throughput amounts to (8). □

Remark. One can easily see that

$$\lim_{L\to\infty} F(T_{\max}^{(L)}) = \begin{cases} \alpha\mu & \rho < 1 \\ m\mu & \rho \geq 1 \end{cases}$$

where

$$\alpha = \left\{ \sum_{k=1}^{m} \frac{(m\rho)^k}{(k-1)!} + \frac{m^{m+1}}{m!}\frac{\rho^{m+1}}{1-\rho}\right\}\left\{ 1 + \sum_{k=1}^{m} \frac{(m\rho)^k}{k!} + \frac{m^m}{m!}\frac{\rho^{m+1}}{1-\rho}\right\}^{-1} ,$$

and

$$\lim_{L\to\infty} T_{\max}^{(L)} = \begin{cases} \beta\mu & \rho < 1 \\ \infty & \rho \geq 1 \end{cases} ,$$

where

$$\beta = \left\{ \sum_{k=1}^{m} \frac{(m\rho)^k}{k!} + \frac{m^m}{m!}\left[(m+1)\frac{\rho^{m+1}}{1-\rho} + \frac{\rho^{m+2}}{(1-\rho)^2}\right]\right\}$$

$$\cdot \left\{ \sum_{k=1}^{m} \frac{(m\rho)^k}{(k-1)!} + \frac{m^m}{(m-1)!}\frac{\rho^{m+1}}{1-\rho}\right\}^{-1} .$$

Lemma 6. *The throughput time delay function is continuous nondecreasing on R_+. In addition, for all T, $T_{\max}^{(L-1)} \leq T \leq T_{\max}^{L}$, and all $L \in N$, F is convex.*

Proof: The proof can be easily supplied. □

The throughput time delay function of the M/M/2 queueing system with $\mu=10$ and $c=17$ is graphically shown in Fig.2. Fig.3 depicts the throughput time delay function for various values of the parameter c. The proof of the "overall concave" behavior of the throughput time delay function is left to the reader as a simple exercise.

V. Conclusion

In this paper the optimal control of a M/M/m queue has been derived. As in the M/M/1 case the optimal control has been shown to be a window flow control mechanism. A simple relationship between the window size and the maximum allowed time delay in the M/M/m system has been established. Furthermore it has been proven that the throughput time delay function is continuous, piecewise convex and nondecreasing.

Acknowledgement

The author would like to thank Prof. Mischa Schwartz for his advice and encouragement throughout the completion of this work.

References

[1] Bharath-Kummar, K., "Optimum End-to-End Flow Control in Networks," *Conference Record of the International Conference on Communications*, pp. 23.3.1 - 32.3.6, June 1980.

[2] Kleinrock, L., *Queueing Systems, Volume I: Theory*, John Wiley, New York, 1975.

[3] Kleinrock, L., "Power and Deterministic Rules of Thumb for Probabilistic Problems in Computer Communications," *Conference Record of the International Conference on Communications*, pp. 43.1.1 - 43.1.10, June 1979.

[4] Lazar, A.A., *Optimal Information Processing Using Counting Point Process Observations*, Ph.D. Dissertation, Dept. of Electrical Engineering and Computer Science, Princeton University, Princeton, NJ 08544, Oct. 1980.

[5] Lazar, A.A., "Optimum Control of a M/M/1 Queue", in *Proceedings of the Nineteenth Allerton Conference on Communication, Control and Computing*, Univ. of Illinois, Urbana, Sept. 30 - Oct. 2, 1981.

[6] Schwartz, M., *Computer Communication Networks Design and Analysis*, Prentice Hall, Englewood Cliffs, 1976.

[7] Schwartz, M., Routing and Flow Control in Data Networks, *IBM Research Report*, **RC 8353 (#36319)**, IBM T.J. Watson Research Center, Yorktown Heights, 1980.

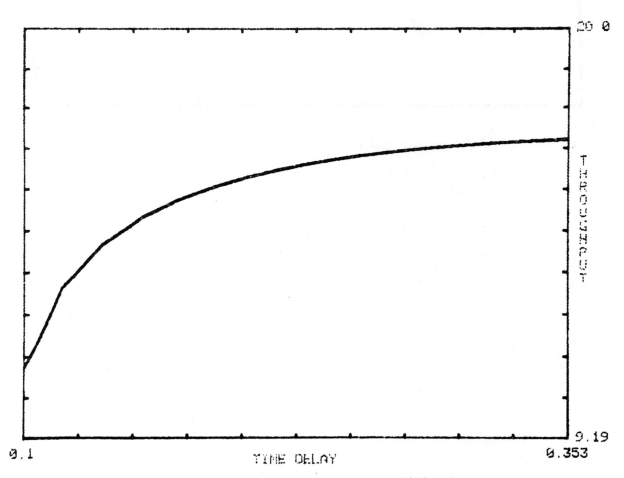

Fig.2 The throughput time delay function of the M/M/2 queueing system

(μ = 10, c = 17)

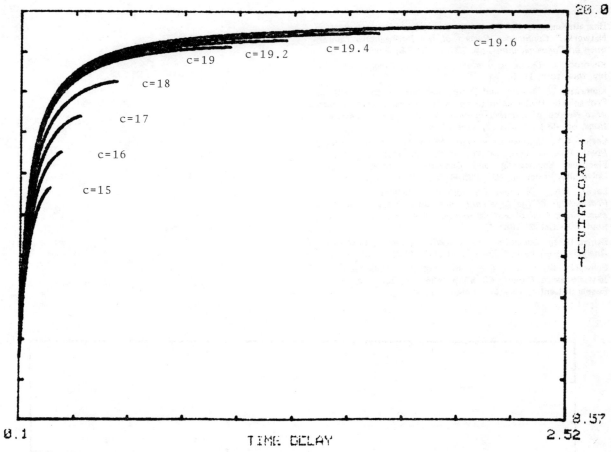

Fig. 3 The dependence of the throughput time delay function on the
parameter c (μ = 10).

NETWORK MODELING WITH BURSTY TRAFFIC AND FINITE BUFFER SPACE

by Jeffrey R. Spirn
Digital Equipment Corporation TW/D16
1925 Andover St., Tewksbury MA 01876

INTRODUCTION

Although there have been very significant advances recently in the state of the art of solvable queueing networks, there are still many phenomena of interest to computer network designers which are not well handled by such methods. Much computer network traffic is bursty [2], and therefore poorly approximated by a Poisson process, but only Poisson arrivals are admissible for solvable queueing networks. In this respect, conventional queueing network models of computer networks can be expected to be optimistic in their performance predictions, often extremely optimistic as we will indicate. A second difficulty with such models is that they require infinite-length queues, and so cannot predict packet loss rates due to finite buffer capacity, a performance measure of principal interest. Although a closed queueing network allows one to limit the total number of packets in transit along a given path, this is not the same as restricting the number of packets which can be queued at each node of a multi-hop path. Contention for buffer space among multiple paths at a given node is also difficult to model by conventional techniques.

Several models have been proposed for congestion and buffer overflow in store-and-forward networks but with non-bursty traffic; overviews appear in [3] (chapter 11) and in [4], for example. To see the significance of bursty traffic, consider a simple finite-length, exponential service queue with bulk arrival, so that each Poisson arrival is a cluster of one or more simultaneous packets. We shall call each such cluster a message, although there is no requirement that there be any correspondence between these and actual network messages. Let the number of packets in an arriving message be geometrically distributed with mean $B>1$, and let ρ have the usual meaning of arrival rate divided by service rate. Then it is straightforward to demonstrate that the mean number of packets queued or in service at equilibrium will be:

$$\frac{\rho B}{1-\rho}$$

which is exactly B times that which would be obtained in an ordinary M/M/1 queue with no input clustering. More generally, if the number in a message has mean B and variance σ^2, the mean queue length will be:

$$\frac{\rho}{1-\rho}\left[1 + B + \sigma^2/B\right]/2$$

so that the greater the average size of the messages, or the greater their variance, the larger will be the mean queue length. By Little's result, the mean waiting time is similarly expanded, by a factor equal to the mean message size in the case of geometric messages.

In this paper, we propose a class of queueing network models, and a method for their approximate solution, for computer networks with bursty traffic and finite buffer space. The model is open, implying no population limit except for buffer size limits and therefore no window-type flow control mechanism. Each node of the computer network is represented as a finite-length queue with exponential service and an arrival process which is initially bulk Poisson, but becomes less and less clustered from hop to hop. Elaborations are possible to account for varying mean packet sizes and certain buffer pooling schemes, although these involve further approximation. The approximations of the method were validated against several simulations, with reasonable agreement, and certainly with much less error than is obtained by modeling a bursty traffic source as Poisson.

NODE MODEL

Consider a queue with capacity for N customers (including the one, if any, in service) which arrive as a bulk Poisson process. Each arriving message consists of one or more packets, distributed in number as follows:

$$\text{Pr[k packets in message]} = (1-1/B)^{k-1}/B \quad , \qquad k \geq 1$$

so that there are a mean B packets per message. Messages arrive as a Poisson process with rate λ messages/second, and packet service is exponentially distributed with mean p/μ, p the mean packet size in bytes. It is straightforward to demonstrate that the following expressions give the probability of finding n packets in such a queue at equilibrium:

$$P(n) = \begin{cases} \dfrac{1-\rho}{1-\rho\alpha^N} & \text{if } n = 0 \\[2em] \dfrac{1-\rho}{1-\rho\alpha^N}\dfrac{\rho}{B}\alpha^{n-1} & 1 \leq n \leq N \end{cases}$$

where:

$$\rho = \lambda B p/\mu$$
$$\alpha = 1 - (1-\rho)/B$$

If $B=1$, then the above distribution reduces to the classical solution for a space-limited M/M/1 queue, but with $B>1$ the arrival process is not Poisson and the probability function decays much more slowly with increasing argument. As one would expect, the loss rate in the clustered case is much higher than with ordinary Poisson arrival. Let $L(k)$ denote the expected number of packets lost in an arriving message, given that k packets are in the queue just ahead of the arrival. Then

$$L(k) = \sum_{i=N-k}^{\infty} (i-N+k) \, \text{Pr[i in message]}$$

$$= B(1-1/B)^{N-k} \tag{1}$$

after manipulation. Multiplying $L(k)$ by $P(k)$ and summing, we obtain the unconditional expected number of rejected packets per message. Dividing by B, the mean number of packets per message, we finally obtain:

$$\text{Pr[arriving packet lost]} = P(N)(B-1+\rho)/\rho$$

after manipulation. (This is the probability that an arbitrary packet is lost; several losses within a single message are possible so the loss probability exceeds $P(N)$ for $B>1$.)

This type of queue is a reasonable model for packet queueing at the <u>originating node</u> of a path*. We assume packets at a source are likely to be highly clustered; for example, when transferring a file the entire file is likely to be transmitted almost at once as a series of packets. The server corresponds to a physical line between nodes in

----

*In this case, however, packet "losses" may be treated differently, since packets may not actually become lost at the originating node. But the buffer here may still fill up, reducing the transmission rate as if some packets were lost.

the computer network, and serves packets at a rate equal to the transmission speed of the modeled line. The exponential service assumption may be interpreted to mean that packet lengths (hence their transmission times) are variable, although they each occupy a single fixed-size buffer at the host. (We make no claim that the exponential distribution is a realistic description of packet lengths.)

But this model is not valid for intermediate nodes in a path through the network, because the packets will be less clustered at the input to such nodes. If the output of the queue of this section were bulk Poisson, we could simply string together an open network of such queues and obtain an exact solution. But packets do not exit the queue simultaneously; they are separated by at least a packet serving interval of mean p/μ. If the server is nearly saturated, the output will be nearly Poisson. Furthermore, if packets of more than one path share a given physical line, the output of that line for a particular path will be even less clustered due to the intermingling of packet types. We shall describe a procedure for modeling this de-clustering of packets after formulating a means of building computer network models out of the queues of this section.

NETWORK MODEL

Let there be a number of finite length queues and their physical line servers connected together in some specified fixed manner. All lines are unidirectional (simplex); a full-duplex line is effected by two parallel, but opposite, lines and their queues. One or more open (infinite-source) virtual circuits (packet transmission paths) exist in the network, where a virtual circuit is specified by giving its sequence of physical lines. Each such line will be termed a hop. The routing of the ith virtual circuit will be given as the sequence of lines and queues $h(i,1), h(i,2), \ldots$ We shall assume here that each virtual circuit has a single path, but this is easily generalized to multiple parallel paths. Messages of this circuit are inserted at rate $\lambda(i)$ into the node which is the sending end of line $h(i,1)$. Each message consists initially of an average $B(i,1)$ packets, geometrically distributed, of mean length p each. For the time being, we will assume that all circuits share the same mean packet size.

The nth physical line has speed $\mu(n)$, so that at its jth hop a packet will experience a transmission time $p/\mu(h(i,j))$. The queue for line n has capacity $N(n)$ packets, including the one, if any, in service. We will assume that packet losses affect the length, rather than the rate, of messages, and so will use $B(i,1)$, $B(i,2)$, ... to denote the mean lengths in packets of messages arriving to line queues $h(i,1)$, $h(i,2)$, ..., respectively. As an approximation, we will assume that message lengths remain geometrically distributed throughout. We will assume that a packet does not enqueue --- become ready for transmission over the jth hop --- until it has been completely transmitted over hop j-1. Packets arriving to a full queue are simply discarded, there is no attempt to "backpressure" the preceding node as is often done for congestion control in real networks.

DE-CLUSTERING PROCEDURE

At this point we shall introduce several additional approximations. While it is quite possible to specify a queue with a kind of "semi-clustered" input, for which packets of a given message are separated by at least a packet serving interval of mean $p/\mu(h(i,j-1))$, this would likely have a very complicated solution, particularly with finite waiting room. Instead, we propose the following simple strategy. Each queue is solved two ways --- assuming bulk Poisson arrival, and assuming ordinary Poisson arrival, in each case at the same packet arrival rate. A clustering statistic is developed to characterize the degree of burstiness of the arrival process or processes. This statistic is then used to interpolate between the two solutions. While this may appear a crude technique, it has had acceptable success in our tests (to be described).

To calculate such a clustering statistic, a running estimate of the delay between successive packets in a message is kept for each path. Let $d(i,j)$ denote the estimated mean delay between successive packets of virtual circuit i upon arrival to the jth hop of this circuit. (Specifically, $d(i,j)$ is the mean interval between successive completions of transmission over hop j-1.) By the bulk Poisson arrival assumption, we have $d(i,1)=0$. To calculate $d(i,j+1)$ from $d(i,j)$, we argue as follows: If the line for the jth hop is lightly loaded, then there will be negligible queueing delay and $d(i,j+1)=d(i,j)$. But under heavier load, the output interval will be the time to process each packet $[p/\mu(h(i,j))]$, plus the time to process packets of any other circuits sharing this line which arrived during the interval represented by $d(i,j)$. When performing this computation, the queue for line $h(i,j)$ has been solved, so that $B(i,j+1)$, the successfully arriving mean message length to hop j, is known. Then:

$$d(i,j+1) \simeq \max[d(i,j), (d(i,j)*s(i,j)+p)/ (h(i,j))]$$

where $s(i,j)$ is the total successful arrival rate (in bytes per unit time) to line $h(i,j)$ of all circuits <u>except</u> circuit i.

If we compare $d(i,j)$ with a standard for queue $h(i,j)$, we can decide how clustered is this message stream from the point of view of this queue and server. The obvious standard is the mean packet transmission time over this line. If $d(i,j)<<p/\mu(h(i,j))$, then the packets of a circuit i message arrive (in effect) simultaneously to this queue; if $d(i,j)>>p/\mu(j(i,j))$, there is insignificant clustering as each packet can be processed before the next arrives. Then the clustering statistic is computed as a function $c(p/\mu(h(i,j)), d(i,j))$, where function c has the following properties:

$$c(x,y) = \begin{cases} 0 & \text{if } x<<y \\ 1 & \text{if } x>>y \end{cases}$$

The following function was chosen, with little justification other than xy symmetry (in the case $\gamma=0$) and programming convenience:

$$c(x,y) = .5 + .3183*\arctan(\theta*(x-y)/\min(x,y) - \gamma)$$

for parameters θ and γ, with suitable adjustments if $x=0$ or $y=0$.

To determine good values for the parameters, a series of simulations was performed on the simple two-stage, single virtual circuit network of figure 1. The first queue has infinite capacity whereas the second has capacity 50 packets; this ensures that the only losses will occur in the second queue as determined by the degree of clustering at its input. Speeds of 100, 200, and 400 packets/second were tried for the first line, but the second line had speed 100 packets/second in all cases. (Observe that with a first-line speed of 100 only parameter γ affects the predicted result, but at higher speeds both parameters are significant and the input to the second queue becomes more and more bursty.) Over several input streams representing various loadings and degrees of burstiness, the following parameters yielded acceptable results: $\theta=4$ and $\gamma=3.1$. With these values, we have $c(x,x)\simeq 0.10$, implying that if two equal-speed lines are in series, the second will see (in effect) almost Poisson output from the first*.

Several clustering statistics must be computed for each line queue. Each input stream to a given queue will have a different $d(i,j)$, hence a distinct clustering statistic. To calculate each queue length distribution, we shall assume a single aggregate input process for the queue as an approximation. The aggregate clustering statistic is then a weighted (by packet arrival rate) average of the individual statistics.

SOLUTION PROCEDURE

Unlike conventional solvable open queueing networks, the arrival rate to each queue is not known a priori, because of packet losses, so a different solution procedure must be used. For each virtual circuit, the solution program maintains a <u>frontier</u> f(i), initially equal to 1, such that all queues $h(i,1)...h(i,f(i)-1)$ have been solved. A count of <u>internal</u> (i.e., non-first-hop) <u>inputs</u> is maintained for each queue, and decremented as the inputs are determined one by one. When the count becomes zero, the queue is eligible for solution, and all frontiers of circuits using the queue are incremented by one.

There are network topologies, for example that of figure 2, for which this procedure will fail. Such multi-hop looping topologies, which are analogous to deadlocked processes, have the property that each queue in a certain set has an input which is the output of another member of the set. There is no linear order in which the queues can be solved; in fact, there seems to be no reasonable method of solving such a system other than by successive iteration. Although it appears straightforward to do such iteration, this was not included in the program we describe, as it seems unlikely that such a topology would arise in practice. Since the program can easily count the queues it has solved, and test whether any more are eligible to solve, this "deadlock" is easily detected by the program.

----

*On the other hand, $c(2x,x) \simeq 0.73$, so there can be significant clustering on input to a slow line preceded by a faster one.

When the program determines that a queue, say queue i, is eligible for solution, an aggregate input process is obtained by taking a weighted average of each of the input streams, their mean message lengths and clustering statistics. (The aggregate message rate is the sum of the input rates.) Two queue length distributions are calculated for the finite-length queue, assuming bulk Poisson and ordinary Poisson input, respectively. The aggregate clustering statistic C is employed to determine an interpolated mean queue length:

$$E(q) = E(q|\text{bulk Poisson}) * C + E(q|\text{ordinary Poisson}) * (1-C)$$

which can be used to determine mean waiting times as we will indicate. The calculation of mean output message length $B(i,j+1)$ from mean input message length $B(i,j)$ can then be performed for each individual input circuit via a two-dimensional linear interpolation, assuming all four combinations of clustered/unclustered input stream with clustered/unclustered queue-length distribution. Thus, for example:

$P_{nc,nc}$ = Pr[Poisson arrival rejected from a queue whose distribution is calculated assuming Poisson arrival]
= Pr[N in queue assuming Poisson arrival]

$P_{c,nc}$ = Pr[bulk Poisson arrival rejected from a queue whose distribution is calculated assuming Poisson arrival]

$$= \frac{1}{B}\sum_{k=0}^{N} L(k)\, \Pr[k \text{ in queue under Poisson arrival}]$$

$P_{nc,c}$ = Pr[Poisson arrival rejected from a queue whose distribution is calculated assuming bulk Poisson arrival]
= Pr[N in queue assuming bulk Poisson arrival]

$P_{c,c}$ = Pr[bulk Poisson arrival rejected from a queue whose distribution is calculated assuming bulk Poisson arrival]

$$= \frac{1}{B}\sum_{k=0}^{N} L(k)\, \Pr[k \text{ in queue, bulk Poisson arrival}]$$

where $L(k)$, the expected number of rejected bulk Poisson arrivals given k in the queue, appears in (1). Let $C(i,j)$ and $C(h(i,j))$ denote, respectively, the clustering statistic of the given input stream and the aggregate input clustering statistic. The output mean message length is then approximately:

$$B(i,j+1) \simeq B(i,j)*[1 - P_{c,c}*C(i,j)*C(h(i,j)) - P_{nc,c}*(1-C(i,j))*C(h(i,j))$$
$$- P_{c,nc}*C(i,j)*(1-C(h(i,j))) - P_{nc,nc}*(1-C(i,j))*(1-C(h(i,j)))]$$

There is a potential difficulty: we have required B>1 and it is possible for some $B(i,j)$ to become smaller than one. Actually, it is straightforward to reformulate the foregoing analysis to use the geometric distribution starting at zero:

$$\Pr[k \text{ packets in message}] = (B/(B+1))^{k} /(B+1) , \quad k \geq 0$$

but this would eliminate ordinary Poisson arrival as a special case. Since losses in practical systems should be small, on the order of one per cent or less, and since the above procedure seems (without apparent mathematical basis) to still work even with mean slightly less than one in our experiments, we did not take this latter approach.

Because the several input streams to a queue are aggregated for the purpose of calculating the queue-length distribution, the distribution of the number of a particular virtual circuit in the queue cannot be directly determined. But we can determine $W(i,j)$, the mean waiting time (including service time) of stream i over hop j, by the following argument. Since messages arrive as a Poisson process, the mean number in queue ahead of an arriving message (in the clustered input case) is the number $E(q)$ at a random instant, computed above as a one-dimensional interpolation. Then:

E(number of packets ahead of an arriving packet)
= $E(q)$ + E(packets in this message ahead of a successful arrival)
= $E(q)$ + $.5*[B(i,j+1)-1]$

since B(i,j+1) is the mean number of successful arrivals per message.   Therefore

W(i,j|clustered arrivals) = (E(q) + 1 + .5*[B(i,j+1)-1]) * p/μ (h(i,j))

and similarly for the case of ordinary Poisson arrivals, so that:

W(i,j) = (E(q) + 1 + .5*C(i,j)*[B(i,j+1)-1]) * p/μ (h(i,j)) .

In this way, the model can predict the loss probability and waiting time for each hop of each virtual circuit, and therefore the total circuit loss rate and waiting time.

EXTENSIONS

In this section we shall briefly discuss relaxation of two assumptions made so far --- that there is a single queue (and queue capacity) for all virtual circuits sharing a given physical line, and that all virtual circuits share the same mean packet length.

One alternative buffer allocation scheme which can be handled, perhaps even with improved accuracy, is a complete partitioning strategy in which each virtual circuit has a separate, finite-length buffer for each physical line. Since each queue will then have only a single input stream, no input aggregation is required and this form of inaccuracy is eliminated. But a different kind of approximation then appears necessary, since the single-server line must be allocated as, in effect, multiple servers, one per queue. In the case of queues having an exact product-form solution [1], this can be done quite simply. Consider, for example, a Processor-Sharing server for a queue containing open customers of several classes. Then the distribution of (say) class 1 customers is exactly the same as if class 1 customers only had a private server of rate

$$\mu(1) \left[1 - \sum_{j \neq 1} \lambda(j) \ B(j,1) \ p/\mu(j) \right]$$

where λ(j) and μ(j) are, respectively, the arrival rate of class j customers, and the service rate of class j customers on the original server. This method can be used in our case as well, to create an effective private server for each virtual circuit queue, although here the decomposition must be considered an approximation.

Therefore, either complete sharing or complete partitioning of line buffer space among virtual circuits can be modeled. But it appears very difficult to model limited sharing strategies which fall between these two extremes, or to treat any kind of buffer sharing strategy at the node level.

It would appear possible to use the input aggregation technique to allow a distinct mean packet length for each virtual circuit, and this has been done. We assume in this case that buffer space is allocatable at the character level, so that the queue capacity is given in total stored packet bytes (or an equivalent unit). The chief difficulty was in specification of an aggregate mean packet size; ordinary weighted average (weighted by packet arrival rate) gave poor results, often an order of magnitude error in predicted loss rate. Weighting by character arrival rate, which skews the average toward the larger size packets seems to have performed reasonably well so far, but the results are as yet inconclusive. Since queue lengths in this case need not be multiples of the aggregate packet size, it was decided to specify the queue-length distribution at the byte level. A distribution having the same cumulative as that obtained by assuming all packet sizes are equal to the aggregate value was used for this purpose. (This may be an unnecessary complication.)

VALIDATION

To test the approximations in the model solution, a simulation program which takes the identical input was written. It was therefore very convenient to construct a given modeling case and compare the analytical and simulated results. The simulation reproduced all assumptions of the queueing model, bulk Poisson arrival, exponentially-distributed packet service times, and allocation of buffer space only upon completion of transmission from the previous hop. Several representative four node test cases were tried, with path lengths ranging up to three hops, with good agreement in both total waiting time and end-to-end loss rate for each virtual circuit. Errors ranged as high as about 100 per cent in certain individual loss probabilities or waiting times, but typically tended to be in the vicinity of 10-30 per cent, some of which can be ascribed to simulation error.

A typical validation result appears in figure 3. The line speeds are, respectively, 200, 100, 200, and 100 packets/second, and all line queues have capacity 50 packets. The simulation was run until 100,000 packets succesfully completed transmission. To estimate simulation error, each virtual circuit was modeled as three parallel virtual circuits, each with one-third the transmission rate*. Each simulation result is reported as the average of the three individual results, ± their empirical standard deviation.

The analytical results tended to be less accurate when transmission lines were nearly saturated, typically 30-60 per cent or so error, although the simulations were more suspect in this case. These experiments are for a single mean packet size common to all circuits. Preliminary testing using distinct packet sizes, with packet size aggregation skewed as described above, has thus far given comparable, perhaps not quite as good, agreement with simulation. Further testing of all features is in progress.

DISCUSSION AND CONCLUSIONS

This form of model appears to be a useful tool in the design or configuration of long-haul or certain types of local-area computer networks. While only approximately solved, it directly addresses two of the most significant omissions of conventional, topologically general queueing models of such systems. Bursty traffic, in particular, may yield very different results than Poisson traffic. The solution procedure presented here is very fast --- linear-time in the number of lines and number of virtual circuits.

Nevertheless, the fact that the solution is approximate should be kept in mind, and therefore viewed with some suspicion. The simulator mentioned above has a second useful purpose: to confirm that the method is indeed accurate in any given case. It would be prudent, in particular, to confirm any model prediction by simulation which is to be used as the basis for an actual system design.

ACKNOWLEDGEMENT Madhav Marathe provided many useful comments on this manuscript.

REFERENCES

[1]   Basket, F., Chandy, K.M., Muntz, R.R., and Palacios, F.G. Open, closed, and mixed networks of queues with different classes of customers. J. ACM 22 2 (April 1975)

[2]   Lam, S.S. A new measure for characterizing data traffic. IEEE Trans Commun. COM-26 (Jan. 1978)

[3]   Schwartz, M. Computer-Communication Network Design and Analysis Prentice-Hall, Englewood Cliffs N.J. (1977)

[4]   Schwartz, M. and Saad, S. Analysis of congestion control techniques in computer communication networks. in Flow Control in Computer Networks, Grange and Gien eds., North-Holland, Amsterdam (1979)

----

*This is not as effective as several simulation runs, or a run over several regeneration points, since errors in the three lines are likely correlated. But this method was very quick to implement, requiring only input data modification.

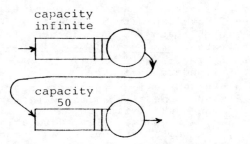

FIGURE 1   Two lines, one virtual circuit

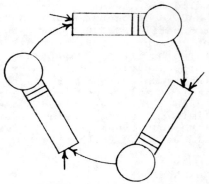

FIGURE 2   "Deadlocked" network. There are three virtual circuits, each beginning at a different queue, and each two hops long.

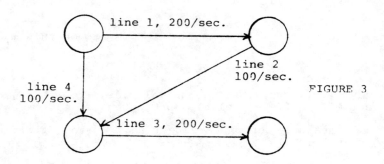

FIGURE 3

VIRTUAL CIRCUITS: circuit 1 uses lines 1,2,3;   rate = 8, B = 4
                   circuit 2 uses lines 1,2;   rate = 5, B = 8
                   circuit 3 uses lines 4,3;   rate = 10, B = 2
                   circuit 4 uses line 3;   rate = 1, B = 20

CIRCUIT	PCT LOSS		WAIT TIME	
	ANALYSIS	SIMULATION	ANALYSIS	SIMULATION
1	0.905	1.69+0.30	.148	.196+.002
2	2.581	2.41+0.28	.161	.210+.005
3	0.0002	0.14+0.08*	.030	.045+.001
4	8.217	10.27+0.82	.054	.088+.004

POISSON EQUIVALENT

1	0.0003		.066	
2	0.0003		.058	
3	0.0000		.022	
4	0.0000		.009	

----

*Doubtful significance

SESSION 3: LOAD BALANCING AND ROUTING

Chair: David A. Ault
The MITRE Corporation
McLean, VA

PASSAGE TIMES IN COMPUTER COMMUNICATION NETWORKS WITH NON-DETERMINISTIC ROUTING

L. Donatiello, G. Iazeolla, S. Tucci*

Department of Computer Science
University of Pisa
Corso Italia, 40
56100–Pisa
Italy

Abstract

Passage times are the times for a job or a message to traverse a portion of the network. Networks with dynamic routing can be modeled by the use of mathematical models based on the theory of queueing networks. This theory allows the derivation of performance indices for certain passage times called response times (or the times for a job to traverse the _entire_ network). This is generally unsatisfactory for multistation system architectures, where analysts are required to evaluate the time to communicate from a given node to any other node, in _a_ portion of the network. This paper deals with the mathematical derivation of the mean passage time in general queueing networks and introduces a straight-forward solution to this problem.

1. Introduction

Local or geographically distributed multistation system architectures require the analyst be able to evaluate the time to communicate from a given node i to any other node j of the system. For any pair of nodes (i, j) the _first_ _passage_ _time_ from i to j (denoted t_{ij}) can be defined as the elapsed interval from the time a job (or a message) arrives at node i to the time it arrives at node j for the first time.

Certain passage times (e.g., the time from node i to itself in closed networks, or the time from node i to the sink node in open ones) are interpreted in computer system models as _response_ _times_.

Multistation system architectures require knowledge of both passage and response times. The importance of passage times evaluation in computer/communication networks has been discussed in several papers [CHOW 78, IGLE 78, YU 77]. The mathematical derivation of the distribution of passage times has interested several authors but no general practicable results have been obtained. Namely, the proposed derivations either lead to very cumbersome complexities [YU 77] or stick to very specific models [CHOW 78]. For this reason the interests of some researchers have turned to discovering reliable evaluation techniques based on the use of simulation models [IGLE 78]. On the mathematical front, computation of the mean _response_ time is a generally known procedure in open and closed networks. It is done by use of Little's Theorem in the so called General Response Time Law (GRTL) [DENN 78]. The extension of this law to the computation of mean _passage_ times in open networks

* At present he is visiting IBM T. J. Watson Research Center, Yorktown Heights, NY.

is generally unfeasible. Namely, the extension is impossible whenever jobs may encounter a sink node on the path from node i to node j. This will be proved in the paper and an alternate procedure will then be suggested.

Let us consider the computer/communication network illustrated in Figure 1. Each node represents either a hardware piece with processing and storage capabilities (computer, minicomputer, intelligent terminal, etc.) or a piece with transmission capabilities (channel). Nodes of the first type are denoted by letters (h through *l*) in the figure, while nodes of the second type are numbered (1 through 4). Users of the computer network may originate, at each node, transactions of different types: e.g., they may require to perform queries or update transactions against a data-base that is stored at any of a designated set of nodes, or they may require to transmit a message to users residing at different nodes, or first to update and then send a message, etc. A known volume of transactions will be assumed to enter some nodes (this is modeled by the arrival source in the Figure 1).

Some other nodes are assumed to permit exit of messages (the sink nodes). Knowledge of average passage times in this example provides a means to evaluate the execution of the system transactions.

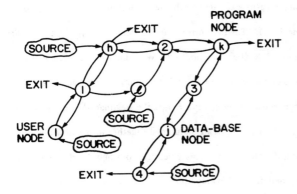

Figure 1: Example of Computer/Communication Network

A query transaction, for example, originated at node i, may require to read information from the data-base copy residing at node j by the use of the program copy residing at node k (Figure 2).

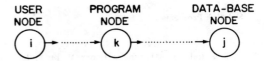

Figure 2: Query Processing

For this transaction then there will be a flow of data from node i to k, from k to j, from j back to k, and from k back to i, respectively in order 1) to wake up the program residing in k 2) to access to the data-base residing in j 3) to transfer data to the program, and 4) to give the answer back to the user.

From our abstraction-level point of view, this process can be modeled by a service request (job) entering node i from the arrival source and first requiring to be destined to node k; once in k, it requires to be destined to node j and, then, from j back to k and from k back to node i. The request from i to k (and similarly for the others) does not follow a predetermined path from the source to the destination node, but is dynamically routed according to convenience, channel availability or error resuming criteria (the case of feed-back loops) as modeled by the probabilistic branching matrix of the network. The four associated services will be rendered to the job, 1) the first time it hits node k starting from i; 2) the first time it hits node j starting from k; 3) the first time it hits node k starting from j; 4) the first time it hits node i starting from k. The average time to complete the query transaction is thus given by the sum of the respective average passage times, namely $E(t_{ik}) + E(t_{kj}) + E(t_{jk}) + E(t_{ki})$, each one of which is computed according to relations we shall give in the paper. Note that if nodes 1, h, k, 4 of the network did not allow for exit routes then the derivation of the four passage times above would have been possible by use of the classical General Response Time Law. It is exactly the existence of possible outflow routes that makes the derivation of point-to-point transaction times a non-trivial task in computer/communication networks with stochastic routing.

2. Solution Problems

Let an N node BCMP type network W be given and let $E(t_k)$ denote the average sojourn time (waiting plus service) jobs experience at node k. This time can be computed according to conventional procedures [REIS 78, REIS 80]. Let $R = ||r_{hk}||$ h, k = 0,1,...,N be the network branching matrix, r_{hk} denoting the probability for a job or message leaving the node h to join node k. Node h = 0 denotes the sink node, i.e., the environment customers enter when departing from the network and from which they never come out ($r_{00} = 1$, $r_{h0} = 1 - \sum_{k=1}^{N} r_{hk}$). The stochastic nature of the network branching matrix implies that jobs do not follow a predetermined path from the source to the destination node. In addition, feedback loops are admitted, so that some nodes (including the source) may be visited more than once before reaching the destination node. Therefore, algorithms available for the evaluation of passage times for the case of static or fixed routing, or for the case of feedforward networks, cannot be extended to our case.

BCMP type queueing networks can be solved for single or multiple class jobs circulating in the network. The addition of the multiclass feature does not help in the solution of our problem as discussed in the text. For the sake of conciseness the discussion will thus be limited to single class BCMP networks. Extension to the multiclass case is straightforward.

The branching matrix R of W can be seen as the one-step transition matrix of a Markov chain X with state space E = { 0,1,...,N}, state 0 being an absorbing state. Let us follow an individual job J during its journey through the network. We can say that whenever job J is in node i of network W then the stochastic process is in state i of chain X. When W is an open network then the chain X has one absorbing state (state 0), while states 1,2,...N are transient states.

Let i and k denote two transient states and define the matrix

$$V = ||V(i,k)|| \quad i,k = 1,...,N \tag{1}$$

V(i,k) denoting the expected number of visits the stochastic process X makes to state k starting at state i before joining the absorbing state. Then according to [CINL 75]

$$V = (I - Q)^{-1} \tag{2}$$

where I is the identity matrix and Q is the matrix obtained from R by deleting the row and the column corresponding to the absorbing state. By the similarity of network W and process X from a flow-point of view, one can then say that the network mean response time starting at node i (i.e., the elapsed interval from the time a job arrives to i, to the time it arrives to the sink node 0) is given [GELE 80] by:

$$E(t_{i0}) = \sum_{k=1}^{N} V(i,k) \ E(t_k) \tag{3}$$

Relation (3), holding for the evaluation of the expected response time, is easily extended to the derivation of the expected passage time $E(t_{ij})$. To this purpose, let us denote by $\{j_i, j_2, ..., j_p\}$ the states of X (i.e., the nodes of W) which can be reached only through j. According to the definition of passage time t_{ij}, for the purpose of evaluating $E(t_{ij})$, the destination state j and the states $\{j_i, j_2, ..., j_p\}$ can be lumped together into a new absorbing state, denoted by A. This gives rise to a new Markov chain X_1, obtained from X by combining states $\{j, j_i, j_2 ..., j_p\}$ into the unique state A.

In the simplest case, let us assume that the original absorbing state 0 is included in the set $\{j_1, j_2, ..., j_p\}$. In this case let us denote by $E_1 = E - \{j, j_1, j_2, ..., j_p\} + \{A\} \triangleq \{A, 1, 2, ..., N'\}$, $N' \leq N$, the state space of chain X_1, where $\{1, 2, ..., N'\}$ denotes the set of states of X which survived in X_1. By an easy extension of (3) one can then say that

$$E(t_{ij}) = E(t_{iA}) = \sum_{k=1}^{N'} V_1(i,k) \, E(t_k) \qquad (4)$$

where $V_1 = (I-Q_1)^{-1}$ and matrix Q_1 is obtained from R by deleting the rows and the columns corresponding to nodes $\{j, j_1, j_2, ..., j_p\}$, as in Figure 3.

In the general case, unfortunately, the sink node is not included in the set $\{j_1, j_2, ..., j_p\}$. Let us then denote by X_2 new Markov chain obtained from X by combining states $\{j, j_1, ..., j_p\}$ into the unique state A. The state space of X_2 becomes:

$$E_2 = E - \{j, j_1, j_2, ..., j_p\} + \{A\} =$$
$$= \{A, 0, 1, 2, ..., N'\} \; N' \leq N$$

Where $\{0, ..., N'\}$ are the states of X which survived in X_2 and A is the absorbing state that lumps together states $\{j, j_1, j_2, ..., j_p\}$ of X. In this case, there are, then, two absorbing states (0 and A). Let Q_2 be the matrix obtained from R by deleting the rows and the columns corresponding to state 0 and to states $\{j, j_1, j_2, ..., j_p\}$, as in Figure 4.

The entries $V_2(i,k)$ of matrix $V_2 = (I - Q_2)^{-1}$ will give the expected number of visits to k, starting at i, before reaching either 0 or A. Therefore by application of (3) now one obtains

$$E(t_{i,0A}) = \sum_{k=1}^{N'} V_2(i,k) \, E(t_k) \qquad (5)$$

which gives the average time to get from node i to any one of the absorbing nodes, 0 or A. This time, in other words, is the weighted mean between the time $E(t_{i,0})$ and the time $E(t_{i,A})$.

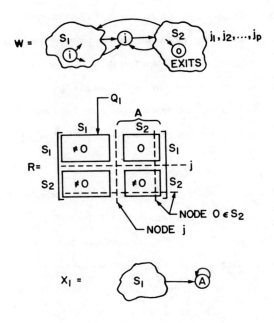

Figure 3: Solution Procedure for the Simplest Case

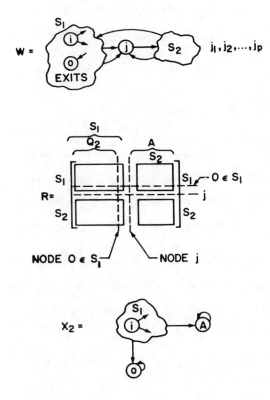

Figure 4: Solution Procedure for the General Case

The question is: how can the time $E(t_{i,A})$ be computed separately? Indeed, this time is the average passage time $E(t_{ij})$ we are looking for. The answer is that this separation is not immediate, since within each term $V_2(i,k)$ in (5) there appear two contributing terms: namely, there appear both the average number of visits to k before reaching state 0 and that before reaching state A.

This observation leads to a more general conclusion. Relation (3) is nothing else than the GRTL [DENN 78], provided one replaces terms $V(i,k)$ by the node visit ratios X_k/X_i introduced in [DENN 78], or the job flow through node k relative to the job flow through node i. But, according to (2), the terms $V(i,k)$ are trivial functions of the network branching matrix R (as are the visit ratios) and therefore cannot take into account the different contributions given by jobs exiting at 0 and by those exiting at A. In other words, some more algebra has to be applied to R in order to find the percentage of jobs that, starting at node i, are absorbed by the sink node 0, before reaching the destination node j*. This is the scope of the next section.

3. Solution Procedure

Let X_2 denote the Markov chain obtained from network W according to the procedures described above. In the following we shall denote by i the starting state of the Markov chain walk, by j the final absorbing state (j≡A), by k any intermediate transient state, and by 0 the intermediate absorbing state of X_2.

Let us denote by $F(i,k)$ the conditional probability that, starting at i, the Markov chain X_2 _ever_ visits k (i.e., conditional that neither state 0 nor state A are entered before). It is easy to see [CINL 75, DONA 81] that:

$$F(i,k) = r_{ik} + \sum_{b \in E_2 - \{k\}} r_{ib} F(b,k) \quad i,k \in E_2 \quad (6)$$

and that various elements are computed as follows:

$$F(h,h) = 1 - \frac{1}{V_2(h,h)}$$

$$F(h,k) = \frac{V_2(h,k)}{V_2(k,k)} \quad \text{for } h,k \neq 0,A, h \neq k \quad (7)$$

$$F(h,0) = \sum_{i=1}^{N'} V_2(h,i) r_{i0}$$

$$F(h,A) = \sum_{i=1}^{N'} V_2(h,i) r_{iA} \quad (8)$$

where $V_2(h,k)$ are the elements of matrix $(I - Q_2)^{-1}$, and $r_{i0} = 1 - \sum_{k=1}^{N'} r_k$ and $r_{iA} = r_{ij}$.

It now remains to separate $V_2(h,k)$ into two components $V_2^0(h,k)$ and $V_2^A(h,k)$ where $V_2^0(h,k)$ is the expected number of times that, starting from state h, the Markov chain X_2 visits state k before being absorbed by state 0. $V_2^A(h,k)$ has a corresponding definition. Note:

$$V_2(h,k) = V_2^0(h,k) F(h,0) + V_2^A(h,k) F(h,A).$$

Definition (6) does not exclude that the chain X_2, starting at state i, visits the same state i more than once before reaching state k.

Another possibility for X_2 is that starting at i and after m steps, it is absorbed by either state 0 or state A before any return to state i. Let us denote by $H_m(i,u)$, where $u = \{0,A\}$, this probability. Then:

$$H_m(i,u) = \begin{cases} r_{i0} + r_{iA} & \text{for } m = 1 \\ \sum_{b \in E_2 - \{i,0,A\}} r_{ib} H_{m-1}(b,u) & \text{for } m \geq 2 \end{cases} \quad (9)$$

For the pair (i,u) we can define:

$$H(i,u) = \sum_{m=1}^{\infty} H_m(i,u) \quad (10)$$

---

* The separation of the weighted means above by introducing fictitious job classes of the BCMP type is not even possible. Indeed, by their own definition, the BCMP job classes do not allow knowing in advance what percentage of jobs will certainly join the destination node j without being before absorbed by sink nodes.

According to (6), F(k,k) denotes the probability that, starting at k, the Markov chain even returns to k. It is then easy to demonstrate that the following relationships hold for the F and the H:

$$F(k,0) + F(k,A) = 1 \qquad (11)$$

$$H(k,0) + H(k,A) = 1-F(k,k) \qquad (12)$$

$$H(k,0) = F(k,0)(1-F(k,k)) \qquad (13)$$

$$H(k,A) = F(k,A)(1-F(k,k)) \qquad (14)$$

Let us denote by N_k the total number of visits to state k and by P_{iA} ($N_k = n$) the probability that, starting from i, state k is visited n times given the process X_2 is absorbed by state A. Then one can write:

$$
\begin{aligned}
P_{iA} (N_k = n) &= \\
&= \frac{\text{Prob } \{i \rightarrow k, \text{ then } k \rightarrow k \quad n-1 \text{ times and } k \rightarrow A \text{ directly}\}}{\text{Prob } \{i \rightarrow A\}} \qquad (15)
\end{aligned}
$$

$$= \frac{F(i,k) \ F(k,k)^{n-1} \ H(k,A)}{F(i,A)}$$

The average number of visits to state k for the process starting at i and exiting at A, will then be:

$$
\begin{aligned}
E_{iA}(N_k) &= \sum_{n=1}^{\infty} n P_{iA} (N_k = n) = \\
& \qquad\qquad\qquad\qquad (16) \\
&\quad \frac{1}{(1-F(k,k))^2} \ \frac{F(i,k) \ H(k,A)}{F(i,A)}
\end{aligned}
$$

On the other hand, by definition is

$$V_2^A(i,k) = E_{iA}(N_k)$$

and then, by refining (16) according to (7) and (14) we can write

$$V_2^A(i,k) = V_2(i,k) \ \frac{F(k,A)}{F(i,A)} \qquad (17)$$

This quantity is the contributing term to the average number of visits $V_2(i,k)$ in case the process exits at state A. (By introduc-

ing the probability P_{i0} ($N_k = n$) in place of (15), and then proceeding similarly, on might obtain the remaining contributing term $V_2^0(i,k)$ which, however, is not of direct interest in this work). Quantities F(k,A) and F(i,A) in formula (17) are computed according to (8).

By refining equation (5) we thus obtain

$$E(t_{ij}) = \sum_{k=1}^{N'} V_2^A(i,k) E(t_k) \qquad (18)$$

which solves our problem.

4.   **Solution Example**

We shall now apply the theory above for the computation of the four passage times, $E(t_{ik})$ through $E(t_{ki})$, mentioned in the example in Figure 1. For the sake of conciseness we shall show the complete derivation of $E(t_{ik})$, while giving only final results for the remaining three times.

We assume the following data hold for the Figure 1 example:

Source input rates = 0.5   (poissonian)

Node service rates = 10   (FIFO exponential)

Branching matrix R, as in Figure 5b).

by application of conventional procedures we first derive the node sojourn times, obtaining:

$$E(t_i) = 0.141; \ E(t_1) = 0.141; \ E(t_h) = 0.204;$$

$$E(t_2) = 0.395; \ E(t_l) = 0.116; \ E(t_k) = 0.414;$$

$$E(t_3) = 0.435; \ E(t_j) = 0.459; \ E(t_4) = 0.179$$

Next we define the state A, lumping together states corresponding to nodes K, j, 3, 4 of the original network, this obtaining the Markov chain X_2 shown in Figure 5a). The average number of visits the chain X_2 makes to its own states is given by matrix V_2 derived in Figure 5c) according to relation $V_2 = (I-Q_2)^{-1}$, where Q_2 is part of matrix R as shown by Figure 5b).

35

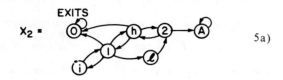

5a)

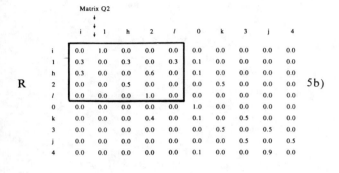

Matrix Q2

	i	1	h	2	l	0	k	3	j	4
i	0.0	1.0	0.0	0.0	0.0	0.0	0.0	0.0	0.0	0.0
1	0.3	0.0	0.3	0.0	0.3	0.1	0.0	0.0	0.0	0.0
h	0.3	0.0	0.0	0.6	0.0	0.1	0.0	0.0	0.0	0.0
2	0.0	0.0	0.5	0.0	0.0	0.0	0.5	0.0	0.0	0.0
l	0.0	0.0	0.0	1.0	0.0	0.0	0.0	0.0	0.0	0.0
0	0.0	0.0	0.0	0.0	0.0	1.0	0.0	0.0	0.0	0.0
k	0.0	0.0	0.0	0.4	0.0	0.1	0.0	0.5	0.0	0.0
3	0.0	0.0	0.0	0.0	0.0	0.0	0.5	0.0	0.5	0.0
j	0.0	0.0	0.0	0.0	0.0	0.0	0.0	0.5	0.0	0.5
4	0.0	0.0	0.0	0.0	0.0	0.1	0.0	0.0	0.9	0.0

R ... 5b)

	i	1	h	2	l
i	1.97183	1.97183	1.26760	1.35211	0.59155
1	0.97183	1.97183	1.26760	1.35211	0.59155
h	0.84507	0.84507	1.97183	1.43662	0.25352
2	0.42253	0.42254	0.98591	1.71831	0.12676
l	0.42253	0.42254	0.98591	1.71831	1.12676

V_2 ... 5c)

Figure 5: Solution Example for the Computation

of Passage Time $E(t_{ik})$ from Figure 1.

We now apply the (8) to obtain

$$F(i,A) = \sum_{s=1}^{N'} V_2(i,s)\, r_{sA} =$$
$$= V_2(i,i)\, r_{iA} + V_2(i,1) r_{1A} + V_2(i,h) r_{hA} +$$
$$+ V_2(i,r)\, r_{2A} + V_2(i,l) r_{lA} = V_2(i,2) r_{2A} = 0.676$$

and similarly, be denoting w any intermediate state in X_2

$$F(w,A) = \sum_{s=1}^{N'} V_2(w,s) r_{sA} = V_2(w,2) r_{2A}$$

namely, for w=1, h, 2, l.

$$F(1,A) = 0.676, \quad F(h,A) = 0.718,$$
$$F(2,A) = 0.860, \quad F(l,A) = 0.860$$

By application of (17) and (18) we finally obtain

$$E(t_{ik}) = \sum_{s=1}^{N'} V_2^A(i,s)\ (E(t_s) = V_2^A(i,l)E(t_l) +$$
$$V_2^A(i,1)E(t_1) + V_2^A(i,h)\ E(t_h) +$$
$$V_2^A(i,2)\ E(t_2) + V_2^A(i,l)\ E(t_l) = 1.596$$

which gives the first of the passage times we were looking for.

By similar reasoning, one can derive the remaining passage times $E(t_{kj})$, $E(t_{jk})$, $E(t_{ki})$ obtaining $E(t_{kj}) = 2.594$, $E(t_{jk}) = 2.596$, $E(t_{ki}) = 7.615$. The total query transaction time in the example in Figure 1 thus amounts to

$$E(t_{ik}) + E(t_{kj}) + E(t_{jk}) + E(t_{ki}) = 14.401$$

and this ends the example.

Acknowledgements

The authors would like to thank Ms. Patricia Carvalho for preparing the camera-ready copy of the paper. They are also grateful for the many constructive suggestions given by the anonymous referees.

5.   **References**

[CINL 75]   Cinlar, E. "Introduction to Stochastic Processes" Prentice Hall, 1975.

[CHOW 78]   Chow, W-M. "The Cycle Time Distribution of Exponential Central Server Model" AFIPS Conf. Proc. 43 (1978 NCC).

[DENN 78]   Denning P.J., Buzen J. P. "The Operational Analysis of Queueing Network Models" Comp. Surv. 10, 3 (Sept., 1978).

[DONA 81]   Donatiello L., Iazeolla G., Tucci, S. "Passage Times in Queueing Networks," Computer Performance Vol. 2, No. 4, Dec. 1981.

[IGLE 78]   Iglehart D. L., Shedler, G. S., "Regenerative Simulation of Response Times in Networks of Queues" J. ACM 25, 3 (July 78).

[GELE 80]   Gelenbe E., Mitrani, I., "Analysis and Synthesis of Computer Systems," Academic Press 1980, pp. 84-85.

[REIS 78]   Reiser, M., Sauer, C. H. "Queueing Network Models: Methods of Solution and their Program Implementation" Current Trends in Programming Methodology, Vol. III K. Mani Chandy, R. T. Yeh Ed., Prentice Hall, 1978.

[REIS 80]   Reiser, M., Lavenberg, S. S.   "Mean Value Analysis of Closed Multichain Queueing Networks" J. ACM 27, 2 (April 80).

[YU 77]   Yu, P.S., "Passage Time Distributions for a Class of Queueing Networks: Closed, Open or Mixed, with Different Classes of Customers, with Application to Computer System Modeling" SEL-77-017, Stanford Electronics Laboratories, Stanford, CA (March 77).

OPTIMAL ROUTING IN NETWORKS WITH FLOW-CONTROLLED VIRTUAL CHANNELS*

Simon S. Lam   and   Y. Luke Lien

Department of Computer Sciences   IBM T. J. Watson Research Center
University of Texas at Austin   Yorktown Heights, New York 10598
Austin, Texas 78712

Abstract

Packet switching networks with flow-controlled virtual channels are naturally modeled as queueing networks with closed chains. Available network design and analysis techniques, however, are mostly based upon an open-chain queueing network model. In this paper, we first examine the traffic conditions under which an open-chain model accurately predicts the mean end-to-end delays of a closed-chain model having the same chain throughputs. We next consider the problem of optimally routing a small amount of incremental traffic corresponding to the addition of a new virtual channel (with a window size of one) to a network. We model the new virtual channel as a closed chain. Existing flows in the network are modeled as open chains. An optimal routing algorithm is then presented. The algorithm solves a constrained optimization problem that is a compromise between problems of unconstrained individual-optimization and unconstrained network-optimization.

1. INTRODUCTION

The early store-and-forward packet switching networks are mostly datagram networks. In these networks, each packet carries its own source-destination addresses. It is treated as an independent entity with regard to its acceptance into the network and subsequent movement through the network. The current generation of packet switching networks, however, are mostly virtual channel networks [ROBE 78]. In these networks, packets are associated with logical source-destination connections called virtual (or logical) channels. Each packet is identified by its virtual channel ID. Among other attributes, virtual channels are individually end-to-end flow-controlled. Examples of flow controls are SNA pacing [IBM 75], RFNM in ARPANET [OPDE 74] and various window mechanisms

[POUZ 73, CERF 74]. All of them work by limiting the number of packets that a virtual channel can have in transit within the network. (This number will be referred to as the virtual channel window size.) An important function of end-to-end flow controls is the synchronization of the data source input rate to the data sink acceptance rate. They also provide, to some extent, a form of congestion control capability for the network.

We will not dwell upon the details and relative merits of datagram and virtual channel networks [ROBE 78]. Our main interest here is on models for network performance analysis and design. Datagram networks are naturally modeled as open-chain queueing networks given the independence assumption of Kleinrock [KLEI 64]. Such a model forms the basis of extensive studies on the design and analysis of store-and-forward packet switching networks [KLEI 64, KLEI 76, GERL 77, SCHW 77, GALL 77].

Packet switching networks with flow-controlled virtual channels, on the other hand, are naturally modeled as queueing networks with closed routing chains [BASK 75]; each closed chain represents a flow-controlled virtual channel and the chain population size is equal to the virtual channel window size [REIS 79, LAM 82]. In practice, virtual channel networks are becoming the dominant form of networks. However, available tools for network analysis and design are still mainly based upon open-chain queueing network models. A serious drawback of closed-chain models is the large computational time and space needed to calculate network performance measures (chain throughputs and mean end-to-end delays). Some progress has been made recently to reduce these computational requirements and the solution of networks with many virtual channels is feasible [LAM 81a, LAM 81b]. Nevertheless, the computational requirements remain substantially more than those of open-chain models.

We propose an approach to incorporate the behavior of flow-controlled virtual channels in network design and optimization tools using a combination of both closed-chain and open-chain models. A closed-chain model is first solved to provide chain throughputs and mean end-to-end delays. Given chain throughputs, an open-chain model is then employed for a sequence of intermediate optimization steps (such as, for example, the routing of incremental flows to be considered later on in this paper). To avoid the accumulation of errors, the closed-chain model is applied at

* This work was supported by National Science Foundation Grant No. ECS78-01803.

various checkpoints of the optimization procedure to re-calculate chain throughputs and mean delays.

Two related problems are investigated in this paper. First, we examine the traffic conditions under which an open-chain model accurately predicts the mean end-to-end delays of a closed-chain model having the same chain throughputs. We found that in general the approximation is fairly accurate when communication channels in the network are not heavily utilized. Second, we consider the problem of optimally routing a small amount of incremental traffic corresponding to the addition of a new virtual channel (with a window size of one) to a network. We model the new virtual channel as a closed chain. Existing flows, on the other hand, are modeled as open chains. An optimal routing algorithm to solve a constrained optimization problem is presented.

Our optimization problem is similar to the classical flow deviation problem [FRAT 73, GERL 73, KLEI 76, GALL 77] in that the objective is to minimize the impact of a small amount of incremental flow on the mean transit delay of all packets in the network. But unlike flow deviation the incremental flow in our model is not infinitesimal, and our optimization is constrained by a bound on the mean end-to-end delay of the new virtual channel.

The balance of this paper is organized as follows. In Section 2, open-chain and closed-chain queueing network models are described. The accuracy of approximating a closed-chain model by an open-chain model is then examined. In Section 3, the optimal routing problem is formulated. In Section 4, an optimal routing algorithm is presented.

2. OPEN-CHAIN AND CLOSED-CHAIN MODELS

In a packet switching network, communication channels and nodal processors can be modeled as FIFO queues with exponentially distributed service times given the independence assumption of Kleinrock [KLEI 64]. We shall assume that the packet switching network has sufficient buffers so that blocking due to buffer overflow has negligible probability. (The problem of buffer requirements and loss probabilities have been considered in [LAM 76].)

Suppose that there are K uni-directional virtual channels between pairs of nodes. Packets in the same virtual channel follow a fixed route (which may be chosen probabilistically from a finite set of routes between source and sink).

Open-chain model

A model in which each virtual channel is represented as an open chain assumes that the external packet arrivals to the source node of a virtual channel constitute a Poisson process at a known constant rate. (An open-chain model also assumes that the number of packets belonging to a virtual channel that are travelling within the network is not limited.) Let the rate of all packet arrivals to server m be λ_m packets/second. The work rate of server m is C_m bits/second and the average length of a packet is $1/\mu$ bits. The traffic intensity of server m is defined to be $\rho_m = \lambda_m/(\mu C_m)$. Given that $\rho_m < 1$ for all m, the throughput of each virtual channel is the same as its external input rate and the mean end-to-end delay of its packets is the sum of mean delays of the servers along its route. The mean delay of server m is given by the M/M/1 mean delay formula and is equal to $1/(\mu C_m - \lambda_m)$. Thus, both the throughputs and mean end-to-end delays of virtual channels can be obtained very easily for an open-chain model.

Closed-chain model

The flow-control window size of a virtual channel limits the maximum number of packets that it can have in transit within the communication network at the same time. Let there be K virtual channels and N_k denote the window size of virtual channel k, for k = 1,2,...,K. We model the handling of external arrivals before they are admitted into the network by an additional FIFO server that works at a rate of γ_k packets/second. (See Figure 1.) If the number of packets in transit within a virtual channel is equal to its window size, then the source server is "blocked." A blocked source server is later unblocked when an end-to-end acknowledgment returns from the sink indicating receipt of a packet. It is assumed that the queue of external arrivals waiting to enter the network is never empty. Thus, the actual input rate of virtual channel k is determined by γ_k and the fraction of time its source server is unblocked.

The blocking behavior is naturally modeled in a queueing network by a closed chain with a fixed number of circulating customers. Each customer corresponds to an "access token." Initially, N_k tokens are placed at the source server of virtual channel k. Each packet admitted into the network carries a token with it. When there is no more token at the source server, it is blocked. A packet arriving at the sink node of the virtual channel releases its token which is then carried back by the end-to-end acknowledgment to the source server to be reused again. Thus, the N_k circulating tokens of a virtual channel correspond to N_k circulating customers of a closed chain.

We model the delay incurred by the return of an end-to-end acknowledgment from the sink to the source by an infinite-server (IS) service center [REIS 79, LAM 82]; the distribution of such random delays may be different for different virtual channels. It is not really important to model the route of the acknowledgments explicitly because these acknowledgements typically either are piggybacked in data packets, or if sent separately, are very short. Thus, they consume relatively small amounts of buffer and channel resources in the network, which may be accounted for separately in a straightforward manner.

To solve for the performance measures (virtual channel throughputs and mean end-to-end delays) of a closed-chain model, the computational time and space requirements of both the (sequential) convolution algorithm [REIS 75] and the MVA algorithm [REIS 80] grow exponentially with K; specifically, they are proportional to $\prod_{k=1}^{K} (N_k+1)$. These requirements are thus beyond the limits of present computers when network models with 10 or more virtual channels are considered.

The tree convolution algorithm, developed by these authors [LAM 81a, LAM 81b], is intended for the solution of networks in which chains do not visit all servers in the network. In models of communication networks and distributed systems, it is often true that chains visit only a small fraction of all queues in the network (sparseness property). Furthermore, chains are often clustered in certain parts of the network and their routes are constrained by the network topology (locality property). By making use of the routing information of chains, the time and space requirements of the tree convolution algorithm can be made substantially less than those of the (sequential) convolution and MVA algorithms. The number of closed chains that can be handled varies depending upon the extent of sparseness and locality present in their routes. We have solved numerically many network examples with 32-50 routing chains. In some extreme cases, the solution of networks with up to 100 routing chains has been found to be possible [LIEN 81].

Network design using both open-chain and closed-chain models

The large computational requirements of closed-chain models make them unattractive for use in network design procedures. Both Pennotti and Schwartz [PENN 75] and Gerla and Nilsson [GERL 80] suggested the use of open chains to approximately model flow-controlled virtual channels. The difficulty encountered is that the throughputs of the flow-controlled virtual channels needed as input parameters of an open-chain model are not known. We propose to use a combination of both open-chain and closed-chain models in design procedures for networks with flow-controlled virtual channels. A closed-chain model is first employed and chain throughputs and mean delays are computed exactly using the tree convolution algorithm. An open-chain model with the same chain throughputs is then employed for a sequence of intermediate optimization steps in the network design procedure (e.g., the routing of incremental flows to be studied below). To avoid the accumulation of errors, the closed-chain model is employed at various checkpoints of the design procedure to recompute chain throughputs and mean delays.

Traffic conditions under which an open-chain model is applicable

With the tree convolution algorithm we can solve models with many closed chains. Suppose that the throughputs of flow-controlled virtual channels in a network are first computed using a closed-chain model and an open-chain model with the same throughputs is specified. The mean end-to-end delays predicted by the open-chain model can then be compared with those given by the closed-chain model. The results of such a comparative study for a network example with 64 communication channels and 32 virtual channels are next presented.

In the network example, the source server work-rate is assumed to be $\gamma = 1$ packet/second for all chains. The service rate of each communication channel is assumed to be $\mu C = 10$ packets/second. The mean end-to-end acknowledgment delay for virtual channel k is assumed to be $h_k/\mu C$, where h_k is the number of communication channels in the route of virtual channel k. The virtual channel window size is $N_k = 3$ for all k. The average utilization of the 64 communication channels is 0.185, with a maximum utilization of 0.281 and a minimum utilization of 0.082 and a standard deviation of 0.066. Table 1 shows the throughputs, mean delays and delay estimates of the 32 virtual channels. The mean delays are given by the closed-chain model. The delay estimates are mean delays given by the open-chain model. The percentage errors in the delay estimates are quite small in this case.

We next proceed to investigate the effect of varying the relative source and channel speeds, γ and μC. We vary γ from 10 to 0.5 while keeping μC and all the other parameters constant. The results are shown in Table 2. Note that the channel utilizations are highest at $\gamma = 10$ and lowest at $\gamma = 0.5$. The accuracy of the open-chain model is very poor for $\gamma = 10$ (same value as μC) and improves as γ decreases.

Observe that when $\gamma \ll \mu C$, the source server is the "bottleneck" in each routing chain; thus, it behaves like a Poisson source at rate γ much of the time (i.e., like an open chain). However, when γ approached μC in magnitude, the open-chain model gave very large errors. This behavior may be explained as follows. When γ is almost the same as μC, the bottleneck in each routing chain is at one of the communication channels within the network. Note that when the utilization of an M/M/1 queue is high, its delay distribution has a long tail, which gives rise to a poor estimate of the delay in a closed-chain model where the queue lengths are bounded.

The effect of varying the virtual channel window size was also investigated. Window sizes of 2, 3 and 4 were considered. It was found that as the window size was increased, the accuracy of the open-chain model improved, despite increases in the channel utilizations.

We also considered the effect of routing. In general, we found that the accuracy of the open-chain model suffers from the presence of highly utilized servers within the packet switching network, either due to poor routing or due to a high-level of input traffic (large γ).

It was also found that in almost all cases considered, the delay estimates of the open-chain model were larger than the mean delays of the closed-chain model. There are two possible reasons for the overestimates. First, the delay estimates are obtained from M/M/1 delay distributions that have long tails. Second, the mean-value analysis shows that the mean delay encountered by a closed-chain customer is determined by the mean queue lengths of a network with that customer removed [REIS 80]. The open-chain model as described above does not account for this behavior. A consequence of the overestimation of delays is that the impact of bottlenecks on chain delays in an open-chain model is exaggerated compared to that in a closed-chain model. This means that if an open-chain model is used for the routing of incremental flows (see the following section), bottlenecks will be avoided more "rigorously" than if a closed-chain model is employed.

3. OPTIMAL ROUTING OF INCREMENTAL FLOWS

We consider the problem of introducing a small amount of incremental flow from a source node to a destination node into a network with existing flows. Several optimal routing problems may be formulated depending upon the nature of the incremental flow and the optimization objective. We next review the underlying objectives of ARPANET routing and flow deviation in this context. A new optimal routing problem is then formulated.

The objective of the ARPANET routing algorithm [MCQU 78] is to minimize the (estimated) delay of an individual packet from its source node to its destination node. Let t_m be the (estimated) delay of communication channel m. The optimal route is given by the path Q for which $\sum_{m \varepsilon Q} t_m$ is minimized over all paths from the given source node to the given destination node. In other words the (estimated) communication channel delays constitute the distance metric for shortest path routing. We observe that in ARPANET routing, the incremental flow is an individual packet and the individual-optimization objective is pursued.

It has been observed by several authors [AGNE 76, GALL 77] that routing algorithms with the objective of individual-optimization do not necessarily lead to network-optimization, i.e., minimizing the mean delay of all packets in the network. The flow deviation method [FRAT 73, GERL 73, KLEI 76] considers an incremental flow that is infinitesimal relative to existing flows in the network. The network-optimization objective is pursued; specifically, the route for the incremental flow is chosen to minimize the (infinitesimal) increase ΔT in the mean network transit delay T of all packets. Let f_m denote the flow in communication channel m (in bits per second) and d_m denote the value of the partial derivative of T with respect to f_m evaluated at the existing flow value. It was shown that the optimal route for the incremental flow is given by the shortest path using $\{d_m\}$ as the distance metric.

We next pose a similar problem for networks with flow-controlled virtual channels. The incremental flow corresponds to the addition of a new virtual channel with a window size of one (not necessarily an infinitesimal amount of flow). The network-optimization objective is first considered.

One method to evaluate ΔT is to calculate T using the tree convolution algorithm for the network both with and without the additional virtual channel (given a specific route for it). However, to determine the optimal route with this approach would require numerous applications of the tree convolution algorithm and would be very expensive in terms of computation time.

We shall adopt the solution approach proposed in Section 2. A closed-chain model is initially used to calculate the throughputs of the existing flow-controlled virtual channels. These are then modeled as open chains. The new virtual channel to be added is modeled as a closed chain.

Let the aggregate arrival rate of the existing traffic in the network to communication channel m be denoted by λ_m packets/second. The service rate of channel m is μC_m packets/second where $1/\mu$ is the average length of a packet in bits and C_m is the channel speed in bits/second. Define $\rho_m = \lambda_m/(\mu C_m)$. The total throughput rate at which open chain packets leave (or enter) the network is γ_o packets/second. The closed chain representing the virtual channel being added has a population size of one (i.e. window size is one), a source server work-rate of γ packets/second and a mean end-to-end acknowledgment delay of τ seconds. The source and sink nodes of the virtual channel are known but its route is to be determined.

Let Q denote the set of communication channels constituting a route chosen for the new virtual channel. From the arrival theorem [SEVC 79, LAVE 80], the mean delay encountered by the new virtual channel's packet at channel $m \varepsilon Q$ is $1/(\mu C_m - \lambda_m)$. The mean network transit delay of the new virtual channel is

$$T_c = \sum_{m \varepsilon Q} \frac{1}{\mu C_m - \lambda_m} \tag{1}$$

Applying Little's formula [LITT 61], the throughput rate of the new virtual channel is

$$\gamma_c = \frac{1}{(1/\gamma) + \tau + T_c} \tag{2}$$

Let T_o be the mean network transit delay and $\bar{n}_o$ be the mean number of packets in the network before the addition of the new virtual channel. The increase in the mean delay due to the new virtual channel is

$$\Delta T = \frac{\sum_{m \varepsilon Q} \Delta \bar{n}_{m,o} + \bar{n}_o + \gamma_c T_c}{\gamma_o + \gamma_c} - T_o \tag{3}$$

where $\Delta \bar{n}_{m,o}$ is the increase in the mean queue length of the open chains at channel m due to the new virtual channel, and is given by

$$\Delta \bar{n}_{m,o} = \frac{\lambda_m}{\mu C_m - \lambda_m} \bar{n}_{m,c} \tag{4}$$

where $\bar{n}_{m,c}$ is the mean number of new packets (belonging to the added virtual channel) at channel m. A derivation of (4) is given in [PENN 75]. It may also be obtained by differentiating the moment generating function of the product-form solution for networks with both open and closed chains [REIS 75, LAM 82]. An application of Little's formula yields

$$\bar{n}_{m,c} = \gamma_c/(\mu C_m - \lambda_m). \tag{5}$$

Finally, we have

$$\Delta T = \frac{\sum_{m \varepsilon Q} \frac{\lambda_m \gamma_c}{(\mu C_m - \lambda_m)^2} + \gamma_c T_c - \gamma_c T_o}{\gamma_o + \gamma_c}$$

$$= \frac{\sum_{m \varepsilon Q} [\frac{\lambda_m}{(\mu C_m - \lambda_m)^2} + \frac{1}{\mu C_m - \lambda_m}] - T_o}{(\gamma_o/\gamma_c) + 1}$$

$$= \frac{\sum\limits_{m \epsilon Q} \frac{\mu C_m}{(\mu C_m - \lambda_m)^2} - T_o}{\gamma_o (\frac{1}{\gamma} + \tau + \sum\limits_{m \epsilon Q} \frac{1}{\mu C_m - \lambda_m}) + 1} \qquad (6)$$

To minimize ΔT, the route should be chosen to try to minimize the numerator and to maximize the denominator if possible. Minimizing the numerator implies the choice of a shortest path from source to destination using $\mu C_m / (\mu C_m - \lambda_m)^2$ as the distance metric. Note that this is essentially the same as the distance metric of

$$\frac{C_m}{(C_m - f_m)^2} \qquad \text{where } f_m = \lambda_m / \mu \qquad (7)$$

given by the flow deviation method for an open-chain model. This similarity is interesting since the derivation of (6) above and the derivation of (7) in the flow deviation method are based upon different models.

Maximizing the denominator, on the other hand, implies that the longest path should be chosen with $1/(\mu C_m - \lambda_m)$ as the distance metric. Note that the incremental flow γ_c is much smaller than the existing network throughput γ_o in the objective function ΔT in (6). To minimize ΔT, a route may possibly be selected with a very long delay for the incremental flow. Since we are considering an amount of incremental traffic that is not infinitesimal, it makes sense to impose a maximum delay bound τ_{max} on the mean delay of the new virtual channel. (Most likely, the user requesting for the new virtual channel will want his mean delay to be bounded.) Hence, we formulate the following constrained optimization problem:

$$\min_{Q} \Delta T \qquad \text{subject to } \sum\limits_{m \epsilon Q} \frac{1}{\mu C_m - \lambda_m} < \tau_{max}. \quad (8)$$

A dual of the above problem is

$$\min_{Q} \sum\limits_{m \epsilon Q} \frac{1}{\mu C_m - \lambda_m} \qquad \text{subject to } \Delta T < \Delta_{max} \quad (9)$$

where Δ_{max} is a bound on ΔT. An algorithm to solve the problem in (8) is presented in Section 4.

We can interpret the constrained problem in (8) or (9) as a compromise between the objectives of individual-optimization and network-optimization. Note that the individual-optimization objective of ARPANET routing does not consider the impact of the incremental flow on the network. On the other hand, the network-optimization objective of flow deviation ignores the performance of the incremental flow (since it is assumed to be infinitesimal). The constrained problems in (8) and (9) take into account both considerations.

Let us reexamine the mean end-to-end acknowledgment delay which has been assumed to be a constant τ. This corresponds to the assumption that virtual channels (in opposite directions) between any two nodes employ routes that are chosen independently. A different but equally plausible assumption that one can make is that flows in the network are symmetric and virtual channels between any two nodes employ the same route (traversed in opposite directions). In this case, τ in Eqs. (2) and (6) should be changed to T_c.

4. AN OPTIMAL ROUTING ALGORITHM

Our algorithm to solve the constrained problem in (8) is based upon a branch-and-bound technique.

Consider the packet switching network as a directed graph described by (V, E) where V is a set of vertices (network nodes) and E is a set of directed arcs (communication channels). A path in the network is a sequence of <u>distinct</u> nodes $Q = v_0, v_1, \ldots, v_n$ such that (v_i, v_{i+1}) is an arc in E for $i = 0, 1, \ldots, n-1$. We shall only consider acyclic paths.

Let v_s be the source node and v_d be the destination node of the virtual channel for which a path (or route) is desired. We shall consider only those paths that originate at v_s and either end at v_d or do not contain v_d. A path is said to be <u>complete</u> if it ends at v_d. A path is said to be <u>incomplete</u> if it does not contain v_d.

Each complete path Q from v_s to v_d is associated with two measures:

  (i) its cost COST(Q) given by Eq. (6), and
  (ii) its mean end-to-end delay DELAY(Q) given by

$$\text{DELAY}(Q) = \sum\limits_{m \epsilon Q} \frac{1}{\mu C_m - \lambda_m} \qquad (10)$$

Each incomplete path Q is also associated with two measures:

  (i) its estimated cost ECOST(Q) given by

$$\text{ECOST}(Q) = \frac{\sum\limits_{m \epsilon Q} \frac{\mu C_m}{(\mu C_m - \lambda_m)^2} - T_o}{\gamma_o (\frac{1}{\gamma} + \tau + \tau_{max}) + 1} \qquad (11)$$

  (ii) its mean end-to-end delay DELAY(Q) given by Eq. (10).

If the network is assumed to have symmetric flows and symmetric routes so that τ is replaced by T_c in (2) and (6), then τ should be replaced by τ_{max} in (11).

The following data structures are used in the algorithm below:

C_PATHS the set of complete paths constructed

I_PATHS the set of incomplete paths constructed

R_NODES the set of nodes that have not been visited by an incomplete path.

Given a path $Q = v_0, v_1, \ldots, v_n$, it is said to be <u>extendable</u> to v_{n+1} to form a new path $v_0, v_1, \ldots, v_n, v_{n+1}$ if v_{n+1} is not already in the path, a communication channel exists from v_n to v_{n+1}, and DELAY of the extended path is less than τ_{max}.

Algorithm {to find an optimal path}

begin
    use a shortest path algorithm to find a mini-
       mum delay path Q' from v_s to v_d;

    if DELAY(Q') $\geq \tau_{max}$ then

       quit {comment: no feasible solution exists};
    initialize C_PATHS to be the empty set,
       I_PATHS to contain the path consisting of
       v_s only, and R_NODES to be $V - \{v_s\}$;

    repeat

    Consider all paths that can be formed by
      extending a path in I_PATHS to a node in
      R_NODES and select Q in I_PATHS that is
      extendable to v in R_NODES to form Q_{new}
      such that ECOST(Q_{new}) is minimized;

    if Q_{new} is incomplete then
      begin
         add Q_{new} to I_PATHS;
         delete v from R_NODES
      end
    else {comment: Q_{new} is complete and v is v_d}
      begin
         add Q_{new} to C_PATHS;
         label Q in I_PATHS to be nonextendable
           to v_d
      end
    until one of the following conditions is true
    or both are true:

    1. Q_{new} is complete and COST of Q_{new} is
       less than COST of any path in C_PATHS
       and is less than ECOST of any extendable
       path in I_PATHS
       {comment: Q_{new} is the optimal solution}

    2. no more path in I_PATHS is extendable
       to a node in R_NODES
       {comment: the path in C_PATHS with
         minimum COST is the optimal solution}
end

    Theorem. If a feasible solution exists, the
algorithm terminates with an optimal path Q* for
the problem in (8).

    We provide only a proof outline of the above
theorem. If a feasible solution exists, termination of the algorithm is due to the assumption of
a finite graph with a finite number of acyclic
paths from v_s to v_d. The optimality of the path
Q* is guaranteed by the termination conditions of
the algorithm. It is sufficient to show that Q*
is better than all complete paths that may be
extended from the paths in I_PATHS. Consider Q in
I_PATHS. Suppose that it is extendable by channel
f to a new path Q'. Consider two cases. First,
Q' is a complete path. We have

$$COST(Q') = \frac{\sum_{m \in Q} \frac{\mu C_m}{(\mu C_m - \lambda_m)^2} + \frac{\mu C_f}{(\mu C_f - \lambda_f)^2} - T_o}{\gamma_o(\frac{1}{\gamma} + \tau + \sum_{m \in Q'} \frac{1}{\mu C_m - \lambda_m}) + 1}$$

$$> \frac{\sum_{m \in Q} \frac{\mu C_m}{(\mu C_m - \lambda_m)^2} - T_o}{\gamma_o(\frac{1}{\gamma} + \tau + \tau_{max}) + 1} = ECOST(Q) > COST(Q*)$$

The second case is that Q' is incomplete. We
then have

$$ECOST(Q') = \frac{\sum_{m \in Q} \frac{\mu C_m}{(\mu C_m - \lambda_m)^2} + \frac{\mu C_f}{(\mu C_f - \lambda_f)^2} - T_o}{\gamma_o(\frac{1}{\gamma} + \tau + \tau_{max}) + 1}$$

$$> ECOST(Q) > COST(Q*)$$

In this case, Q' is added to I_PATHS. Extend
incomplete paths in I_PATHS to nodes in R_NODES
until all paths in I_PATHS become nonextendable.
The proof is completed by applying induction.

5. CONCLUSIONS

    Both open-chain queueing networks and
closed-chain queueing networks have been employed
in the past to model packet switching networks
with flow-controlled virtual channels. A closed-
chain model is the more natural of the two.
Despite some recent advances in computational
techniques (such as the tree convolution algorithm), the computational requirements of a
closed-chain model are still too large to be used
in network design procedures. An open-chain
model, on the other hand, encounters the difficulty that the throughputs of flow-controlled
virtual channels, needed as input parameters for
the model, are not known.

    We examined the traffic conditions under
which an open-chain model accurately predicts the
mean end-to-end delays of a closed-chain model.
We then proposed an approach to employ both
closed-chain and open-chain models in network
design procedures. A closed-chain model is used
to compute virtual channel throughputs. An open-
chain model is used for intermediate optimization
steps.

    The problems of optimally routing incremental
flows were explored. We observed that the underlying objectives of ARPANET routing and flow
deviation correspond to unconstrained individual-
optimization and network-optimization problems
(respectively). We formulated a constrained
optimal routing problem that is a compromise
between the two objectives. An algorithm that
finds an optimal solution to the problem has
been presented.

REFERENCES

AGNE 76 Agnew, C. E., "On Quadratic Adaptive
          Routing Algorithms," Comm. ACM 19 (1976)
          pp. 18-22.

BASK 75 Baskett, F., K. M. Chandy, R. R. Muntz
          and F. Palacios, "Open, Closed, and
          Mixed Networks of Queues with Different
          Classes of Customers," JACM, April 1975.

CERF 74 Cerf, V. and R. Kahn, "A Protocol for
          Packet Network Intercommunication,"
          IEEE Trans. on Communications, COM-22
          (1974), 637-648.

FRAT 73   Fratta, L., M. Gerla and L. Kleinrock, "The Flow Deviation Method: An Approach to Store-and-forward Network Design," Networks 3 (1973), 97-133.

GALL 77   Gallager, R., "An Optimal Routing Algorithm Using Distributed Computation," IEEE Trans. on Commun., Vol. COM-25, Jan. 1977, pp. 73-85.

GERL 73   Gerla, M., "The Design of Store-and-forward Networks for Computer Communications," Ph.D. dissertation, Department of Computer Scienes, UCLA (Jan. 1973).

GERL 77   Gerla, M. and L. Kleinrock, "On the Topological Design of Distributed Computer Networks," IEEE Trans. on Communications, COM-25 (1977), pp. 48-60.

GERL 80   Gerla, M. and P. O. Nilsson, "Routing and Flow Control Interplay in Computer Networks," Proc. Fifth ICCC, Atlanta, Oct. 1980.

IBM 75   IBM Corp., Systems Network Architecture General Information, GA27-3102-0 (Jan. 1975).

KLEI 64   Kleinrock, L., Communication Nets--Stochastic Message Flow and Delays, (McGraw-Hill, New York, 1964).

KLEI 76   Kleinrock, L., Queueing Systems, Volume 2: Computer Applications (Wiley-Interscience, New York, 1976).

LAM 76   Lam, S. S., "Store-and-forward Buffer Requirements in a Packet Switching Network," IEEE Trans. on Communications COM-24 (1976) pp. 394-403.

LAM 81a   Lam, S. S. and Y. L. Lien, "A Tree Convolution Algorithm for the Solution of Queueing Networks," Dept. of Computer Sciences, University of Texas at Austin, Technical Report TR-165, January 1981.

LAM 81b   Lam, S. S. and Y. L. Lien, "Modeling and Analysis of Flow Controlled Packet Switching Networks," Proc. 7th Data Communications Symposium, Mexico City, Oct. 1981.

LAM 82   Lam, S. S. and J. W. Wong, "Queueing Network Models of Packet Switching Networks, Part 2: Networks with Population Size Constraints," Performance Evaluation, Vol. 2, No. 2, 1982 (to appear).

LAVE 80   Lavenberg, S. S. and M. Reiser, "Stationary State Probabilities of Arrival Instants for Closed Queueing Networks with Multiple Types of Customers," J. Applied Probability, Dec. 1980.

LIEN 81   Lien, Y. L., "Modeling and Analysis of Flow-controlled Computer Communication Networks," Ph.D. Thesis, Dept. of Computer Sciences, University of Texas at Austin, Dec. 1981.

LITT 61   Little, J. D. C., "A Proof of the Queueing Formula: $L = \lambda W$," Operations Research 9 (1961) pp. 383-387.

MCQU 78   McQuillan, J. M., G. Falk and I. Richer, "A Review of the Development and Performance of the ARPANET Routing Algorithm," IEEE Trans. on Commun. COM-26 (1978), pp. 1802-1811.

OPDE 74   Opderbeck, H. and L. Kleinrock, "The Influence of Control Procedures on the Performance of Packet-switched Networks," Proc. National Telecommunications Conference, San Diego (Dec. 1974).

PENN 75   Pennotti, M. and M. Schwartz, "Congestion Control in Store and forward Tandem Links," IEEE Trans. on Communications COM-23 (1975), pp. 1434-1443.

POUZ 73   Pouzin, L., "Presentation and Major Design Aspects of the CYCLADES Computer Network," Proc. Third Data Communications Symposium, St. Petersburg, Florida (Nov. 1973).

REIS 75   Reiser, M. and H. Kobayashi, "Queueing Networks with Multiple Closed Chains: Theory and Computational Algorithms," IBM Journal of Research and Development 19 (1975).

REIS 79   Reiser, M., "A Queueing Network Analysis of Computer Communication Networks with Window Flow Control," IEEE Trans. on Communications COM-27 (1979) pp. 1199-1209.

REIS 80   Reiser, M. and S. Lavenberg, "Mean Value Analysis of Closed Multi-chain Queueing Networks," JACM 27 (1980) pp. 313-322.

ROBE 78   Roberts, L. G., "The Evolution of Packet Switching," Proc. IEEE, Vol. 66, Nov. 1978.

SCHW 77   Schwartz, M., Computer-Communication Network Design and Analysis, Prentice-Hall, 1977.

SEVC 79   Sevcik, K. C. and I. Mitrani, "The Distribution of Queueing Network States at Input and Output Instants," Proc. 4th Intl. Symp. on Modeling and Performance Evaluation of Computer Systems, Vienna, Austria, 1979.

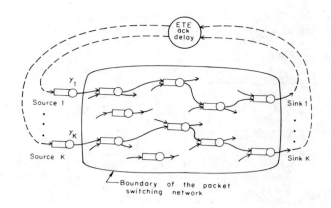

Fig. 1. An illustration of the closed-chain queueing network model.

chain	throughput rate	mean delay	delay estimate	% error
1	9.20e-01	6.02e-01	6.15e-01	2.28e+00
2	9.20e-01	6.02e-01	6.15e-01	2.28e+00
3	9.17e-01	6.25e-01	6.41e-01	2.49e+00
4	9.17e-01	6.25e-01	6.41e-01	2.49e+00
5	9.20e-01	6.03e-01	6.17e-01	2.27e+00
6	9.20e-01	6.03e-01	6.17e-01	2.27e+00
7	9.47e-01	4.96e-01	5.07e-01	2.11e+00
8	9.47e-01	4.96e-01	5.07e-01	2.11e+00
9	9.41e-01	5.36e-01	5.49e-01	2.57e+00
10	9.41e-01	5.36e-01	5.49e-01	2.57e+00
11	9.45e-01	5.06e-01	5.18e-01	2.29e+00
12	9.45e-01	5.06e-01	5.18e-01	2.29e+00
13	8.18e-01	9.91e-01	1.02e+00	2.85e+00
14	8.18e-01	9.91e-01	1.02e+00	2.85e+00
15	9.86e-01	2.73e-01	2.78e-01	1.74e+00
16	9.86e-01	2.73e-01	2.78e-01	1.74e+00
17	9.88e-01	2.44e-01	2.47e-01	1.21e+00
18	9.88e-01	2.44e-01	2.47e-01	1.21e+00
19	9.89e-01	2.33e-01	2.35e-01	1.01e+00
20	9.89e-01	2.33e-01	2.35e-01	1.01e+00
21	9.89e-01	2.32e-01	2.35e-01	1.03e+00
22	9.89e-01	2.32e-01	2.35e-01	1.03e+00
23	9.97e-01	1.23e-01	1.24e-01	7.36e-01
24	9.97e-01	1.23e-01	1.24e-01	7.37e-01
25	9.17e-01	6.25e-01	6.40e-01	2.50e+00
26	9.17e-01	6.25e-01	6.40e-01	2.50e+00
27	9.70e-01	3.79e-01	3.86e-01	1.84e+00
28	9.70e-01	3.79e-01	3.86e-01	1.84e+00
29	8.56e-01	8.46e-01	8.68e-01	2.60e+00
30	8.56e-01	8.46e-01	8.68e-01	2.60e+00
31	8.84e-01	7.57e-01	7.78e-01	2.73e+00
32	8.84e-01	7.57e-01	7.78e-01	2.73e+00

Errors in delay estimates
            Average : 2.02e+00
           Variance : 4.32e-01
 Standard Deviation : 6.57e-01

Table 1. Mean delays and delay estimates for the network example.

Case of	utilizations of communication channels				% errors in delay estimates			
	mean	max.	min.	st. dev.	mean	max.	min.	st. dev.
$\gamma = 10$	0.466	0.808	0.134	0.188	40.3	127	15.3	26.3
$\gamma = 2$	0.299	0.469	0.112	0.107	7.34	9.86	4.74	1.37
$\gamma = 1$	0.185	0.281	0.082	0.066	2.02	2.85	0.74	0.66
$\gamma = 2/3$	0.130	0.195	0.061	0.047	0.80	1.39	0.22	0.34
$\gamma = 1/2$	0.100	0.148	0.048	0.036	0.40	0.77	0.09	0.19

Table 2. Channel utilizations and errors in delay estimates for different values of γ.

Case of	utilizations of communication channels				% errors in delay estimates			
	mean	max.	min.	st. dev.	mean	max.	min.	st. dev.
window size = 2	0.159	0.248	0.064	0.057	4.02	4.73	2.94	0.46
window size = 3	0.185	0.281	0.082	0.066	2.02	2.85	0.74	0.66
window size = 4	0.197	0.294	0.092	0.070	0.88	1.72	0.18	0.45

Table 3. Channel utilizations and errors in delay estimates for different window sizes.

Load Balancing
in
Homogeneous Broadcast Distributed Systems

Miron Livny and Myron Melman
Department of Applied Mathematics
The Weizmann Institute of Science
Rehovot, Israel

ABSTRACT

Three different load balancing algorithms for distributed systems that consist of a number of identical processors and a CSMA communication system are presented in this paper. Some of the properties of a multi-resource system and the balancing process are demonstrated by an analytic model. Simulation is used as a mean for studying the interdependency between the parameters of the distributed system and the behaviour of the balancing algorithm. The results of this study shed light on the characteristics of the load balancing process.

INTRODUCTION

Distributed processing systems are characterized by resource multiplicity and system transparency [1]. Every distributed system consists of a number of autonomous resources that interact through a communication system. From the user's point of view this set of resources acts like a 'single virtual system'. As he submits a task for execution he does not and should not consider either the internal structure or the instantaneous load of the system. It is the duty of the system's load balancing algorithm to control the assignment of resources to tasks and to route the tasks according to these assignments.

The stochastic properties of the tasks - arrival and execution times - cause resource contentions that lead to the establishment of queues. The existence of queues of waiting tasks demands dynamic reconsideration of previous assignments.

The assignment algorithm is motivated by the desire to achieve better overall performance relative to some selected metric of system performance. The strategy of the load balancing algorithm has a strong effect on the utilization of the system resources and determines its overall performance. The purpose of this paper is to investigate the behaviour of the load balancing process in broadcast distributed systems.

The problem of resource allocation in an environment of cooperating autonomous resources and its relationship to system performance is a major issue associated with the design of distributed systems [2]. A number of studies of this issue have been reported [3] [4] [5] [6]. Most of these studies deal with distributed systems that utilize central elements, such as a job dispatcher, a shared memory , a main processor, or with systems that consist only of two processors. This paper deals with distributed load balancing algorithms for homogeneous distributed systems whose communication system consists of a broadcast medium. There are no central elements in the system and the balancing algorithm is distributed among the resources. The policy of the algorithm is to minimize the expected turnaround time of the tasks.

Initially a simple analytic model is used for demonstrating some of the properties of a multi-resource system and the balancing process. Then three different load balancing algorithms for broadcast distributed systems are defined and discussed. The last part of the paper presents results of the simulation study. In the study, the three algorithms were simulated under various operating conditions. The results demonstrate the interdependency between the parameters of the distributed system and the behaviour of the balancing algorithm.

LOAD BALANCING

In a distributed system it might happen that a task waits for service at the queue of one resource while at the same time another resource which is capable of serving the task is idle. A load balancing algorithm whose goal is to minimize the expected turnaround time of the tasks will tend to prevent the system from reaching such a state.

Assume a system of N identical[1] and independent M/M/1 queueing systems [7]. Let P_{wi} be the probability that the system is in a state in which at least one customer waits for service and at least one server is idle then

$$P_{wi} = \sum_{i=1}^{N} \binom{N}{i} Q_i H_{N-i} = (1-Po^N)(1-Po^N-(1-Po)^N)$$

where

$Q_i = Po^i$ is the probability that a given set of i servers are idle

$H_i = (1-Po)^i - (Po(1-Po))^i$ is the probability that a given set of i servers is not idle and at one or more of them a task waits for service

$Po = 1 - \frac{\lambda}{\mu}$ is the probability that a server is idle.

Fig. 1 shows the value of P_{wi} for various values of server utilizations, $\rho = 1-Po$, and number of servers N. The curves of the figure indicate that for practical values of ρ, P_{wi} is remarkably high and that in systems with more than ten servers almost all the time a customer is waiting for service and another server is idling.

The high value of P_{wi} indicates that by balancing the instantaneous load of the multi-resource system their performance can be considerably improved. Note that the average load of a server is the same for all servers. The shape of the curves shows that for a given number of servers P_{wi} reaches its maximum value when the servers are utilized during 65% of the time. As the utilization of the servers increases past the level of 65% P_{wi} decreases. This property of P_{wi} indicates that a 'good' load balancing algorithm should work less when the system is heavily utilized. It is clear that the same thing is true for systems that are idle most of the time.

A reduction in P_{wi} of a multi-resource system will cause an improvement of the expected turnaround time, W, of the tasks. If the servers are interconnected by a communication system P_{wi} can be

---

[1] All the systems have the same arrival, λ, and service, μ, rates.

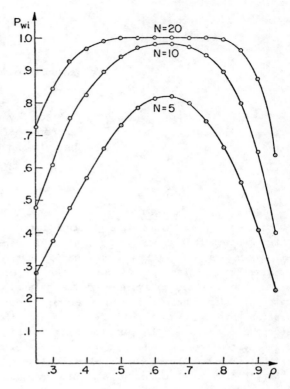

figure: 1 P_{wi} as a function of ρ

reduced by transfering tasks from one queue to another. These transfers affect the utilization and consequently the performance of the communication system and can be considered as the price paid for the reduction of W.

The expected turnaround time of the above multiresource system will be minimal if P_{wi} will be zero. In such a case the system will behave like an M/M/N (single queue N servers) system [7]. P_{wi} can be reduced to zero only if the servers are inter-connected by a communication system whose task transfer rate is much higher than the service rate of the servers. In a system where P_{wi} is zero a task will be transferred from one queue to another when one of the following events occurs:

1. A task arrives at a busy server and there are less than N tasks in the system.

2. A server completes the service of a task, no other tasks are waiting in its queue and there are more than N tasks in the entire system.

Therefore a lower bound to the rate of tasks transferred in order to minimize W is given by

$$LT = \sum_{i=1}^{N-1} (\lambda i P_i + \mu(N-i)P_{N+i})$$

where P_i is the probability of having i tasks in an M/M/N system [7]. The first element of the summation is the rate of transfers caused by the arriving tasks (the first event). The second element is part of the transfer rate caused by the departing tasks (the second event).

Fig. 2 gives the values of the lower bound LT as a function of the number of servers for various arrival rates, λ . Note that a considerable number of tasks has to be transferred in order to achieve the performance of a M/M/N system. For systems with more than ten servers almost one out of λ^{-1} tasks are transferred.

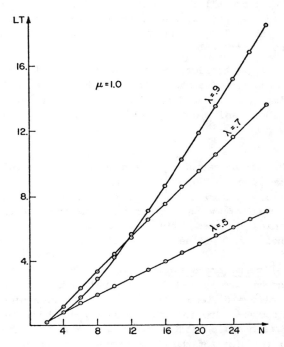

figure: 2 Lower Bound on task transfer rate in an M/M/N like system vs. nuber of servers

These results indicate that in systems where task transmission time is not negligable the load balancing process will utilize a large portion of the capacity of the communication system. The utilization of the communication system will determine the delays associated with the transmission of a task or any other message. These delays will cause an increase in P_{wi} and therefore an increase in W. The amount of traffic generated by the balancing algorithm has a major effect on its ability to improve the performance of the system. Fig. 2 shows that in order to achieve the optimal performance, $P_{wi} = 0$, a large portion of the tasks have to be transferred.

THE DISTRIBUTED SYSTEM MODEL

The model describes a homogeneous N-server distributed system. The system consists of N identical nodes and a communication channel. Every node has a processor P, a communication processor CP and a queue, Fig. 3. The channel is a passive broadcast medium (radio or coxial/fiber cable) with a CSMA-CD (carrier sense multiple access collision detection) access method. The access to the channel and the transmission of messages is controlled by the CP according to the ETHERNET protocol [8] [9].

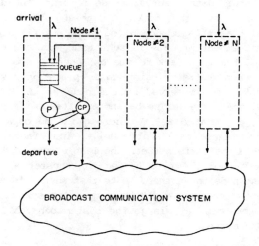

figure: 3 The Broadcast Distributed System

Tasks arrive independently at each node and join the queue. The queueing discipline at all the nodes is FIFO (first-in-first-out). The arrival rate of each stream of tasks is λ and the inter-arrival time has a negative exponential distribution. The task arrival process to the entire system consists of N identical independent poisson processes with a total rate of N .

The service time demand of the tasks has a negative exponential distribution and the mean service time is μ^{-1}. The tasks leave the system after being served, and depart from the same node at which they had entered the system. It is assumed that the system operates in steady-state conditions ($\lambda < \mu$). The utilization of the servers is $\rho = \frac{\lambda}{\mu}$.

The number of tasks at node i (waiting for service or being served) is denoted by N_i and $ST = (n_1, \ldots, n_N)$ describes the state of the system. A state of the system is defined as unbalanced if there are two servers i and j such that $n_i - n_j > 1$. The unbalance factor of a state ST is defined as

$$UBF = \begin{cases} \underset{0 < i, j \leq N}{\text{MAXIMUM}}((n_i - n_j)n_j^{-1}) & \text{if ST is UNB} \\ 0 & \text{otherwise} \end{cases}$$

Note that if the system is in an unbalanced state and one of the servers is idle the UBF of the state is infinite.

The purpose of the channel, Fig. 3, is to transfer tasks from one node to the other in order to improve the expected turnaround time of a task. The flow of tasks via the channel is governed by a distributed load balancing algorithm.

A node that wants to transfer one of its waiting tasks to another node will send it a message that describes the task. The message has to contain all the external data a server needs in order to identify and serve the task. In this model it is assumed that this amount of data, T, is fixed and the same amount of data is sent from the node that executed the task back to the entrance node of the task. Such a transmission takes place only when the task was not served by the node at which it entered the system. The balancing rate of the system, β, is defined as $\frac{\mu^{-1}}{CT}$ where C is the capacity of the communication channel. The factor β expresses the ratio between the mean execution time of a task and the time needed to transfer a task from one node to another. Note that when β is zero the system becomes an $N(M/M/1)$ queueing system and when β becomes very large the system behaves like an $M/M/N$ system.

LOAD BALANCING ALGORITHMS

A distributed load balancing algorithm is composed of two main elements - the control law element and the information policy element. The control law determines when, from where and to whom to transfer a waiting task. The decision is made according to the current available information on the state of the system. It is the function of the information policy to collect data for the control element concerning the load of the system resources. Both elements use the communication system for carrying out their functions. The control element sends messages that describe tasks and the information element sends 'status messages' that contain data on the system's load.

The delays associated with the transmission of a message may lead to the execution of a wrong operation by the balancing algorithm. As a result of such an operation a task is placed in a queue that has more waiting tasks than the queue from which the task has been removed. The balancing process faces a 'transmission dilemma' because of the two opposing impacts the transmission of a message has on the overall performance of the system. On the one hand the transmission improves the ability of the algorithm to balance the load. On the other hand it raises the expected queueing time of messages because of the increase in the utilization of

the channel. The net impact of a message transmission on the overall performance of the system depends on the balancing rate of the communication system, the number of nodes and the rate at which tasks arrive at the system.

Three different distributed load balancing algorithms for broadcast distributed system are defined in this study. From the load balancing point of view broadcast communication systems have two advantages:

1. Uniform distance - the expected time that is needed to transfer a message from one node to another is the same for all pairs of nodes. Therefore all the nodes are equal-priority candidates for receiving a waiting task. Only the relative load of the nodes has to be considered by the control law.

2. Messages broadcast - the capability of the communication system to broadcast messages improves the ability of the algorithm to get a global and updated description of the system status.

The communication system consists of a single transmission resource and therefore it can not transfer a number of messages simultaneously. The high rate of message transfers generated by the balancing process (fig. 2) requires that the balancing rate of the system will be high.

The state broadcast algorithm - STB. The STB balancing algorithm utilizes both the broadcast and the uniform distance properties of the communication system. The information policy of the algorithm is based on status broadcast messages. Whenever the state of the node changes, because of the arrival or departure of a task, the node broadcasts a status message that describes its new state. This information policy enables each node to hold its own updated copy of the system state vector, SSV, and guarantees that all the copies are identical. The information contained in the $SSV = (s_1, .. , s_N)$ gives the node a global and updated picture of the system state and enables the control law to base its decisions on the state of the whole system. Note that SSV may differ from ST due to transmission delays. The distributed control law of the STB algorithm will transfer a waiting task from node i to node j if the following conditions are fulfilled.

1. $s_i - s_j > 1 + (BT \cdot s_j)$ where BT is a parameter that controls the balancing threshold of the algorithm.

2. $((s_i > s_k)$ or $(s_i = s_k$ and $i \geq k))$ for all $k = 1,\ldots,N$.

3. $s_j \leq s_k$ for $k = 1,\ldots,N$.

When more than one node has a minimal number of waiting tasks the selection of the destination node is made randomly.

The <u>broadcast idle algorithm – BID</u> . The BID algorithm is based on a less liberal information policy. Under this policy a node broadcasts a status message when it enters an idle state. The message alerts all the other nodes and causes them to activate the control element of the algorithm. The control law of the BID algorithm consists of the following steps:

1. If $n_i > 1$ go to step 2, else terminate the algorithm.

2. Wait $D \cdot n_i^{-1}$ units of time. D is a parameter of the algorithm. Its value depends on the properties of the communication system.

3. Broadcast a reservation message if no other node has broadcasted such a message during the time-out period.[2] If another node has succeeded to broadcast a reservation message terminate the algorithm.

4. Wait for a reply message. The reply will be positive if the node that has broadcasted the idle message is still idle. The node will send a reply in any case.

5. If the reply is positive and $n_i > 1$ transfer a task to the idle node, else terminate the algorithm.

The purpose of the state-dependent time-out period is to give nodes with greater load a better chance to transfer a task to the idle node.

The <u>poll when idle algorithm – PID</u>. The information policy of both previous algorithms is based on broadcast messages. The information policy of the PID algorithm is based on polling . The node starts to poll a subset of the system nodes whenever it enters an idle state. The sequence of the polling operation of the PID algorithm is the following:

1. Randomly select a set of R nodes $(a_i, \ldots, a_R)$ and set $J = 1$. R is a parameter of the algorithm.

_____

2

If the transmission of the message is delayed because of collisions the same condition is tested before an attempt to retransmit the message is made.

2. Send a message to node a_j and wait for a reply.

3. Receive the reply message. Node a_j will either send back one of its waiting tasks, if there are any, or an 'empty queue' reply.

4. If the node is still idle and $j < R$, increment j and go to step 2 else terminate the polling.

The STB algorithm attempts to prevent the system from being in a state in which the UBF is greater than BT whereas the two other algorithms decide to transfer a task only when the UBF of the state is infinite. The STB algorithm is motivated by the assumption that by keeping the UBF of the system below BT the probability that the system will be in a state with an infinite UBF will decrease. The IDB and PID algorithms assume that because of the 'transmission dilemma' it is more important to minimize the channel utilization than to keep the UBF below a finite level.

SIMULATION STUDY

All the above algorithms aspire to improve the performance of the distributed system by balancing the instantaneous load of the system resources, each one in its own way. In order to evaluate the algorithms their performance has to be predicted and the relation between their behaviour and the parameters of the system studied.

The balanced distributed system can be modeled as a queueing network. Because of the dynamic routing of the tasks the queueing model has no feasible numerical solution. Therefore simulation has to be used as a means to predict the performance of the model.

For this study three discrete time simulation models were written using SIMSCRIPT II.5. Each model describes a different algorithm. In all the models it was assumed that there are no delays associated with the control operations of the balancing algorithm. The only delays considered are communication delays. The communication is carried out according to the ETHERNET protocol and the effect of collisions is included in the simulation model. Table 1 lists the numerical values of the simulation parameters.

The expected turnaround time, W, of a task in an M/M/N queueing system with a task arrival rate of $N \cdot \lambda$ is a monotonic decreasing function of N [7]. Although the addition of another server increases the rate at which tasks arrive at the system the supplemental node decreases the expected queueing time of a task.

The effect of the number of nodes, N, on the W of the distributed system is demonstrated by Fig.

STB - □ ; IDB - ▲ ; PID - ● ; M/M/N - △ ; M/M/1 - ○ ;

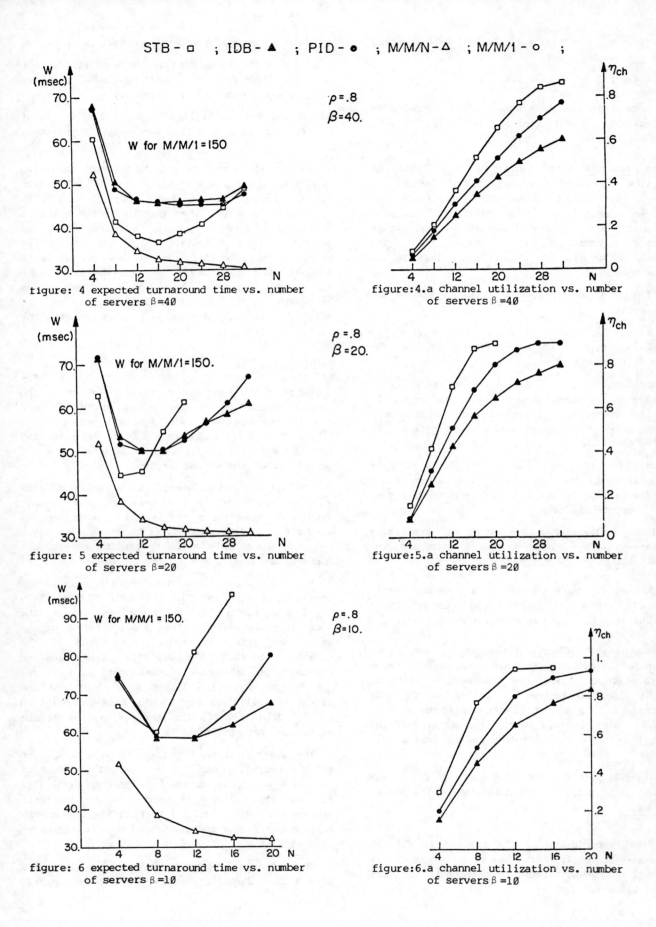

figure: 4 expected turnaround time vs. number of servers β=40

figure:4.a channel utilization vs. number of servers β=40

ρ =.8
β =40.

W for M/M/1 = 150

figure: 5 expected turnaround time vs. number of servers β=20

figure:5.a channel utilization vs. number of servers β=20

ρ =.8
β =20.

W for M/M/1 = 150.

figure: 6 expected turnaround time vs. number of servers β=10

figure:6.a channel utilization vs. number of servers β=10

ρ =.8
β =10.

W for M/M/1 = 150.

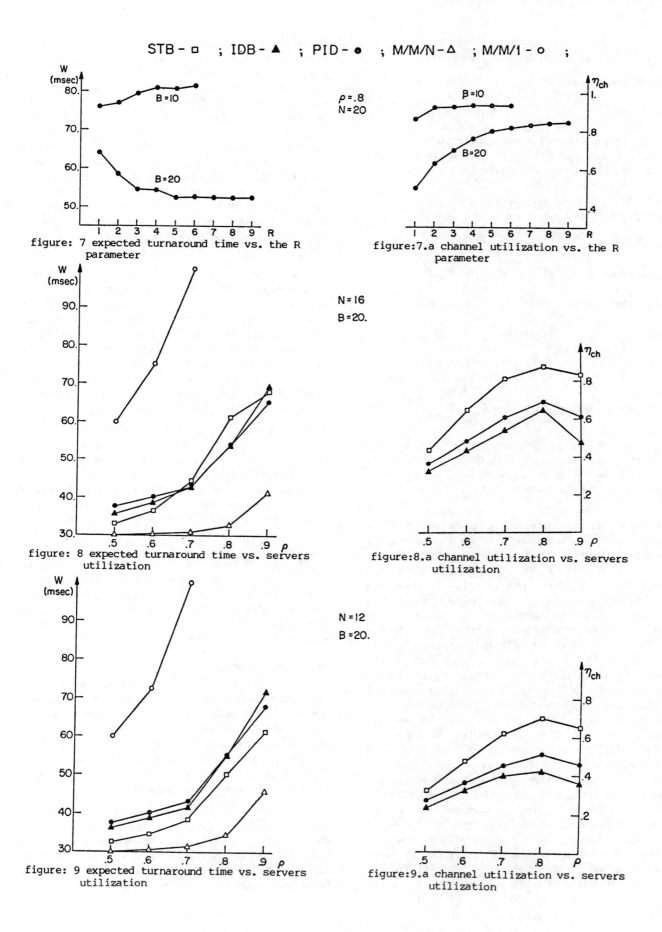

STB - □ ; IDB - ▲ ; PID - ● ; M/M/N - △ ; M/M/1 - ○ ;

figure: 7 expected turnaround time vs. the R
parameter

ρ = .8
N = 20

figure:7.a channel utilization vs. the R
parameter

N = 16
B = 20.

figure: 8 expected turnaround time vs. servers
utilization

figure:8.a channel utilization vs. servers
utilization

N = 12
B = 20.

figure: 9 expected turnaround time vs. servers
utilization

figure:9.a channel utilization vs. servers
utilization

TABLE 1
Values of simulation parameters

channel transmission rate	3 Mbit/sec
slot length (see [8])	3.2 μ sec
retransmission delay uniformly distributed between 28. CN sec and 50. CN sec where CN is the collision counter (see [9])	
transmission time of status/ reservation/polling message	50 μ sec
expected task service time (μ^{-1})	30 msec
BT parameter of STB algorithm	1.9
D factor of IDB algorithm	1.0 msec
R parameter of PID algorithm	5
balancing rate β	10,20,40 (β =10 means T=1Kbyte)
simulation length $\cdot \lambda^{-1}$	30.0 sec

4, 5, 6. The figures give the W of the three algorithms for three different balancing rates, β. In all the cases the balanced system has a considerably better W then the unbalanced system, M/M/1.

For a system with β =10 the expected waiting time of a task is decreased by at least 70%. The degree to which the balancing algorithm approaches the optimal W of an N server system (M/M/N) depends both on the balancing rate of the system and on the number of nodes. The turnaround time curves show that an increase in the number of nodes in a balanced distributed system has two counteracting effects. On the one hand it improves the probability that a waiting task will be transferred to an idle server, as in an M/M/N system. But on the other hand it raises the utilization of the communication channel, Fig. 4a, 5a, 6a. Higher channel utilization causes a slow-down in the balancing process resulting from an increase in message queueing delays. The net result of these two effects will determine whether the increase in N improves, does not affect, or deteriorates the expected turnaround time of a task. Every algorithm reaches a point, N_m, at which an addition of another server will cause an increase in W. The value of N_m depends on the algorithm and balancing rate of the system. Note that in all cases when N is less than the N_m of the STB algorithm the W of this algorithm is the smallest. After it reaches its minimal value the W of the STB algorithm

increases in a steep slope until it becomes greater than the W of the other algorithms. The degradation in the performance of the STB algorithm is caused by the increase in transmission delays. The BID and STP algorithms are less sensitive to the utilization of the channel. Therefore there is a wide range of N values for which they have almost the same performance. The reservation mechanism of these algorithms helps them to prevent 'wrong operations'. On the other hand the two algorithms transfer tasks only when at least one of the servers is idle. Therfore an increase in transmission delays increases the P_{wi} of the system. The IDB and PID algorithms have almost the same W under all the conditions simulated.

The balancing process utilizes a large portion of the communication channel capacity, Fig. 4a, 5a, 6a. The STB algorithm has the highest channel utilization and the IDB the smallest. The communication activity of the PLI algorithm can be easily controlled by the value of the R parameter. Fig. 7, 7a show how both channel and W depend on the size of the polling set of the algorithm. Note that for β = 10 a decrease in R causes a reduction in both W and the channel utilization.

Fig. 8 and 9 show how the balancing process reacts to changes in the utilization of the servers, ρ. For all values of ρ that were simulated the balanced algorithms improve considerably the expected turnaround time of the tasks. Note that the relative performance of the algorithms depend on the utilization of the servers.

Fig. 8a, 9a show that when the system is heavily utilized , ρ >.8, an increase in the utilization of the system causes a decrease in the channel utilization. Although the throughput of the system increases, the amount of transfers needed to balance the system decreases.

CONCLUDING REMARKS
In the opening analysis it was shown that the expected queueing time of a task in a distributed system can be reduced by means of load balancing. The results obtained from the simulation studies give a quantitative description to this ability. The results presented demonstrate the strong dependency between the performance of the balancing algorithm and the system parameters.

The purpose of the study was to shed light on the load balancing process in homogeneous broadcast distributed systems. The three algorithms that were defined in the course of the study represent three different approaches to the distributed load balancing problem. The simulation results show that each approach is the 'best' under certain conditions. The dependency between the behaviour of the algorithm and the parameters of the system deters from any attempt to select the ultimately 'best' algorithm. For these algorithms, as for other distributed control algorithms, there is no absolute answer to the question 'is algorithm A better then B' (see [10]). Therefore getting a better uderstanding of the processes involved in distributed load balancing has to be the aim of a study of this type of algorithms.

Three main conclusions can be derived from the simulation study:

1. Higher resource multiplicity does not necessarily result in better turnaround time. Every algorithm reaches a point at which an increase in the number of servers decreases the performance of the system. Therefore when a number of servers is given it might be better, from the W point of view, to assemble them into two or more systems than to integrate them into one system.

2. The balancing process has a high communication activity. This has been predicted by the analytic analysis and is demonstrated by the results of the simulation runs.

3. The selection of the control law and information policy should depend on the expected transmission delays of the balanced system. The 'transmission dilemma' is an important element of the balancing process.

This study is a part of an ongoing research in distributed load balancing systems. In the coming stages some of the restrictions of the model presented here will be released and distributed systems with other communication disciplines will be considered.

REFERENCES

(1) P. H. Enslow, Jr. "What is a Distributed Data Processing System ," Computer, January 1978, pp. 13-21.

(2) R. H. Echhouse, Jr., J. A. Stankovic, "Issues in Distributed Processing - An Overview of Two Workshops," Computer, January 1978, pp. 22 - 26.

(3) H. S. Stone, "Multiprocessor Scheduling with the Aid of Network Flow Algorithms," IEEE Trans. of Software Engin., Vol. SE-3, No. 1, January 1977, pp. 85-93.

(4) A. Kratzer, D. Hammerstrom, "A Study of Load Leveling," Proceedings of COMPCON, Fall 1980, pp. 647-654.

(5) Y. C. Chow, W. H. Kohler, "Dynamic Load Balancing in Homogeneous Two-Processor Distributed Systems," International Symposium on Computer Performance, Modeling, Measurement and Evaluation, Augast 1977, pp. 49-52.

(6) Y. Eran, M. Livny, M. Melman, "Modeling and Evaluation of a Tree Structured Network: a Case Study," Proceedings of MELECON 1981.

(7) L. Kleinrock, "Queueing Systems Vol. 1: Theory," Wiley, New york, 1975.

(8) R. M. Metcalfe, D. R. Boggs, "Ethernet: Distributed Packet Switching for Local Computer Networks," Xerox Research Report, csl-80-2, 1980.

(9) A. K. Agrawala, R. M. Bryant, J. Agre, "Analysis of an Ether-Like Protocol," Computer Networking Symposium 1977, pp. 104-111.

(10) J. M. Mcquillan, I. Richer, E. C. Rosen, "The New Routing Algorithm for the ARPANET," IEEE Trans. on Communications, vol. COM-28, No. 5, May 1980, pp. 711-719.

SESSION 4: PANEL: PERFORMANCE OF GLOBALLY DISTRIBUTED NETWORKS

Chair: Stuart Wecker
Technology Concepts Inc.
Sudbury, MA

Issues in the Performance of Globally Distributed Networks

PANEL MEMBERS

Robert L. Gordon, Prime Computer, Inc., *Framingham, MA*
  Operational Measurements on a High Performance Ring

James P. Gray, *IBM Corporation, Research Triangle Park, NC*
  Performance of SNA's LU-LU Session Protocols

James G. Herman, *Bolt Beranek and Newman, Inc., Cambridge, MA*
  ARPANET Performance Tuning Techniques

Raj Kanodia, *GTE Telenet Communications Corporation, Vienna, VA*
  Performance Related Issues in Packet Switched Networks

Don Seligman, *Digital Equipment Corporation, Tewksbury, MA*

Note: Not all abstracts were available at the time of printing.

PERFORMANCE OF GLOBALLY DISTRIBUTED NETWORKS

Stuart Wecker
Technology Concepts Inc.
Sudbury, Massachusetts

In the design and implementation of computer networks one must be concerned with their overall performance and the efficiency of the communication mechanisms chosen. Performance is a major issue in the architecture, implementation, and installation of a computer communication network. The architectural design always involves many cost/performance tradeoffs. Once implemented, one must verify the performance of the network and locate bottlenecks in the structure. Configuration and installation of a network involves the selection of a topology and communication components, channels and nodes of appropriate capacity, satisfying performance requirements.

This panel will focus on performance issues involved in the efficient design, implementation, and installation of globally distributed computer communication networks. Discussions will include cost/performance tradeoffs of alternative network architecture structures, methods used to measure and isolate implementation performance problems, and configuration tools to select network components of proper capacity. The panel members have all been involved in one or more performance issues related to the architecture, implementation, and/or configuration of the major networks they represent. They will describe their experiences relating to performance issues in these areas. Methodologies and examples will be chosen from these networks in current use. There will be time at the end of the session for questions to the panel.

Panel members include:

Robert Gordon, Prime Computer Inc.
James Gray, IBM Corp.
James Herman, Bolt, Beranek, & Newman
Raj Kanodia, GTE Telenet Corp.
Dan Seligman, Digital Equipment Corp.

OPERATIONAL MEASUREMENTS
ON A
HIGH PERFORMANCE RING

R. L. GORDON

PRIME COMPUTER, INC.

Abstract:

Application and system software architecture can greatly influence the operational statistics of a local network. The implementation of a transparent file system on top of a high bandwidth local network has resulted in generating a high degree of file traffic over the local network whose characteristics are largely fixed and repeatable. These statistics will be presented along with arguments for and against designing mechanisms that optimize specifically for that class of traffic.

Keywords: local networks, remote files, performance

The authors address is:
Prime Computer, Inc.
500 Old Conn Path
Framingham, Massachusetts 01701

Performance of SNA's LU-LU Session Protocols

James P. Gray

IBM Corporation
P. O. Box 12195
Research Triangle Park, N. C.

SNA is both an architecture and a set of products built in conformance with the architecture (1,2,3). The architecture is layered and precisely defined; it is both evolutionary and cost effective for implementing products. Perhaps the largest component of cost effectiveness is performance: transaction throughput and response times. For SNA, this involves data link control protocols (for SDLC and S/370 channel DLC's), routing algorithms, protocols used on the sessions that connect logical units (LU-LU session protocols), and interactions among them.

SNA's DLC and routing protocols have been discussed elsewhere (4,5,6); this talk examines protocols on sessions between logical units (LU-LU session protocols) and illustrates the results of design choices by comparing the performance of various configurations.

LU-LU session protocols can be categorized as

*   Startup (including restart after failure), versus

*   Steady State

and as

*   Control, versus

*   Application

Performance, as discussed here, applies to steady state, application data flows. LU-LU session protocols connect application programs (including microcode) and meet several requirements, with all layers contributing. The transport layers provide these services to the session layer:

*   FIFO and error-free delivery of data

*   Notification of loss of connectivity: failure of partner LU or failure of session

*   Full duplex flow of data

*   Selective admission of traffic (management of shared buffer resources, or "flow control")

*   Selectable class of service (priority, route, delay ...)

The session layer adds services for use by transaction programs that use a particular session (terminals have "built-in" transaction programs):

*   Maintenence of connection state

*   Selective receipt of data (management of LU buffer resources)

*   Matching of sizes of request units

*   Representation of "Messages" as chains of request units

*   Reset of session states ("purging") preparatory to ERP by transaction programs

*   Maintenance of "Conversation" State: Half-duplex flow of data between transaction programs.

*   "Interrupt" flow between transaction programs

*   Serial session sharing amongst transaction programs

*   Resolution of contention (avoids "polling")

*   Data "mapping" or presentation services

*   Controlled termination or "shutdown" of sessions

*   Data encryption (optional)

*   Full duplex flows of data between transaction programs (optional)

Transmission performance benefits are created by
efficient link controls; with care these benefits are preserved and enhanced in upper layers:

- Path control enhances DLC with multi-link
  transmission group scheduling for control of
  errors, increases in throughput, and priority transmission.

- Path control manages buffers with an adaptive algorithm.

- Path control's explicit routing avoids flow
  "turbulence" (a fluid mechanics analogy).

- Session flow control (pacing) is adjustable;
  it can even be turned off.

- Session protocols avoid polling, thus avoid-
  ing both extra traffic and needless latency.

- Session protocols are "pipelined", with
  implied responses.

- Presentation services (compression, compaction, outboard formatting) and distributed processing reduce the amounts of data
  that flow.

- When desirable (e.g., at the access link
  between a controller and a major SNA node
  (e.g., NCP/VS)), link scheduling and session
  scheduling are interlocked (e.g., a session
  pacing message will release traffic on the
  very next link service opportunity).

Experience with actual networks confirms that
properly configured SNA networks provide significant performance benefits over available alternatives, e.g., BSC networks.

Various detailed performance results, assembled
from work done by several groups in IBM, will be
presented at the conference.

REFERENCES

1. E. H. Sussenguth, "Systems Network Architec-
    ture: A Perspective," ICCC 1978 Conference
    Proceedings, Kyoto, Japan (1978).

2. Systems Network Architecture Format and Pro-
    tocol Reference Manual: Architecture Logic,
    SC30-3112; available through the local IBM
    Branch Office. This is a definitive refer-
    ence for details of SNA.

3. Systems Network Architecture: Concepts and
    Products, GC30-3072; available through the
    local IBM Branch Office.

4. J. P. Gray and T. B. McNeill, "SNA
    multiple-system networking," IBM Systems
    Journal 18, No. 2, pp. 263-297, 1979.

5. R.A. Donnan and J. R. Kersey, "Synchronous
    data link control: A perspective," IBM
    Systems Journal 13, No. 2, pp. 140-162,
    1974. The requirements for, and benefits
    of, SDLC.

6. G. A. Deaton and D. J. Franse, "Analyzing
    IBM's 3270 Performance Over Satellite
    Links," Data Communications, October 1980.

ARPANET Performance Tuning Techniques

James G. Herman
Bolt Beranek and Newman Inc.

As part of its operation and maintenance of the
ARPANET for the past twelve years, BBN has been
asked to investigate a number of cases of
degradation in network performance. This
presentation discusses the practical methods and
tools used to uncover and correct the causes of
these service problems. A basic iterative method
of hypothesis generation, experimental data
gathering, and analysis is described. Emphasis is
placed on the need for experienced network analysts
to direct the performance investigation and for the
availability of network programmers to provide
special purpose modifications to the network node
software in order to probe the causes of the
traffic patterns under observation. Many typical
sources of performance problems are described, a
detailed list of the tools used by the analyst are
given, and a list of basic techniques provided.
Throughout the presentation specific examples from
actual ARPANET performance studies are used to
illustrate the points made.

SESSION 5: APPLIED MODELS

Chair: Walter C. Roehr
*ConTel Information Systems, Inc.
Reston, VA*

The Determination of Upper Bounds
for Economically Effective Compression
in Packet Switching Networks*

Avner Aleh
K. Dan Levin

Department of Decision Sciences
The WHARTON School
University of Pennsylvania
Philadelphia, PA 19104

I. Introduction

"Whtd: Comp. Sci. w/exp. in data comm."
(The New York Times, Thursday, September 10,
1981). When people and organizations pay to
communicate by the word, number, line or page, the
decimal system and the English language suddenly
become very inefficient. This holds true for data
communication networks, where different methods
can be used to get the same message across the
network, in compact form without losing the
information content. Many techniques have been
developed since 1948, ([Huffman 52], [Alsberg
75]), when Claude E. Shanon mathematically derived
the maximum amount of information that can be sent
through a given channel. However, data
compression (and decompression) require computing
resources at the sending and receiving ends of the
communication line. Only when the processing
costs are lower than communication costs, data
compression can be applied economically.

Taking into account the forecasted expenditure on
computer communication of 4.5 billion dollars in
1986 [Cerf 77], substantial savings could be
realized by applying compression.

Currently, high-quality television signals
can be compressed from more than 100 million bits
per second to about 28 million bits per second
without quality loss. Lower quality video, used
for teleconferencing, can be condensed to as
little as 1.5 to 3 megabits per second, and
facsimile transmission can be compressed by a
factor of 50 with only slight degradation in
quality. With the growing trend towards
data/text, electronic mail and image services
[Lurin 78], the performance analysis of computer
communication networks should focus on the
handling of longer data strings (as compared to
current patterns).

This paper deals with the economic tradeoffs
associated with data compression in a packet
switching environment. In this transmission

---

*This research was supported by the Office of
Naval Research, ONR Grant N00014-75-C-0462.

technique, a string of data denoted by L is broken into a set of packets, according to the following transformation: $L \to S \to M \to P$. S stands for segments, where a segment represents the collection of data which was generated by a single command (like read or write) at point A, and is transmitted over the network to point B. Clearly, the segment size (number of characters) can vary. The segments are consequently decomposed by the network to messages, denoted by M, which represent the logical building blocks for data transmission. Every message M is then broken into packets P, the physical transport units, that travel independently over the network from point A to B.

In section II we present the data profile concept and the compression analysis of typical file-transfer data strings. This is followed by a compression cost saving model that is developed in section III. Upper bounds for an economically effective compression service are derived there, and the paper concludes with an example of these bounds based on state of the art technology.

II. The Data Profile Concept

A data profile is defined as: "The number and size of segments, messages and packets generated from the data collection L."

Let

S_k - The k(th) segment length in terms of information bits.

K - The number of segments compressed in a given period.

M_{jk} - The number of information bits in the j(th) message in the k(th) segment.

Q_k - The number of messages generated from segment k.

P_{ijk} - The number of information bits in packet i of message j in segment k.

N_{jk} - The number of packets generated from message j in segment k.

For given network standards, of message and packet sizes, the parameters $\{Q_k, M_{jk}, N_{jk}, P_{ij}\}$ can be directly derived from K and $\{S_k\}$.

Let

$$N_M = \sum_{k=1}^{K} Q_k \qquad = \quad \text{the number of messages generated from a given profile.}$$

$$N_P = \sum_{k=1}^{K} \sum_{j=1}^{Q_k} N_{jk} \qquad = \quad \text{the number of packets generated from that profile.}$$

Then, when a compression process with a compression ratio α is applied to the profile, the compressed profile parameters (denoted by superscript c) are determined as a function of α, i.e.,

$$L^c = L/\alpha$$

$$N_M^c = \sum_{k=1}^{K} Q_k^c \qquad \text{where } Q_k^c \text{ is the number of messages generated from segment k after the compression}$$

$$Q_k^c \leq Q_k, \quad N_M^c \leq N_M$$

$$N_p^C = \sum_{k=1}^{K} \sum_{k=1}^{Q_k^C} N_{jk}^C \qquad \text{where } N_{jk}^C$$

is the number of packets generated from message j in segment k after the compression

$$N_{jk}^C \leq N_{jk} \rightarrow N_p^C \leq N_P$$

In order to evaluate the effect of compression in "effective" terms, i.e., the number of packets (which are the basic charge units) generated from given data, one has to take into account the additional overhead components. In a packet switching environment these components consist of:

1. RFNM (Request For Next Message) message for each data message

$$\sum_{k=1}^{K} \sum_{j=1}^{Q_k} \ell_R = \ell_R \sum_{k=1}^{K} Q_k$$

where ℓ_R is the length of the RFNM message and also the length of the packet control overhead (168 bits in ARPANET).

2. Control overhead for each packet

$$\sum_{k=1}^{K} \sum_{j=1}^{Q_k} \sum_{i=1}^{N_{jk}} \ell_R = \ell_R \sum_{k=1}^{K} \sum_{j=1}^{Q_k} N_{jk}$$

The effective reduction in the number of packets is also affected by the number of control packets. Since the number of control packets in the compressed data string is a function of the compression level, i.e., segment compression, message compression or packet compression, the profile parameters for the different compression

levels can be derived as follows:

A. Segment compression – denoted by superscript SC

$$L^{SC} = L/\alpha$$

$$N_M^{SC} = \sum_{k=1}^{K} Q_k^C \leq N_M$$

$$N_P^{SC} = \sum_{k=1}^{K} \sum_{j=1}^{Q_k^C} N_{jk}^C \leq N_P$$

Clearly, the compression at this level results both in a reduction in data length, number of messages and number of packets.

B. Message compression – denoted by superscript MC

$$L^{MC} = L/\alpha$$

$$N_M^{MC} = \sum_{k=1}^{K} Q_k = N_M$$

$$N_P^{MC} = \sum_{k=1}^{K} \sum_{j=1}^{Q_k} N_{jk}^C \leq N_P$$

A reduction in data length and number of packets.

C. Packet compression – denoted by superscript PC

$$L^{PC} = L/\alpha$$

$$N_M^{PC} = \sum_{k=1}^{K} Q_k = N_M$$

$$N_P^{PC} = \sum_{k=1}^{K} \sum_{j=1}^{Q_k} N_{jk} = N_P$$

A reduction only in data length.

In our analysis we have tested various types of data profiles starting with the ARPA type profile [Kleinrock 74]. Figures 1 to 3 illustrate the compression analysis of a typical "file transfer" data profile, i.e., a data profile characterized by relatively long segments. This specific data profile consists of 1006 segments with an average segment length of 67.1 packets. The total number of messages is 7196, with an average message length of 9.4 packets (we have departed here from ARPA specification by allowing a maximum of 10 packets per message). The total number of packets in the original profile is 67476 packets. The compression analysis in Figures 1 to 3 is performed with compression ratios of 1.25, 2.00 and 2.5.

To explore the compression efficiency, let us define an effective compression ratio - α_E - as the ratio of the number of packets of a given profile (before compression) to the number of packets after the application of a compression process,

i.e., $\quad \alpha_E = N_P/N_p^C =$

$$(\sum_{k=1}^{K} \sum_{j=1}^{Q_k} N_{jk}) / (\sum_{k=1}^{K} \sum_{j=1}^{Q_k^C} N_{jk}^C)$$

This effective compression ratio reflects the actual decrease in the number of packets transmitted over the network. Its importance is evident both to network utilization and to cost/delay analysis.

The effective compression ratio, α_E, is a function of three factors:

- The data profile - F.
- The compressor's compression ratio - α.
- The compression level - CL = {SC,MC,PC}.

i.e., $\alpha_E = \alpha_E(F, \alpha, CL)$, where the following relation generally exists:

$$\alpha_E(F, \alpha, SC) \geq \alpha_E(F, \alpha, MC) \geq \alpha_E(F, \alpha, PC)$$

Table 1 summarizes the compression analysis of Figures 1 to 3 and defines the "effective" compression ratios for the various "nominal" compression ratios.

III. The Cost-Savings Model

The cost-savings tradeoffs of a data compression service, provided free of charge by the network operator, are modeled in this section.

Let

P_C = A per unit (1000 bits) cost of data compression/decompression.

P_T = A per unit (1000 bits) cost of data transmission (leased lines).

P_M = A per message processing cost in the network's nodal processor.

P_P = A per packet processing cost in the network's nodal processor.

ANALYSIS OF PROFILE 28   ALPHA= 1.25

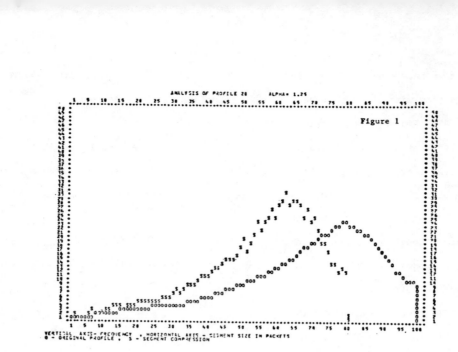

Figure 1

VERTICAL AXIS- FREQUENCY , HORIZONTAL AXIS - SEGMENT SIZE IN PACKETS
0 = ORIGINAL PROFILE , S = SEGMENT COMPRESSION

ANALYSIS OF PROFILE 28   ALPHA= 2.00

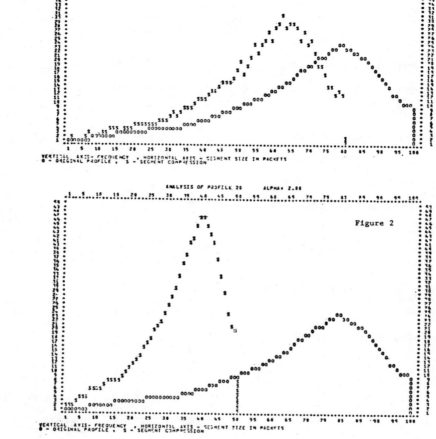

Figure 2

VERTICAL AXIS- FREQUENCY , HORIZONTAL AXIS - SEGMENT SIZE IN PACKETS
0 = ORIGINAL PROFILE , S = SEGMENT COMPRESSION

ANALYSIS OF PROFILE 28   ALPHA= 2.50

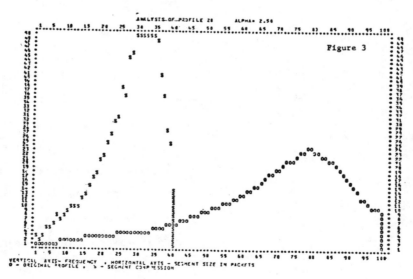

Figure 3

VERTICAL AXIS- FREQUENCY , HORIZONTAL AXIS - SEGMENT SIZE IN PACKETS
0 = ORIGINAL PROFILE , S = SEGMENT COMPRESSION

68

C_D = Cost of the compression service, in terms of a royalty fee per period (we assume that a compression package is available to the network operator for a royalty fee).

Then, the network total cost of transmitting a given data profile, without compression, is:

(1) $TC = P_T \cdot L + P_T \cdot N_M \cdot \ell_R + P_M \cdot N_M + P_T \cdot N_P \cdot \ell_R + P_P \cdot N_P$

where

$P_T \cdot L$ — User's data transmission cost.

$P_T \cdot N_M \cdot \ell_R$ — Transmission cost of N_M RFNM messages, of ℓ_R bits each.

$P_M \cdot N_M$ — Processing cost of N_M messages.

$P_T \cdot N_P \cdot \ell_R$ — Transmission cost of overhead for N_P packets.

$P_P \cdot N_P$ — Processing cost of N_P packets.

α	PROFILE	NUM OF SEGMENTS	NUM OF MESSAGES	NUM OF DATA PACKETS	TOTAL NUM OF PACKETS	α_E	α_{EM}	$\bar{S}$	$\bar{M}$
1.25	ORIGINAL	1006	7196	67476	74672	1.00	1.00	67.1	9.4
	SEG. COMP.	1006	5855	54065	59920	1.25	1.23	53.7	9.2
	MES. COMP.	1006	7196	54065	61261	1.25	1.00	53.7	7.5
1.50	SEG. COMP	1006	4974	45131	50105	1.50	1.45	44.9	9.1
	MES. COMP	1006	7196	47211	54407	1.43	1.00	46.9	6.6
1.75	SEG. COMP.	1006	4333	38766	43099	1.74	1.66	38.5	8.9
	MES. COMP.	1006	7196	40548	47744	1.66	1.00	40.3	5.6
2.0	SEG. COMP.	1006	3844	33991	37835	1.99	1.87	33.8	8.8
	MES. COMP.	1006	7196	33991	41187	1.99	1.00	33.8	4.7
2.5	SEG. COMP.	1006	3177	27281	30458	2.47	2.27	27.1	8.6
	MES. COMP.	1006	7196	27281	34477	2.47	1.00	27.1	3.8

TABLE 1: Statistics for Effective Compression Ratios

When a compression procedure with compression ratio α is applied to the data, the resulting total cost $TC^{c\,(1)}$ is:

(2) $TC^C =$

$$P_T \cdot L/\alpha + P_T \cdot N_M^C \cdot \ell_R + P_M \cdot N_M^C + P_T \cdot N_P^C \cdot \ell_R + P_P \cdot N_P^C + C_D + P_C \cdot L$$

The compression service is economically viable to the network operator if the "after compression" costs do not exceed the regular transmission cost (without compression).

i.e.,

(3) $$TC^C \leq TC$$

Hence,

(4)
$$P_T \cdot L \cdot (\alpha-1)/\alpha + P_M(N_M - N_M^C) +$$
$$P_T \cdot \ell_R(N_M - N_M^C) + P_P(N_P - N_P^C) +$$
$$P_T \cdot \ell_R(N_P - N_P^C) - C_D - P_C \cdot L \geq 0$$

Thus by isolating P_C we can determine the upper bound for economically viable service.

(5)
$$P_C \leq P_T \cdot (\alpha-1)/\alpha + (P_M + P_T \cdot \ell_R) \cdot (N_M - N_M^C)/L +$$
$$(P_P + P_T \cdot \ell_R) \cdot (N_P - N_P^C)/L - C_D/L$$

----

(1) Recall that superscript c denotes the number of messages and packets after compression.

Define: ℓ_M – Average message size in the profile $= L/N_M$

ℓ_P – Average packet size in the profile $= L/N_P$

Substituting in (5) results in:

(6) $$P_C \leq P_T \cdot (\alpha-1)/\alpha + (P_M + P_T \cdot \ell_R)/\ell_M \cdot (1 - N_M^C/N_M) +$$
$$(P_P + P_T \cdot \ell_R)/\ell_P (1 - N_P^C/N_P) - C_D/L$$

Recall that $\alpha_E = N_P/N_P^C$, and denote $\alpha_{EM} = N_M/N_M^C$, the effective compression ratio for messages.

Then

(7) $$P_C \leq P_T \cdot (\alpha-1)/\alpha + (P_M + P_T \cdot \ell_R)/\ell_M \cdot (\alpha_{EM} - 1)/\alpha_{EM} +$$
$$(P_P + P_T \cdot \ell_R)/\ell_P (\alpha_E - 1)/\alpha_E - C_D/L$$

Equation (7) determines the upper bound on the cost of compression/decompression (from the network operator viewpoint) for a free compression service. Consequently, the following conclusions can be drawn:

A. The upper bound on P_C is sensitive to the compression level:

- When compression is performed at the packet level, there is a reduction only in the informational portion of the data (number of packets and messages does not change). Therefore, the upper bound of compression cost is most restrictive.

i.e., $P_C \leq P_T \cdot (\alpha-1)/\alpha - C_D/L$

- Compression at the message level results also in some reduction in the number of packets.

i.e., $P_C \leq (P_T \cdot (\alpha-1)/\alpha - C_D/L) + (P_P + P_T \cdot \ell_R)/\ell_P \cdot (\alpha_E-1)/\alpha_E$

- At the segment compression level there is an additional reduction in the number of packets and messages, and the upper bound on P_C is the least restrictive as in (7).

B. Compression savings are most significant on the long haul routes. This conclusion is based on the fact that tariffs on leased lines are distance dependent and monotonically increasing. The longer the route the packets travel, the higher are the transmission cost and the associated P_T.

C. Savings as a function of the compression level are sensitive to ℓ_R/ℓ_P (the overhead/information ratio).

Let us consider, for example, the following values:

P_T — Transmission cost for 50 KBPS 1500 mile line — 25 cents/1000 packets (based on $5/mile/month).

P_M — 0.2 cents/1000 packets (based on 10 msec per message).

P_P — 0.2 cents/1000 packets (based on 10 msec per packet).

C_D — A royalty fee of 3000 $/year (clearly an inflated figure).

L — $7.8.10^7$ packets/year.

ℓ_P — 1000 bits, typical for file transfer profile.

ℓ_M — 8000 bits.

ℓ_R — 168 bits (ARPA specifications).

Then, with compression ratio of about 2 (which is reasonable in today's technology), the upper bound of (7) is equal to 8.3 cents per 1000 packets. This value is significantly higher than the compression cost of about .2 cents/MBit.[2] This gap is bound to grow as the current trend of faster reduction of computation cost vs. transmission costs continues.

----

(2) Based on 10 seconds/MBit compression/decompression time on a typical communication processor [Gottlieb 75] and at a cost of .02 cents/second.

IV. Conclusions

In this work we examined the economic tradeoffs associated with a data compression service in a packet switching computer communication network. We assume the service to be operationally transparent to the users and provided to the users free of charge. A cost-saving model has been developed based on the characteristics of the data strings transmitted over the network. These characteristics have been represented by a "data-profile," a concept which provided us with a formal tool for describing structure and volume of the data. The analysis focused on a typical file-transfer profile, where long segments of data (long in terms of number of packets) are sent from node to node. This type of profile was analyzed in section II with different compression levels. The results of this analysis have been applied in the cost-saving model of section III. Clearly, significant savings have been realized when the compression has been applied to a file-transfer profile and when state of the art prices have been plugged into the model.

V. References

[Alsberg 75] Alsberg, P. A., "Space and Time Savings Through Large Data Base Compression and Dynamic Restructuring," Proceedings of the IEEE, Vol. 63, No. 8, August 1975, pp. 1114-1122.

[Cerf 77] Cerf, V. G. and A. Curran, "The Future of Computer Communication," Datamation, July 1978, pp. 88-93.

[Gottlieb 75] Gottlieb, D., et al, "A Classification of Compression Methods and their Usefulness for a Large Data Processing Center," AFIPS Conference Proceedings, Vol. 44, SJCC, May 1975, pp. 453-458.

[Huffman 52] Huffman, D. A., "A Method for the Construction of Minimum Redundancy Codes," Proceedings I.R.E., Vol. 40, 1952, pp. 1098-1101.

[Kleinrock 74] Kleinrock, L. and W. E. Naylor, "On Measured Behavior of the ARPA Network," AFIPS Conference Proceedings, Vol. 43, SJCC, May 1977, pp. 767-780.

[Lurin 78] Lurin, E. S. and E. I. Metz, "Get Ready for VAN," Datamation, July 1978, pp. 103-108.

CONCENTRATOR MODELING
WITH
PIPELINING ARRIVALS COMPENSATION

Dr. Patrick V. McGregor
ConTel Information Systems, Inc.

ABSTRACT

A general model of Intelligent Communications Concentrating Devices (ICCD) is presented and analyzed for delay and overflow performance with compensation for the pipelining effect of message arrivals extending over time. The results of the analysis indicate that, for the same trunk utilization, the trend towards buffered terminals with longer messages requires substantially greater buffering in the ICCD. The nominal environment analyzed consisted of 10-40 medium speed terminals (1200 b/s - 9600 b/s) operating over a medium speed trunk (9600 b/s) with trunk utilizations from 20 percent to 80 percent and average message lengths up to 1000 characters. This is a substantially different environment than that typically served by current implementations of ICCDs, which are frequently reported to have throughput improvements of 2-3 times the nominal originating terminal bandwidths, as opposed to the typical factor of 5 for the analyzed environment. This does not reflect on the appropriateness of the ICCDs in serving the new environment, but rather is simply stating that in the new environment the same character volume of traffic may be appearing with different traffic characteristics over higher speed access lines.

If the new environment shows only a difference in traffic characteristics and originating line speed, without change in the traffic control scheme (or lack of scheme), the results indicate essentially reproduction of

a large part of the terminal buffering in the ICCD for adequate overflow performance. Alternatively, with smarter terminals, traffic control schemes (flow control) may enable the ICCD to be reduced to an essentially unbuffered "traffic cop," with the terminal buffering also serving as the shared facility buffering. Several practical implementations of ICCDs have provision for flow control, but require cooperating terminals and hosts. This suggests that ICCD design and application will become more sensitive to the practical operating features of the target environment than has been generally the case to date.

The analysis presented in this paper involves many simplifications to the actual problem. Additional work to accommodate non-exponential message length distributions and heterogeneous terminal configurations are perhaps two of the more immediate problems that may be effectively dealt with.

1. INTRODUCTION

Data communication concentrating devices historically have achieved cost-effectiveness by superposing individual data streams arriving over individual transmission facilities onto one shared transmission facility for long distance connections [MCGR 74]. Early concentrating devices (Time Division Multiplexers and Frequency Division Multiplexers - TDM and FDM respectively) maintained data stream identity by providing a fixed capacity allocation on the shared facility for each of the superposed individual facilities. More recent devices have achieved additional cost-effectiveness through device intelligence to support a greater number of higher-speed terminals by dynamically allocating the capacity of the shared facility on the basis of actual data stream arrival as opposed to the nominal terminal operating speeds. For purposes of this paper, devices with the above capabilities are termed Intelligent Communications Concentrating Devices (ICCDs).

Although early communication concentrating devices were transparent to the data streams, the use of ICCDs to achieve statistical multiplexing economies implies queuing delays for the arriving data stream plus the possibility of service unavailability due to inadequate buffer capacity. To portray the impact of using ICCDs, three basic measures of performance are defined:

$E(W)$ - the average delay introduced by the use of ICCDs. $E(W)$ is defined from when the last character of input to the ICCD is received from the source (terminal or computer) until the last character is transmitted to the destination, normalized to the nominal transmission delay.

$P(W)$ - the probability that the delay introduced by the use of ICCDs is less than a specified value.

$Povf$ - the probability of a buffer overflow condition.

This paper focuses on evaluating such measures as a function of key factors on which they depend. In particular, the impact of a trend from low-speed, unbuffered terminals to high-speed, full-screen buffered terminals is examined. The next section describes a general model for ICCDs covering a wide range of commercial implementations and identifies the factors of interest in analyzing performance. The new analysis approach is neither as sophisticated nor as realistic as other available approaches, but it is considerably easier to implement and serves as a convenient engineering tool to examine the relative performance of alternative devices over a broad range of device and traffic characteristics. The analytical basis of the new approach is given in Section 4, and several results of its application are given in Section 5. Conclusions are presented in Section 6.

2. GENERAL MODEL

The general model of the ICCD is characterized as follows:

(1) individual terminals are connected to the ICCD over individual communication channels operating at a nominal speed S.

(2) When a data stream from an individual terminal begins to arrive, it is absorbed by the ICCD buffer until a "segment" of buffer is filled or an End of Message (EOM) indication is received (such as a carriage return character in line buffered terminals).

(3) The ICCD scans the buffers for each input line, placing filled segments in queue for transmission.

(4) Segments in queue for transmission are assembled as a frame with such overhead as appropriate for addressing and error checking, and are transmitted.

(5) The transmitted frame is retained in memory until a positive acknowledgement is received, after which the memory holding the frame is released. If a negative acknowledgement is received, the frame is returned to the head of the queue for retransmission.

A queuing design of the general model is shown in Figure 1. The general model covers the range of devices commonly known as Intelligent Time Division Multiplexers (ITDMs), Packetized Concentrators (PCs) -- packet switches without switching, and Message Concentrators (MCs), the difference being primarily in the size of segments (very small in ITDMs to whole messages in MCs), and the discipline for frame structure composition (one segment per frame in PCs, while possibly many segments per frame in ITDMs).

The factors affecting performance impact of ICCDs in terms of the above measures can be divided into three broad groups: Device Design, Network Configuration, and Traffic Characteristics.

The primary factors of device design affecting its performance as an ICCD are:

● segment length (Ls) used to trigger buffer contents for transmission (possibly variable);

● frame length (Lf) used to transmit (possibly multiple) segments;

● discipline for scanning line buffers for segments and their assembly as a frame;

- ARQ scheme;

- buffer capacity and allocation scheme;

- flow control provisions;

- compaction technique.

Actual design variations treating each of these factors are numerous and can be very involved. Of interest here are the basic performance differences attributable to rather fundamental design choices, and not the detail of particular refinements.

Perhaps the simplest network configuration of ICCDs is a point-to-point connection of two ICCDs with the original individual facilities at the source end recreated at the destination end. Such a configuration makes the presence of the ICCD basically transparent to the destination, i.e., there is no need to change source and destination support mechanics. Although additional economies can be achieved by a variety of techniques, of interest here is the relative performance of ICCDs as a function of their basic design factors, and not network analysis. Consequently, only this simplest configuration is considered.

A third basic group of factors of interest are traffic related. Two basic dimensions of traffic characteristics are considered: message length and message arrival process. The message length is considered a random variable, ℓ , described by a probability density function, $p(\ell)$. Both input and output traffic is of interest, with the latter usually dominating device performance because of its generally greater length.

Considerable work has been done in characterizing data communications traffic [ABRA 77, DUDI 71, FUCH 70, FISC 72, LAM 78]. The results tend to confirm the generally used geometric probability densities (discrete) with approximation by exponential densities (continuous). Both of these densities are particularly attractive for queuing analysis, with the latter somewhat easier to work with than the former.

The message arrival process is perhaps the most difficult factor to statistically describe. The assumption that messages arrive at random is typical, and leads to description of the arrival process as Poisson (exponential probability density governing

interarrival intervals). However, there are considerable difficulties encountered with such a description in the case of ICCDs and the trend towards buffered terminals. In terms of the general ICCD model, a "message" arrives when a segment becomes ready for transmission. With ITDMs, this may be the arrival of a few characters, and unbuffered, low-speed terminals have been noted to generate such traffic consistent with a Poisson description [FUCH 70]. However, with higher-speed, buffered terminals, the interarrival rate of segments would be a series of constant intervals determined by the segment length and terminal line speed followed by a much longer interval (possibly exponentially distributed) of non-arrivals. Similarly, with PCs and MCs, the arrival process for short messages may appear Poisson with arrival instants defined as the instant of last character arrival, but for long messages (buffered terminals with messages longer than PC segments) the PC arrival process again appears as a sequence of constant interarrival intervals followed by a long interval of no arrrivals.

The significance of the distinctions noted above is examined in Section 3. For purposes of uniformity and simplicity, the arrival process of traffic from the terminal perspective (as opposed to the ICCD perspective) will be viewed as Poisson with a parameter λ message arrivals per second as the average rate. The arrival process from the ICCD perspective will be determined by λ , the ICCD design factors, terminal operating mode, and message length distribution.

3. PREVIOUS WORK

Analysis of ICCDs for both performance assessment and sizing has received considerable attention in the literature. There is no attempt here to present a comprehensive review of such material: rather, basic issues and approaches of delay and buffering analysis are highlighted with selective references and a more extended bibliography to allow the interested reader an opportunity to pursue a more comprehensive review.

The problems of delay distribution and buffering requirements are closely tied in the use of queuing models for ICCD analysis. Both depend on the message length distributions and state probabilities, and finding results for one can generally lead to application of the same analysis technique for finding results for the other. Basic analysis of buffer requirements for ITDMs in the case of Poisson arrivals [CHU 69] and mixed Poisson arrivals and compound Poisson arrivals [CHU 72] have been reported. The analysis approach involves using a Fast Fourier Transform to handle the convolutional part of the problem. More detailed and complex analysis with less constraining assumptions have also been pursued [ANDE 79, KAPL 78, KEKR 78, MASS 78, ZIEG 78]. An intuitive introduction to such analysis and its general applicability is also available [SCHW 77, CHU 73A]. The analysis of PCs and MCs is typically somewhat simpler because of their closer resemblance to the classical M/M/1 queue [BEIZ 75, MCGR 78, MCGR 75, SCHW 78].

In addition to the basic problem of determining buffer requirements, there is the problem of how best to fill the requirement. Several buffer allocation and optimization strategies have been studied [IRLA 78, LAM 79, RICH 77]. However, this work is beyond the intended scope of this paper except to note that quantification of the requirement is not the same as determining if a given storage dedicated to buffering is adequate. Such determination depends on the efficiency with which the storage is used. What can be said is that the requirement is a lower bound on the required storage for its satisfaction. The previous work on delay and buffer requirements analysis generally makes use of the Poisson arrival assumption. However, as noted previously, from the ICCD perspective the arrival process may be considerably different from Poisson. This is illustrated by the three cases synopsized below.

3.1   Case 1

Consider the case of an ICCD serving 20 terminals, each terminal operating with a nominal speed of 30 CPS and each terminal unbuffered. If the ICCD triggers on the carriage return character for forwarding the accumulating buffer for transmission, then the "message" is an input "line," and the arrival instant may be viewed as when the carriage return character is received. In this case, the previous empirical observations support the characterization of the arrival process as Poisson (and geometrically distributed message lengths). If the ICCD uses a segment length of one character, arrivals may still be viewed as Poisson, but with a character viewed as the "message" (constant message length distribution) and a

higher arrival rate (mesage arrival rate times average message length).

3.2   Case 2

Consider the case of an ICCD serving 20 terminals, now each terminal operating with a nominal speed of 120 CPS and each terminal with line buffering. If the ICCD keys on the carriage return character as in Case 1, then the process still looks Poisson and geometric. However, if the ICCD uses a segment much less in length than the average typed line length, then the arrival process is a string of fixed length segments (ending with a small variable   length segment) with constant interarrival times (determined by segment length and line speed), followed by a long interval of no arrivals. Because the ICCD forwards the individual segments as received, it is important to make this distinction. There is not a single instant in which the whole message of several segments is received, but rather a sequence of constant interarrival interval instants at which individual segments are received. The impact of this distinction can be trivially portrayed. Consider the extreme case of zero utilization, an average typed line length of 20 characters, and a segment of one character. Then with a Poisson model, the delay is the transmission time of the message on input (1/6 second) plus the transmission time of the entire message over the trunk (assuming 1200 CPS implies 1/60 second) plus the transmission of the entire message on output (1/6 second), or a total of approximately 1/3 second. With the constant segment model, the transmission of the entire message is only delayed by a single segment delay on the trunk and at the receiving end, or approximately 1/6 second, half the Poisson model. This resulting reduction in delay by segmenting is one of the motivating factors for packet switching as opposed to message switching, and is simply the "pipeline" effect.

3.3 Case 3

Consider the case of an ICCD serving 20 terminals, now each terminal operating with a nominal speed of 960 CPS and each terminal with full screen buffering. If the ICCD keys on the carriage return character as in Case 1, it now sees a sequence of typed lines each following the other with an interarrival time determined by the typed line length distribution, followed by a long interval of no arrivals. Although during the arrival burst the typed line arrivals may be Poisson, they are not in the context of the total time interval. Furthermore, if a fixed size segment is employed, with length less than the average screen size, then the Case 2 situation of arrivals is appropriate. In the full screen buffering case, the impact is more dramatic simply because of the longer forwarding time for the entire screen as opposed to the forwarding time of the last segment.

3.4 Implications

The three cases noted above reflect the general trend in data communications applications: longer messages occurring less frequently on higher speed lines. The implications for ICCDs extends well beyond the inappropriateness of assuming Poisson arrivals. If the aggregate data rate is constant over all three cases at 100 CPS, then a 1200 CPS trunk has very low utilization. In Case 1, there is no possibility of buffer overflow no matter if all terminals are active concurrently. In Case 2, if eleven or more terminals operate concurrently, buffering is required to prevent overflow, and the amount of buffering (plus the traffic statistics) will determine the probability of overflow. In Case 3, any two terminals active concurrently require buffering to prevent overflow. However, the likelihood of concurrent activity is similarly reduced as the nominal input transmission rate increases. The relationship between these factors is not intuitively obvious, and the relative performance of different ICCDs with different segment sizes and buffering is, as has been historically known, not easy. As the evolution trend continues, the removal (or compensation) of the Poisson assumption becomes more critical. Because of the significance of the Poisson assumption in a tractable analysis, the approach here is to simply compensate the classical queuing results to reflect the segment oriented operation of the ICCD rather than to eliminate the assumption.

4. BASIC APPROACH

The problem of interest may be succinctly described as follows:

Given:

(1)	M	–	Number of terminals
(2)	λ	–	Average generation rate of messages for each terminal (messages/second)
(3)	L	–	Average length of messages (characters)
(4)	$p(\ell)$	–	Probability density function of message length
(5)	S	–	Line speed of terminals (characters/second)
(6)	Bc	–	Total buffer capacity of ICCD (characters)
(7)	Bd	–	Amount of buffering dedicated to each terminal (characters)
(8)	Ls	–	Nominal segment length in ICCD operation (characters)
(9)	Lf	–	Nominal frame length in ICCD operation (characters)
(10)	Lfo	–	Overhead in nominal ICCD frame (characters)
(11)	FRD	–	Frame assembly discipline (i.e., one or multiple segments per frame)
(12)	ARQ	–	ARQ discipline (continuous or selective)
(13)	R	–	Shared facility line speed (characters/second)
(14)	PPD	–	Propagation delay on shared facility (second)
(15)	BER	–	Bit error rate on shared facility

- -

Find:

(16)	E(w)	–	Average system delay of messages
(17)	P(w<WMAX)	–	Probability that an arriving message will experience a total system delay less than WMAX
(18)	Povf	–	Probability of buffer overflow, i.e., the required buffer capacity is greater than the available buffer capacity

There is no attempt to provide an in-depth model and analysis treating all of the above factors. As noted in the previous section, such work can be very involved for each individual area. Rather, the approach here is to use a very simple model reflecting what is viewed as the primary factors in order to assess the impact of the traffic trend towards longer, less frequent messages arriving over higher-speed lines. However, the model does depart from previous work with its compensation for the Poisson arrivals assumption.

The simplified version of the problem incorporates only nominal consideration of frame overhead (10), frame assembly technique (11), and excludes consideration of ARQ technique (12), propagation delay (14), bit error rate (BER), and the destination retransmission component of delay.

4.1   Intuitive Description

Intuitive understanding of the model and analysis is facilitated by the following observations:

OBS 1:   The shared facility can serve $N = R/S$ segments before the next full segment arrives over the first line it served.

OBS 2:   As long as the server does not wait for message segment arrival, the service discipline of FIFO will give less delay than if segments of new messages are served before completing old messages. This is simply because the delay measure is based on completion of the last segment transferred and thus all messages could be delayed indefinitely if their last segment was held up for transmission of early segments of new messages.

OBS 3:   The above two observations lead to characterization of the ICCD as an N server FIFO queue.

OBS 4:   As a multiple server queue, note that each server remains occupied throughout the course of the message arrival. Thus, if message arrival initiation instants are Poisson, the state probabilities are the same as for whole message Poisson arrivals.

OBS 5:   When a message arrives to find less than N messages ahead of it, its delay is only the retransmission time of its first segment at the rate of its equivalent individual server (R/N) recalling that the destination retransmission component is excluded.

OBS 6:   When a message arrives to find greater than N messages ahead of it, its delay is determined by the time it spends in the queue plus its own service time. If there are k messages in the system at its arrival, the time in queue is simply the time required for the collection of N servers to complete service on k-(N-1) messages, i.e., only one server has to be free for the message to receive service, not all N servers.

OBS 7:   Analogous to delay, the buffer requirements for messages arriving to find less than N other messages in the queue require only a segment's worth of buffering, whereas the amount required for messages arriving to find more than N messages ahead requires storage determined by the rate at which they fill the buffer (line speed S) and the time before they move into the server.

Based on the above observations, the model may be viewed as a multiple-server queue subject to the ordinary assumptions but with delay and buffering compensated by the significance of segmentizing for the system states less than the number of servers. In particular, the memoryless attribute of exponential message length distributions means that the remaining service delay for messages in transmission (OBS 6 and 7) is independent of the amount already received. Thus, by assuming Poisson arrivals and exponential message lengths, the state probability analysis is the same as for ordinary queuing problems, with buffering and delay results to be compensated for the segmentizing. Note that although message lengths are discrete and generally characterized as geometrically distributed, the exponential approximation is quite reasonable for the longer messages of interest except to the extent that finite buffering in the terminals assures a maximum message length. No claim is made that the compensating measures are exact; only that they are reasonable for the purpose of asssessing the impact of current traffic trends on ICCD performance.

In analyzing the model described above, the message generation rate λ may be interpreted in two ways. If inputs are decoupled from outputs, the rate λ reflects the probability of a terminal generating a message at a random point in time. If, as is often the case, the terminal will not generate a new message until it receives the output corresponding to an old message, then the rate is the probability of a terminal generating a message at a random point in time, given that it has no message in the system. This latter case is called the finite customer population variation, and represents an implicit form of flow control. That is, as messages arrive and occupy buffering, the total arrival rate is reduced accordingly. However, this implicit form of flow control is not to be confused with explicit flow control approaches which dynamically control traffic on an individual terminal basis to match buffer availability. With the finite customer population model, traffic arrivals remain random, with only the average arrival rate dependent on the congestion in terms of the number of customers in the system: it does not directly depend on buffer occupancy, and there is no control over the length of an arriving message. One may anticipate that the case of decoupled inputs and outputs places more severe demands on the system in comparison to the finite customer population case. Analysis for both cases is presented, the former denoted as M/M/N, and the latter as M/M/N/M.

The primary assumptions of the analysis are explicitly stated as:

(A1) The interarrival intervals of messages described by an average arrival rate are governed by the exponential probability density function:

$$p(t) = \lambda e^{-\lambda t}$$

where t is measured from first character received of one message until first character received of the next message.

(A2) Message lengths of messages described by an average length L are governed by the exponential probability density function:

$$p(\ell) = \frac{1}{L} e^{-\ell/L}$$

4.2   M/M/N/M Delay Analysis

For the M/M/N/M queue (Poisson arrivals, exponential service time, N servers, M customers), the arrival rate of messages is dependent on the system state:

$$\lambda_k = (M-k)\lambda$$

The state probabilities are easily determined to be:

$$(1) \quad P_k = \binom{M}{k} \zeta^k P_o \qquad\qquad k \le N$$

$$(2) \quad P_k = \frac{M!}{(M-k)!N!} \frac{\zeta^k}{N^{k-N}} P_o \qquad N < k \le M$$

$$(3) \quad P_k = 0 \qquad\qquad k > M$$

$$(4) \quad P_o = \left[\sum_{k=0}^{N} \binom{M}{k} \zeta^k + \sum_{k=N+1}^{M} \frac{M}{(M-k)!N!} \frac{\zeta^k}{N^{k-N}} \right]^{-1}$$

where $\mu = \frac{R}{NL}$ is the equivalent individual server service rate, and $\zeta = \lambda / \mu$ is the equivalent individual server utilization when serving one terminal. The expected value of delay can be simply approximated as:

$$(5) \quad E(w) = \sum_{k=1}^{N-1} P_k \frac{(k+1)Ls}{R} + \sum_{k=N}^{M} \left(\frac{(k+1-N)L}{R} + \frac{NL}{R} \right) P_k$$

where N = R/S is the equivalent number of servers. The delay factor in the first term reflects the following operations model:

(A3) The ICCD synchronously transmits frames independent of the arrival state of input line segments.

(A4) However, the frame composition is one segment for each active line.

This operational scheme essentially establishes a pro-rated fixed allocation of shared facility capacity for each active line. Thus, a message which arrives to find the system in state $k < N$ receives a $R/(k+1)$ share of the capacity (R). In the second term, the average delay until the message arriving to find the system in state k receives service is the same as for the equivalent single-server case as all servers are busy $((k+1-N)L/R)$. The actual service time of the $k+1$ message remains that of its equivalent individual server (NL/R).

For a specified delay value W, the probability of system delay w being less than the specified value may be written as (for $W \geq Ls/S$):

$$(6) \quad P(w < W) = \sum_{k=0}^{N-1} Pk + \sum_{k=N}^{M-1} P(w < W \mid k) Pk$$

where for all cases of arrivals finding less than N messages in the system, only a segment delay is experienced; and for states N or greater, the condition is satisfied only if the delay of waiting for $(k+1-N)$ messages to complete service plus the delay of the arriving message's own service is less than the specified value. This is simply the probability distribution function of the system time for a given state. Since the interdeparture interval of the departure process is the interval between the collection of servers accepting the next customer, for so long as all servers are busy the departure process is Poisson with parameter μN, and to the waiting customers, the collection of servers appears the same as an equivalent single-server with parameter μN. With this in mind, it can be (not so readily) shown that:

$$(7) \quad P(w < W \mid k) = \left(\frac{N}{N-1}\right)^k \left[(1 - e^{-\mu W}) - \frac{1}{N} \sum_{i=0}^{k-1} \left(\frac{N-1}{N}\right)^i (1 - e^{-N\mu W} \sum_{j=0}^{i} \frac{(N\mu W)^j}{j!}) \right]$$

and for reference

$$(8) \quad p(w \mid k) = \left(\frac{N}{N-1}\right)^k \mu e^{-\mu w} \left[1 - e^{-(N-1)\mu w} \sum_{i=0}^{k-1} \frac{((N-1)\mu w)^i}{i!} \right]$$

The result (7) combined with the state probabilities (1), (2), (3), and (4) gives the needed algebra for (6).

4.2 M/M/N Delay

The M/M/N model is based on a state-independent arrival rate of messages, i.e.,

$$(9) \quad \lambda_k = M\lambda$$

With $N = R/S$ the number of equivalent servers as before, the state probabilities for this case are:

$$(10) \quad Pk = \frac{(N\zeta)^k}{k!} Po \qquad k < N$$

$$(11) \quad Pk = \frac{(N\zeta)^k}{N! \, N^{k-N}} Po \qquad k \geq N$$

$$(12) \quad Po = \left[\sum_{k=0}^{N-1} \frac{(N\zeta)^{k!}}{k!} + \frac{(N\zeta)^N}{(1-\zeta)N!} \right]^{-1}$$

where $\zeta = M\lambda/N\mu$ in this case is the equivalent aggregate server utilization. The expected value of delay is then:

$$(13) \quad E(w) = \sum_{k=0}^{N-1} Pk \frac{(k+1)Ls}{R} + \sum_{k=N}^{\infty} Pk \left(\frac{(k+1-N)L}{R} + \frac{NL}{R}\right)$$

The sum to infinity is computationally burdensome, and can be reduced to:

$$(14) \quad \sum_{k=N}^{\infty} Pk \left(\frac{(k+1-N)L}{R} + \frac{NL}{R}\right) = Po \frac{L}{R} \frac{(N\zeta)^N}{N!\,(1-\zeta)} \left[N + \frac{1}{1-\zeta} \right]$$

This gives:

$$(15) \quad E(w) = \sum_{k=1}^{N} Pk \frac{(k+1)Ls}{R} + Po \frac{L}{R} \frac{(N\zeta)^N}{N!(1-\zeta)} \left[N + \frac{1}{1-\zeta} \right]$$

The waiting time distribution (total communications system time, queuing and being served) for $W > Ls/S$ is:

$$(16) \quad P(w < W) = \sum_{k=0}^{N-1} Pk + P(w < W \mid k \geq N) \sum_{k=N}^{\infty} Pk$$

To determine $P(w < W \mid k \geq N)$, note that:

$$(17) \quad P(w < W \mid k \geq N) =$$

$$\frac{P(w < W) - P(w < W \mid k < N)P(k < N)}{P(k \geq N)}$$

From the perspective of the states of interest, the system is equivalent to an ordinary M/M/N queue in terms of delay. Thus, the $P(w \leq W)$ on the right hand side is the ordinary waiting time distribution which can be (not so readily) determined as:

$$(18) \quad P^O(w < W) \quad =$$

$$1 - e^{-\mu W} - \frac{PB}{N(1-\zeta)-1}\left[e^{-\mu W} - e^{-N(1-\zeta)\mu W}\right]$$

where PB is the probability that all servers are busy:

$$(19) \quad PB \quad = \quad \frac{\dfrac{(N\zeta)^N}{N!}}{\dfrac{(N\zeta)^N}{N!} + (1-\zeta)\displaystyle\sum_{k=0}^{N-1}\dfrac{(N\zeta)^k!}{k!}}$$

Note that in (17), the term $P(w < W \mid k < N)$ must also be that of the ordinary queue. For $k < N$, this is simply the probability that the message service time is less than W, i.e.,

$$(20) \quad P^O(w < W \mid k < N) = \sum_{k=0}^{N-1} Pk\,(1 - e^{-\mu W})\sum_{k=0}^{N-1} Pk$$

Substituting (20) and (18) into (17), and then (17) into (16) gives (after a little manipulation):

$$(21) \quad P(w < W) =$$

$$1 - \frac{PB}{N(1-\zeta)-1}\left[N(1-\zeta)e^{-\mu W} - e^{-N(1-\zeta)\mu W}\right]$$

4.3 M/M/N/M Overflow Analysis

The overflow analysis is a great deal more difficult than the delay analysis as the storage consumption of messages ahead of the arriving message does not depend solely on their waiting time or message length. This is because the arrival process for an individual message is extended over time, and a long message waiting behind short messages may still be arriving at the time it is served, and hence requires less than its length in interim storage. Alternatively, a short message behind long messages may complete its arrival long before it is served. The relationship between these alternative conditions and the other factors, including state probabilities, is not clear (or at least not yet determined by this author). As an approximation, the following is assumed:

(A5) Messages which arrive to find less than N messages in the system require only two segments of storage to accommodate their immediate service;

(A6) Messages which arrive to find N or more messages in the system complete their arrival before service, and hence require the full message length of storage.

This approximation appears conservative by the following argument:

● A short message behind a long message being served will complete its arrival before service, and hence requires its complete message length in storage.

● A long message behind a short message being served will complete only that part of its arrival which is equal to the short message length before being served (and hence requiring no additional storage).

● Consequently, the storage requirement appears determined by the set of k-N minimal length messages out of the entire set of k messages, rather than simply the k-N messages not being served.

The above argument is less than precise. It does not deal with the different starting times of the messages in service, the memoryless attribute to the exponential distribution of message length (and hence service time), or the possible reflection of the argument in the steady-state probabilities of the system states. However, it does provide an intuitive base for understanding the nature of the problem and the assertion of conservative assumptions.

Three different buffering alternatives are considered:

(A7) Pool: A fixed quantity of common storage is used to serve the arriving traffic with allocation on a demand basis.

(A8) Dedicated: A fixed quantity of storage is dedicated to each line to serve its (and only its) arriving traffic.

(A9) Mixed: A fixed quantity of dedicated storage is provided for each line, with a common pool of storage to handle requirements for storage in excess of the dedicated capacity.

For each of these alternatives, the approach to overflow analysis is to determine the probability that storage use in an infinite capacity queue will exceed the actual design capacity. Note that this is not the same as analyzing a truly limited capacity queue. In the former case, all traffic is accepted and eventually served; in the latter case traffic for which there is no capacity is rejected and places no additional demands on the system after rejection. These two cases seem to bound the reality of rejected traffic being resubmitted as soon as practical. However, the former model is easier to analyze, and typically gives negligible differences in results from the latter model for small probabilities of overflow (presumably the design area of interest).

For each of the three types of buffering (pool, dedicated, and mixed), two different perspectives of performance are applicable in defining the probability of overflow:

(A10) The probability that an arriving message will experience an overflow condition;

(A11) The probability that at a random point in time the system is experiencing overflow.

The difference in these two measures is readily illustrated by the case of dedicated buffering. The first measure (A1) depends only on the condition of the buffer serving the arriving message; the condition of other buffers is irrelevant. The second measure depends on the condition of all buffers. The focus here is on the first measure, as it reflects the perspective of the individual user. However, the same basic approach

to the analysis is applicable to both measures, and where notationally convenient, results for both are presented.

4.3.1 M/M/N/M Buffer Pool

This system is particularly easy to analyze under the stated assumptions. The state probabilities are as given in Section 4.1. For given state k (meaning k messages in the system at the time of message arrival), the probability that the arriving message will experience overflow is simply the probability that its message length, when combined with the k-N other messages in queue (recall that messages being served are presumed to require only two "segments" of storage), will be more than the specified capacity. This probability is (with addition of the state summation):

$$(22) \quad Povf = \sum_{k=N}^{M-1} Pk \; e^{-\frac{(Bc-NLs)}{L}} \sum_{i=0}^{k-N} \frac{(\frac{Bc-NLs}{L})^i}{i!}$$

where Bc is the buffer pool capacity, L the average message length, and Ls the segment length. The system overflow probability, Psovf is the same as (22) with the state summation from k=N+1 to M, and the second summation to k-N-1 rather than k-N (i.e., the probability of overflow at a random point in time is the state probability times the probability of overflow given the state -- without event dependence on an arriving message).

4.3.2 M/M/N/M Dedicated Buffering

The dedicated buffering model assumes a fixed allocation of storage (Bd) for each input line. For the finite customer population model, note that after k places a message in the system, it will not generate another message until the first message clears the system. Thus, the probability that an arriving message will cause overflow is, trivially,

$$(23) \quad Povf = e^{-Bd/L} \sum_{k=N}^{M-1} Pk$$

and is independent of state considerations. From the system perspective, overflow at a random point in time depends only on the number of messages in buffers, each with its own independent probability of overflow, i.e.,

$$(24) \quad Psovf = \sum_{k=N+1}^{M} Pk \sum_{i=1}^{k-N} \binom{k-N}{i} Povf^i (1-Povf)^{k-N-i}$$

$$= \sum_{k=N+1}^{M} Pk \left(1-(1-Povf)^{k-N}\right)$$

4.3.3 M/M/N/M Mixed Buffering

The problem of mixed buffering is compounded, naturally, by the joint events of an arriving message experiencing dedicated buffer overflow and buffer pool overflow. In this case, interpret Bc as the storage capacity of the pool minus the fixed requirement of 2NLs storage for the messages in service. The probability of the arriving message experiencing overflow may be written as the joint probabilities:

$$(25) \quad Povf = \sum_{k=N}^{M-1} Pk \; P(Bd \; overflow) \; P(Bc \; overflow \,|\, k)$$

The Pk term is given in (2), and the second term is simply (23). The third term is the probability of Bc overflow, given that the system is in state k when the message arrives. This term depends on how many messages are overflowing and their combined overflow requirement, and can be written as:

$$(26) \quad P(Bc \; overflow \,|\, k) = \sum_{i=1}^{k+1-N} \binom{k+1-N}{i} Pd^i (1-Pd)^{k+1-N-i} \; e^{-Bc/L}$$

$$\sum_{j=0}^{i-1} \frac{\left(\frac{Bc}{L}\right)^j}{j!}$$

where Pd is simply Povf in (23), i.e.,

$$(27) \quad Pd = e^{-Bd/L}$$

For the system perspective, change the k+1-N in (26) to k-N, and

$$(28) \quad Psovf = \sum_{k=N}^{M} Pk \; P(Bc \; overflow \,|\, k)$$

4.4   M/M/N Overflow Analysis

The overflow analysis for the infinite customer population model is structured the same as for the finite customer population model, i.e., the three cases of buffer pool, dedicated buffering, and mixed buffering are considered. The same basic approach of determining the probability of exceeding a specified design storage in an infinite capacity model is applied.

4.4.1 M/M/N Buffer Pool

The probability of a message arriving to find k other messages in the system experiencing an overflow remains given by (22). However, now the summation over the state probabilities gives (with Bc the capacity minus the NLs needed for messages in service):

$$(29) \quad Povf = \sum_{k=N}^{\infty} \frac{(N\zeta)^k}{N! N^{k-N}} Po \; e^{-\frac{(Bc-NLs)}{L}} \sum_{i=0}^{k-N} \frac{\left(\frac{Bc}{L}\right)^i}{i!}$$

With suitable manipulation, this can be reduced to the less computationally burdensome form of:

$$(30) \quad Povf = Po \; \frac{(N\zeta)^N}{N} \; \frac{e^{-(1-\zeta)Bc/L}}{1-\zeta}$$

Note that the system probability of overflow (Psovf) is simply (29) with the summation index on the infinite sum changed to k+N+1 and the limit on the second summation changed to k-N-1. The same type of simplification as seen in (30) is obvious.

4.4.2 M/M/N Dedicated Buffers

For a system in state k, the probability of the arriving message finding exactly i of the k-N queued messages in its buffer is simply the binomial distribution:

$$(31) \quad P(i|k) = \binom{k-N}{i} \frac{1}{M^i} \left(1-\frac{1}{M}\right)^{k-N-i}$$

where M is the number of lines and the homogeneity of the problem is used to argue that all possible distributions of messages are equally likely. To accommodate posssible messages in transmission, the

83

not unreasonable modeling assumption is made that no line has more than one message in service at any point in time, and thus, given i messages in the buffer at the time of arrival, the probability of overflow is:

$$(32) \quad P(ovf \mid k, i) =$$

$$\frac{N}{M} \, e^{-(Bd-Ls)/L} \sum_{j=0}^{i} \left(\frac{Bd-Ls}{L}\right)^j \frac{1}{j!} \; +$$

$$(1-\frac{N}{M}) \, e^{-Bd/L} \sum_{j=0}^{i} \left(\frac{Bd}{L}\right)^j \frac{1}{j!}$$

Note that the above is only an approximation to the extent that the modeling assumption implies that in state k there may be more than k-N messages being queued and not served. However, the simplification does have reasonable basis in reality. The conditional probabilities of (32) and (31) can be combined as below to determine the probability of overflow:

$$(33) \quad Povf = \sum_{k=N}^{\infty} Pk \sum_{i=0}^{k-N} P(i \mid k) \, P(ovf \mid k, i)$$

Simplification of this expression into a closed form has been pursued by the author without fruition to date. The system perspective probability of overflow is somewhat more involved, and can be stated as:

$$(34) \quad Psovf = P(N) \, e^{-Bd/L} \; +$$

$$\sum_{n=1}^{\infty} P(n+N) \left\{ 1 - \left[\sum_{\substack{\Sigma=n \\ i}} \left(\prod_{j=1}^{M} Pij \right) \right] \right\}$$

where

$$(35) \quad Pij =$$

$$\frac{N}{j} (1-e^{-(Bd-Ls)/L} \sum_{m=0}^{i-1} \left(\frac{Bd-Ls}{L}\right)^m \frac{1}{m!}) \; +$$

$$(1-\frac{N}{j}) (1-e^{-Bd/L} \sum_{m=0}^{i-1} \left(\frac{Bd}{L}\right)^m \frac{1}{m!})$$

and Pij=1 for i=0. No simplification has been attempted.

4.4.3 M/M/N Mixed Buffering

As before, the problem of mixed buffering is compounded by the joint events of an arriving message experiencing dedicated buffer overflow and buffer pool overflow. How ever, there is one simplification: the problem of 2NLs storage for messages in service may be viewed as a fixed component of the buffer pool. In this case, interpret Bc as the storage capacity of the pool minus this fixed requirement. The probability of the arriving message experiencing overflow may be written as the joint probabilities:

$$(36) \quad Povf =$$

$$\sum_{k=N}^{\infty} Pk \, P(Bd \, overflow \mid k) \, P(Bc \, overflow \mid k)$$

The Pk term is given in (2), and the second term is readily found from (31) and (32). It is the third term which is of interest.

For i messages in a buffer, the probability that exactly j will overflow into the common pool (from the one buffer) is:

$$(37) \quad P(j \, overflow \mid i \, in \, buffer) =$$

$$\binom{i}{j} \, e^{-Bd/L} \sum_{n=0}^{i-j+1} \left(\frac{Bd}{L}\right)^n \frac{1}{n!}$$

For notational simplicity, let Pjim be (37) with an index m to track particular lines, and define:

$$(38) \quad Pjim = 1 \text{ for } i=0$$

noting $j \leq i$. Then for k+1-N messages in queue, the probability that exactly q messages overflow into the buffer pool is:

$$(39) \quad g_{k+1-N}(q) = \sum_{\substack{\Sigma=q, \; \Sigma \\ j \quad i}=k+1-N} \left(\prod_{m=1}^{M} Pjim \right)$$

The overflow probability is then:

$$(40) \quad P(Bc \, overflow \mid k) =$$

$$\sum_{q=1}^{k+1-N} g_{k+1-N}(q) e^{-Bc/L} \sum_{n=0}^{q-1} \left(\frac{Bc}{L}\right)^n \frac{1}{n!}$$

The above (40) provides the third term for (36) and completes the exercise.

The system probability of overflow is quite analogous in development to the above. Essentially, just remove the requirement of the arriving message overflow (second term in (36)) and change the index from k=N to k=N+1. The rest follows in an ordinary way.

4.5   Segment Size

In the above, the segment size Ls has been somewhat carelessly used to enable simplicity of discussion and notation. Recall that the model permits partially filled segments. This has two impacts. In delay, the segment delay should be dependent on the segment length of the first segment. For buffering, the actual usable capacity should reflect the efficiency of storage, i.e., assuming storage allocated in blocks equal to the segment size, the term Bc should be diminished to Bc(Lsa/Ls) where Lsa is the average segment length. For the assumed exponential message length distribution, the average segment length (and average first segment length) is simply:

$$(41) \quad Lsa \quad = \quad L(1-e^{-Ls/L})$$

5.   RESULTS

The basic model described in the previous section has been implemented in Fortran as an interactive modeling tool and used to produce numerous results. This section summarizes and interprets several of the results. The first part of the discussion focuses on delay characteristics, and the second part on the probability of overflow. In interpreting the results, the reader is cautioned to note the following caveats:

- The model still has many simplifications and assumptions, and has not been validated with actual device performance monitoring: consequently, the results are more appropriately viewed as "ballpark" numbers for comparative analysis then as precise design guidance.

- The use of the exponential message length distribution is more suspect for longer message, buffered terminals as (1) generally the terminal will have limited buffering (albeit comparatively large) and thus a maximum length message, whereas the exponential distribution with a reasonably large mean gives "significant" probability to very large messages, and (2) large messages and smart terminals are more likely to be coupled with some form of blocked message protocol.

The above caveats serve only to caution the reader in interpreting the results. There remains numerous circumstances where the results may be quite applicable, e.g., buffered terminals with floppy disks using the ICCD for error control (as opposed to some form of blocked protocol).

5.1   Delay Results

The normalized average system delay (i.e., average delay divided by nominal transmission delay) versus trunk utilization for both the finite customer population and infinite customer population is shown in Figure 2. Of particular significance is the less than unity delay for utilizations less than .7, whereas in the classical M/M/1 queue unity delay is the minimum, and the occurrence of the "knee" at a higher utilization. Both results are attributable to the use of segmenting. As anticipated, the finite customer population model shows a better performance characteristic than the infinite customer population model.

The normalized delay distribution functions for terminal speeds of 120 CPS and 960 CPS (equal to the trunk speed) are shown in Figure 3. The impact of line speed is obvious and shows the significance of using a normalized measure. The actual delay distribution functions are (intuitively) the same.

The significance of segment length is shown in Figure 4. The strange shape of the curves is readily interpreted. For small segments, variation in segment length has minimal impact because the only significant delay contributors are those messages which are blocked from service until completion of the entire (pipelining) message in transit. For large segments, the system appears essentially as a Message Concentrator, and delay is determined by all message lengths. In between, the segment length impacts the delay in accordance with how much delay it imparts to the pipelining messages.

The insignificance of segment length is shown in Figure 5. Because the model is applicable only to cases where WMAX > Ls/S, the delay distribution function reflects only the delay experienced by messages which must wait for an equivalent server to become available. This waiting time depends only on the lengths of the messages being served, and not the segment length.

The delay distribution functions for several trunk utilization values are shown in Figure 6. The impact of segmenting appears as the relatively high constant component of the distribution, with lesser impact with increasing utilization.

5.2 Overflow

The probability of overflow as a function of buffer pool size for various utilization values is shown in Figure 7. Note that even for very small values of utilization (ζ=.20) there are significant overflow probabilities. This shows the relative significance of the exponential message length distribution and its probabilities of very long messages, in contrast to the effect of multiple simultaneous messages.

The significance of terminal speed is illustrated by the curves of Figure 8. Recall that the terminal speed determines the number of equivalent servers, and hence the degree of pipelining achievable. As seen by the results, over the range considered terminal speed does not appear to have major impact. However, note that this range is essentially that of medium speed terminals (as opposed to 10 CPS low speed terminals). Also note that, as anticipated, the finite customer population model shows a better performance characteristic than the infinite customer population model.

The overflow probability dependence on segment length is illustrated by the curves of Figure 9. Note a much more dramatic dependence than shown for line speed. Indeed, with longer segment lengths there is also an amplification of the line speed dependence. However, the primary contributor to the difference between the results in Figures 7 and 8 is neither segment length nor line speed, but the change in message length (L=1000 in Figure 7, and 200 in Figure 8). This is examined in more detail later.

For the infinite customer population model (M/M/N), there is no dependence of overflow on the number of terminals: only on the total arrival rate of messages. However, for the finite customer population model (M/M/N/M) the number of terminals determines the magnitude of traffic reduction step with each arriving message. The difference is illustrated by the curves in Figure 10. As would be expected, the larger the number of terminals the more the M/M/N/M model resembles the M/M/N model.

The dependence of overflow performance on the buffering scheme is dramatically illustrated by the pooled and dedicated buffer results shown in Figure 11. Although at first glance the curves appear quite comparable, note the order of magnitude difference in the total storage dedicated to buffering for the two cases (as shown on the abscissa).

The last two figures (Figures 12 and 13) show the probability of overflow for various message lengths for both the finite and infinite customer population models. They clearly illustrate that the trend towards longer messages portends a greater magnitude of buffering problem than previously considered, i.e., for the same trunk utilization, longer messages imply a substantially greater buffering requirement than short messages, even with small segments.

6. CONCLUSION

A general model of Intelligent Communications Concentrating Devices has been presented and analyzed for delay and overflow performance with compensation for the pipelining effect of message arrivals extending over time. The results of the analysis indicate that, for the same trunk utilization, the trend towards buffered terminals with longer messages requires substantially greater buffering in the ICCD. The nominal environment analyzed consisted of 10-40 medium speed terminals (1200 b/s - 9600 b/s) operating over a medium speed trunk (9600 b/s) with trunk utilizations from 20 percent to 80 percent and average message lengths up to 1000 characters. This is a substantially different environment than that typically served by current implementations of ICCDs, which are frequently reported to have throughput improvements of 2-3 times the nominal originating terminal bandwidths, as opposed to the typical factor of 5 for the analyzed environment. This does not reflect on the appropriateness of the ICCDs in serving the new environment, but rather is simply stating that in the new environment the same character volume of traffic may be appearing with different traffic characteristics over higher speed access lines.

If the new environment shows only a difference in traffic characteristics and originating line speed, without change in the traffic control scheme (or lack of scheme), the results indicate essentially reproduction of a large part of the terminal buffering in the ICCD for adequate overflow performance. Alternatively, with smarter terminals, traffic control schemes (flow control) may enable the ICCD to be reduced to an essentially unbuffered "traffic cop," with the terminal buffering also serving as the shared facility buffering.

Several practical implementations of ICCDs have provision for flow control, but require cooperating terminals and hosts. This suggests that ICCD design and application will become more sensitive to the practical operating features of the target environment than has been generally the case to date.

The analysis presented in this paper involves many simplifications to the actual problem. Additional work to accommodate non-exponential message length distributions and heterogeneous terminal configurations are perhaps two of the more immediate problems that may be effectively dealt with.

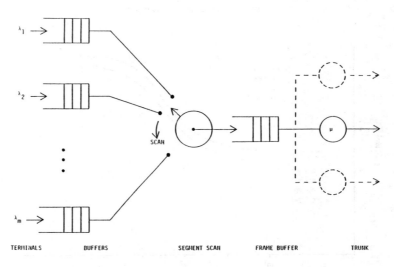

FIGURE 1: ICCD QUEUEING MODEL

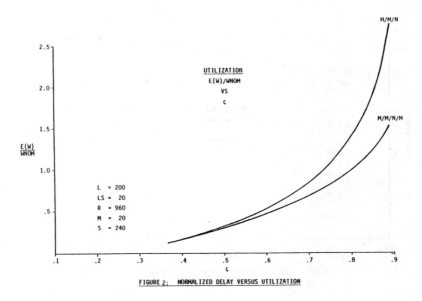

FIGURE 2: NORMALIZED DELAY VERSUS UTILIZATION

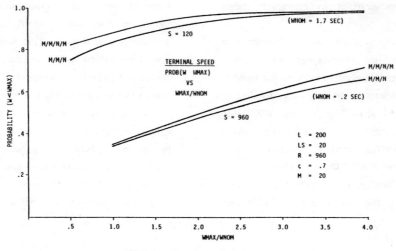

FIGURE 3: DELAY DISTRIBUTION FUNCTIONS

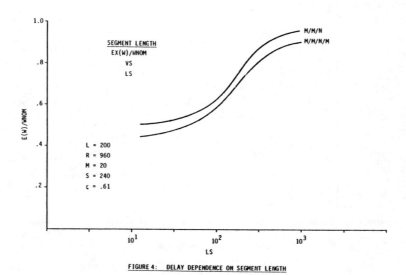

FIGURE 4: DELAY DEPENDENCE ON SEGMENT LENGTH

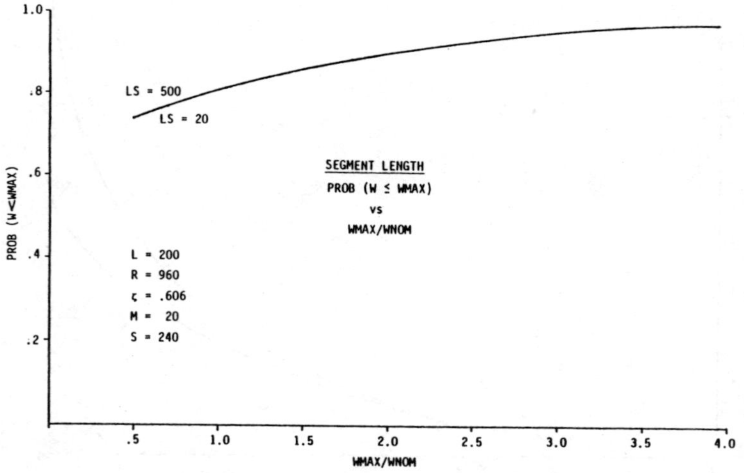

FIGURE 5: DELAY DIST►IBUTION DEPENDENCE ON SEGMENT LENGTH

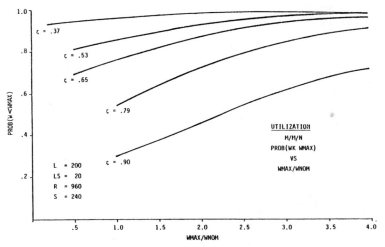

FIGURE 6: DELAY DISTRIBUTIONS FOR VARIOUS VALUES OF UTILIZATION

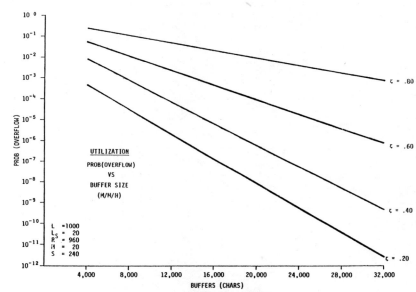

FIGURE 7: OVERFLOW AND UTILIZATION

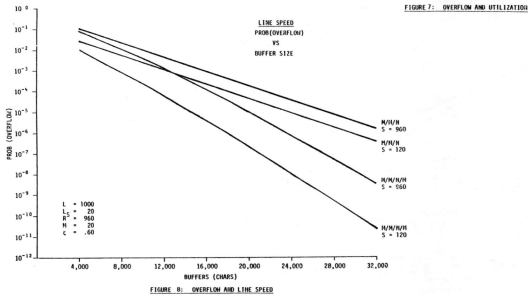

FIGURE 8: OVERFLOW AND LINE SPEED

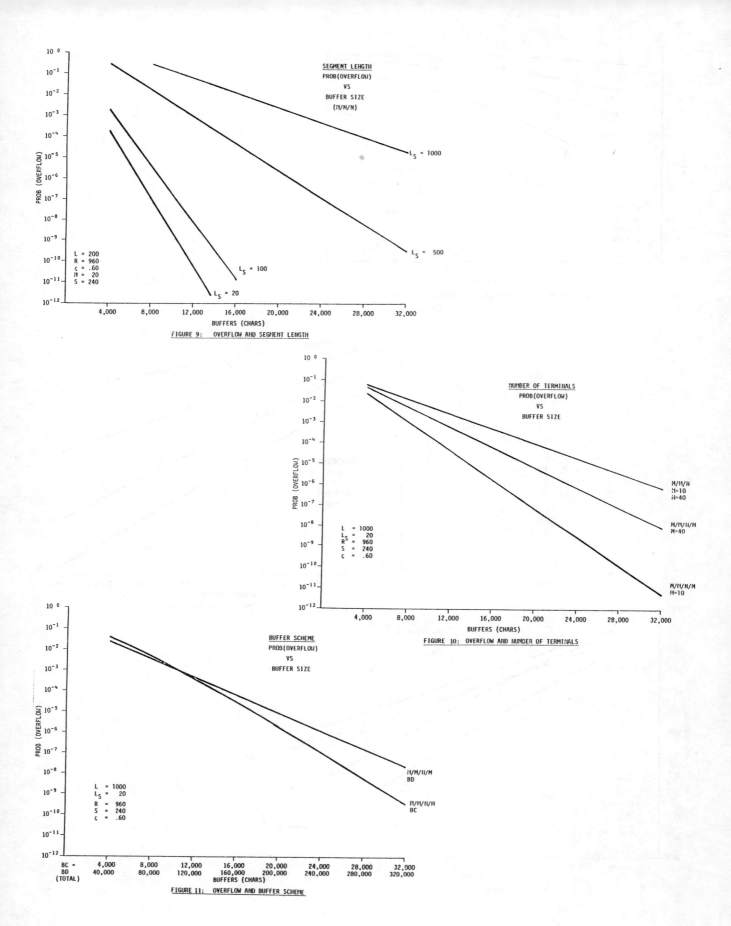

FIGURE 9: OVERFLOW AND SEGMENT LENGTH

FIGURE 10: OVERFLOW AND NUMBER OF TERMINALS

FIGURE 11: OVERFLOW AND BUFFER SCHEME

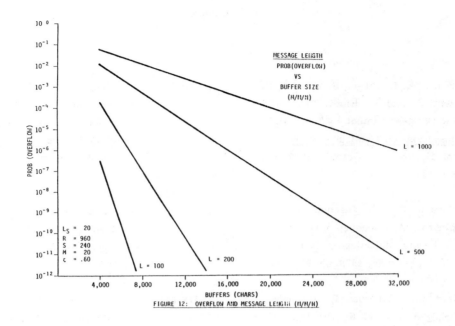

FIGURE 12: OVERFLOW AND MESSAGE LENGTH (H/M/H)

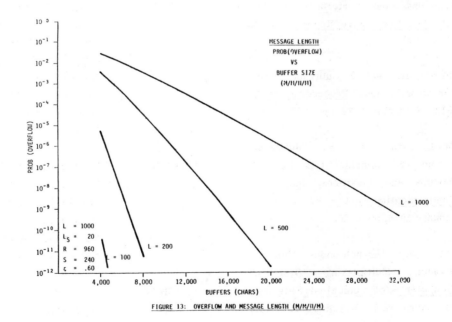

FIGURE 13: OVERFLOW AND MESSAGE LENGTH (M/M/H/M)

[ABRA 77]   Abrams, M., I. Cotton, S. Watkins, R. Rosenthal, and D. Rippy, "The NBS Network Measurement System," IEEE Transactions on Communications, Vol. COM-25, No. 10, October 1977, pp. 1189-1198.

[ANDE 79]   Anderson, R., G. Foschini, and B. Gopinath, "A Queueing Model for a Hybrid Data Multiplexer," BSTJ, Vol. 58, No. 2, February 1979, pp. 279-300.

[BEIZ 75]   Beizer, B., I. Aharoni, R. Rosenberg, E. Shagen, and T. Smith, "Analytic Models of Communications Switching Systems: Purpose, Practice, Problems, and Performance," IEEE Intercom Conference Record, Section 23/4, 1975.

[BURT 72]   Burton, H., and D. Sullivan, "Errors and Error Control," Proceedings of the IEEE, November 1972, pp. 1293-1301.

[CHOU 76]   Chou, W., and P. McGregor, "Computer Communications: Network Devices and Functions," Computer Communication Review, Vol. 6, No. 1, January 1976, pp. 5-26.

[CHU 73]   Chu, W., "Asynchronous Time - Division Multiplexing Systems," Computer -Communication Networks, ed. Abramson, N. and F. Kuo, Prentice-Hall, Inc., Englewood Cliffs, New Jersey, 1973.

[CHU 73B]   Chu, W., "Dynamic Buffer Management for Computer Communications," Proceedings of the Third Data Communication Symposium, Tampa, Florida, November 1973, pp. 68-72.

[CHU 72]   Chu, W., and L. Liang, "Buffer Behavior for Mixed Input Traffic and Single Constant Output Rate," IEEE Transactions on Communications, Vol. COM-2g, April 1972, pp. 230-235.

[CHU 69]   Chu, W., "A Study of Asynchronous Time Division Multiplexing for Time-Sharing Computers," AFIPS Proceedings, Vol. 35, FJCC, 1969, pp. 669-678.

[COX 61]   Cox, D., and W. Smith, "Queues," Champman & Hall, London 1961.

[DUDI 71]   Dudick, A., E. Fuchs, and P. Jackson, "Data Traffic Measurements for Inquiry — Response Computer Communications Systems," Proceedings of the IFIP, Ljubljana, Yugoslavia, August 1971, pp. 634-641 (also Advances in Computer Communications, W. Chu, ed. Artech House, Inc., 1976).

[FISC 72]   Fischer, M., "A Discussion of the Two Basic Assumptions used in Modeling Traffic Behavior in Telecommunications Networks," Technical Comment, No. 4-72, Defense Communications Agency, December 1972.

[FUCH 70]   Fuchs, E., and P. Jackson, "Estimates of Distributions of Random Variables for Certain Computer Communications Traffic Models," CACM, Vol. 13, No. 12, 1970, pp. 752-757.

[HEAR 73]   Heart, F., et. al., "A New Minicomputer/Multiprocessor for the ARPA Network," Proceedings NCC, 1973, pp. 529-537.

[IRLA 78]   Irland, M., "Buffer Management in a Packet Switch," <u>IEEE Transactions on Communications</u>, Vol. COM-26, No. 3, March 1978, pp. 328-337.

[KAPL 78]   Kaplan, M., "The Queue D/D/1 with a Poisson Background," <u>ICC 78 Conference Record</u>, Vol. 3, Toronto, Canada, June 4-7, 1978, pp. 36.5.1-36.5.4.

[KEKR 78]   Kekre, H., and C. Saxena, "Finite Buffer Behavior with Poisson Arrivals and Random Server Interruptions," <u>IEEE Transactions on Communications</u>, Vol. COM-26, No. 4, April 1978, pp. 470-474.

[KLEI 75]   Kleinrock, L., "Queueing Systems - Volume 1: Theory," John Wiley & Sons, Inc., New York, 1975.

[KLEI 64]   Kleinrock, L., "Communication NETS: Stochastic Message Flow and Delay," Dove Publications, Inc., New York, 1972 (also McGraw Hill, 1964).

[KOBA 77]   Kobayashi, H., and A. Konheim, "Queueing Models for Computer Communications Systems Analysis," <u>IEEE Transactions on Communications</u>, Vol. COM-25, No. 1, January 1977, pp. 2-29.

[KUEH 79]   Kuehn, P., "Approximate Analysis of General Queueing Networks by Decomposition," <u>IEEE Transactions on Communications</u>, Vol. COM-27, No. 1, January 1979, pp. 113-126.

[LAM 79]   Lam, S., and M. Reiser, "Congestion Control of Store-and-Forward Networks by Input Buffer Limits - An Analysis," <u>IEEE Transactions on Communications</u>, Vol. COM-27, No. 1, January 1979, pp. 127-133.

[LAM 78]   Lam, S., "A New Measure for Charactering Data Traffic," <u>IEEE Transactions on Communications</u>, Vol. COM-26, No. 1, January 1978, pp. 137-140.

[MASS 78]   Massey, W., and J. Morrison, "Calculation of Steady-State Probabilities for Content of Buffer with Correlated Input," <u>BSTJ</u>, Vol. 57, No. 9, November 1978, pp. 3097-3117.

[MCGR 78]   McGregor, P., and R. Kaczmarek, "Modeling Network Architectures," <u>Proceedings Compcon 78</u>, September 5-8, 1978, Washington, D.C., pp. 419-426.

[MCGR 75]   McGregor, P., W. Chou, and R. Kaczmarek, "Communications Processor Simulation: A Practical Approach," <u>Proceedings NTC</u>, December 1975.

[MCGR 74]   McGregor, P., "Effective Use of Data Communications Hardware," <u>Proceedings NCC</u>, May 1974.

[MOLI 27]   Molina, E., "Applications of the Theory of Probability to Telephone Trunking Problems," <u>BSTJ</u>, 1927, pp. 461-494.

[MORR 79]   Morris, J., "Optimal Blocklengths for ARQ Error Control Schemes," <u>IEEE Transactions on Communications</u>, Vol. COM-27, No. 2, February 1979, pp. 488-493.

[NEWP 77]   Newport, C., and P. Kaul, "Communications Processors for Telenet's Third Generation Packet Switching Network," <u>EASCON-77 Record</u>, September 26-28, 1977, (IEEE Pub. No. 77C1 & 1255-9 EASLOW).

[OPDE 78]   Opderbeck, H., J. Hoffmeier, and K. Spitzer, "Software Architecture for a Microprocessor Based Packet Network," Proceedings NCC, June 1978.

[PAPO 65]   Papoulis, A., "Probability, Random Variables, and Stochastic Processes," McGraw-Hill Book Company, New York, 1965.

[RICH 77]   Rich, M., and M. Schwartz, "Buffer Sharing in Computer-Communication Network Nodes," IEEE Transactions on Communications, Vol. COM-25, No. 9, September 1977, pp. 958-970.

[SCHW 78]   Schwartz, M., "Topological Considerations in Microcomputer Communication Networks: Time Response Analysis," ICC 78 Conference Record, Vol. 2, Toronto, Canada, June 4-7, 1978, pp. 27.4.1-27.4.5.

[SCHW 77]   Schwartz, M., "Computer Communication Network Design and Analysis," Prentice-Hall, Inc., Englewood Cliffs, New Jersey, 1977.

[TOWS 78]   Towsley, D., and J. Wolf, "The Waiting Time Distribution for Statistical Multiplexers with ARQ Retransmission Schemes," ICC 78 Conference Record, Toronto, Canada, June 4-7, 1978, pp. 03.6.1-03.6.4.

[WELD 78]   Weldon, E., "Behavior of a Synchronous Data Link Controlled by a Bit-Oriented Protocol," ICC 78 Conference Record, Vol. 3, Toronto, Canada, June 4-7, 1978, pp. 36.3.1-36.3.6.

[ZIEG 78]   Ziegler, C., and D. Schilling, "Delay Decomposition at a Single Server Queue with Constant Service Time and Multiple Inputs," IEEE Transactions on Communications, Vol. COM-26, No. 2, February 1978, pp. 290-295.

[TIRN 72]   Tirnell, J., "Analysis of the Throughput of a Communications Processor," Computer Design, Part 1, September 1972, pp. 47-51, Part 2, October 1973, pp. 89-93.

Modular Expansion in a Class of Homogeneous Networks

Alan Mink

Inst for Computer Sci & Tech
National Bureau of Standards
Washington, D.C. 20234

and

Charles B. Silio, Jr.

Electrical Engineering Dept.
University of Maryland
College Park, Md. 20742

Abstract

We consider a special class of homogeneous computer network comprising several essentially identical but independent computing systems (ICSs) sharing a single resource. Of interest here are the effects of modularly expanding the network by adding ICSs. We use a previously presented approximate queueing network model to analyze modular expansion in this class of network. The performance measure used in this analysis is the mean cycle time, which is the mean time between successive requests for service by the same job at the CPU of an ICS. In this analysis we derive an intuitively satisfying mathematical relation between the addition of ICSs and the incremental increase in the service rate of the shared resource required to maintain the existing level of system performance.

Introduction

We consider an increasingly important special class of computer network consisting of a number of independent computing systems (ICSs) sharing a single resource. This class includes both inexpensive microcomputers sharing expensive devices and large mainframe computers sharing large on-line data bases or other special resources. For example, in a computer based office system environment the configuration is that of a set of individual intelligent work stations (computer systems) sharing a scarce resource through a local area network. This scarce resource could be anything from a shared repository of data (e.g., a shared disk system) to an expensive laser photocomposition printer. Of interest here are the effects of modularly expanding the network by the addition of ICSs. Modular expansion of this type places a heavier load on the shared device, causing degraded service to each ICS. Important design parameters for this type of network are the effect

on performance caused by a modular expansion, and conversely, the amount of increased capability required by the shared resource to maintain a desired level of system performance.

In this paper we make use of existing queueing network models to derive results that determine the effects on performance caused by modularly expanding this special class of network. An approximate queueing network model of this class has been previously presented [8,10]. Exact queueing network models, both general [1,2,4,11,12] and specific [8,9], require exponential growth in computation time as the number of independent systems increases; whereas, the approximate model is both memory space and computation time efficient. The results of this approximate model when compared to those of the exact model have been shown to be within acceptable engineering limits. Thus, the approximate model is used to derive results presented here.

The structure of this class of network model is reviewed in section II. A previously presented approximate solution technique for this model, upon which our analysis is based, is summarized in section III. In our analysis of a modular expansion, presented in section IV, the performance measure considered is the mean cycle time which is the mean time between successive requests on the CPU of an ICS by the same job. Through analysis of the approximate model we derive a useful and intuitively satisfying relation between the addition of ICSs and the incremental increase in the service rate of the shared resource required to maintain system performance. Some hypothetical examples are provided in section V to demonstrate the applicability of this analysis.

II. The Model

The queueing network model considered here (Figure 1) is a network consisting of a set of R independent computing systems (ICSs) and a single shared processing resource (SPR), labelled device 0 with $s_0=1$. The i-th ICS is a central server system [3] consisting of s_i devices (Figure 2), a single central server (CPU), device i,1 , and a number of peripheral processors (PPUs), devices i,j with $2 \leq j \leq s_i$. The total number of devices in the network

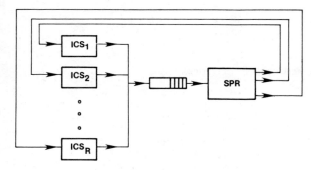

Figure 1. SCS Block Diagram

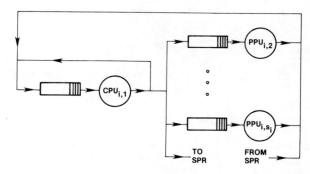

Figure 2. ICS Block Diagram

is $L=\sum_{i=0}^{R} s_i$, and the total number of jobs in this closed queueing network is K. The network state n is defined as the distribution of the various classes of jobs among all the devices, $n=(n_{1,0},$

$\ldots, n_{1,s_1}; n_{2,0}, \ldots, n_{2,s_2}; \ldots, n_{R,s_R})$, where $n_{i,j}$ is the number of class i jobs both waiting and being processed at device j in the i-th ICS.

At each device we assume jobs are processed on a first-come-first-served (FCFS) basis with an exponential service time distribution that is independent and identically distributed (iid) and not dependent on the number of jobs waiting for service. The j-th device of the i-th ICS is characterized by its mean processing service rate $u_{i,j}$, where $u_{i,0}=u_0$ for all i. The job flow is from the i-th CPU to one of the devices within the i-th ICS or to the SPR with a constant known probability, $0<p_{i,j}<1$, where $0\leq j\leq s_i$. Note that the jobs do not change class as they transit between devices. After being processed by a PPU or the SPR the job returns to the i-th CPU with probability equal one. All other transition probabilities are equal to zero.

Each ICS processes a separate job class, while the SPR processes all classes of jobs. A vector description of the job class allocation is $J=(J_1, \ldots, J_R)$, where J_i is the maximum number of (class i) jobs in the i-th ICS. The network job constraints are

$$N_0 = (n_{1,0}, \ldots, n_{R,0})$$

$$\sum_{i=1}^{R} J_i = \sum_{i=1}^{R} \sum_{j=0}^{s_i} n_{i,j} = K, \quad \text{and}$$

$$n_i = \begin{cases} \sum_{j=1}^{s_i} n_{i,j}, & i>0 \\ \sum_{j=1}^{R} n_{j,0}, & i=0 \end{cases}.$$

Class distinction is the means by which the job flow from each ICS is kept segregated. This model is called the Shared Central Server (SCS) Model.

The SPR and the devices within an ICS each represent an intricate subsystem, as do the various communication subsystems interconnecting each of them. The model does not directly incorporate the effects of various strategies that may be used within any of the subsystems, such as the effect of different communication protocols. Within the model the job flow is assumed to occur in zero time, although in an actual system a finite amount of time is required. The communication subsystem for these architectures generally has sufficient excess bandwidth to prevent it from becoming a bottleneck [13,15]. These effects are assumed either to be incorporated into the device processing time or to be insignificant when compared to the overall device processing time.

III. Approximate Solution to the SCS Model

We have previously presented [8,10] an approximate solution technique for the SCS model, which we summarize in this section. This technique is based on representing each device in the network as an independent single server queue (M/M/1), and then approximating flow rates between these devices.

The arrival process in an M/M/1 queue is Poisson with parameter a; therefore, the mean flow rate-in is equal to the mean flow rate-out: rate-in = rate-out = a. The following subscript notation is adopted for clarity: let SPR_i = device i,0 , CPU_i = device i,1 , and $PPU_{i,j}$ = device i,j for j>1. With this notation $a_{SPR_i} = a_{i,0}$ = the mean flow rate to the SPR (device 0) from the CPU of the i-th ICS. For the CPU in each ICS the flow out is decomposed into separate Poisson flows which proceed to the various PPUs and to the SPR. The decomposition of a Poisson flow in this manner is linear [5]. For the SCS this results in the following flow rate relationship

$$(1a) \quad a_{CPU_i} = \sum_{j=2}^{s_i} a_{PPU_{i,j}} + a_{SPR_i},$$

(1b) $\quad a_{PPU_{i,j}} = P_{PPU_{i,j}} a_{CPU_i} = P_{i,j} a_{CPU_i}$,

(1c) $\quad a_{SPR_i} = P_{SPR_i} a_{CPU_i} = P_{i,0} a_{CPU_i}$, and

(1d) $\quad a_{SPR} = \sum_{i=1}^{R} a_{SPR_i}$.

Having postulated a flow relationship between devices, we now consider a relationship between the queueing network parameter K (the total number of jobs circulating in a closed system) and the independent single sever queueing parameter $a_{i,j}$ (the job arrival rate at device i,j). For an M/M/1 queue the mean queue length (including a job in service), given its mean arrival and service rates a and u respectively, is [5]:

(2) $\quad Q = \dfrac{1}{1/\rho - 1}$,

where the traffic intensity $\rho=a/u$. By assuming each device is an independent M/M/1 single server queue we use (1) and (2) to establish the mean queue length balance relation (3). The right side of (3) is the sum of the mean number of jobs at each device in the network. Since each device is being approximated by an M/M/1 queue, the mean number of jobs at that device is given by (2). The left side of (3) represents the number of jobs from the exact closed queueing network model, which is used here to represent the mean number of jobs in the network.

(3a) $\quad K = \sum_{i=1}^{R} \left\{ \dfrac{1}{1/\rho_{SPR}-1} + \dfrac{1}{1/\rho_{CPU_i}-1} + \sum_{j=2}^{S_i} \dfrac{1}{1/\rho_{PPU_{i,j}}-1} \right\}$,

(3b) $\quad J_i = \dfrac{\rho_i}{1/\rho_{SPR}-1} + \dfrac{1}{1/\rho_{CPU_i}-1} + \sum_{j=2}^{S_i} \dfrac{1}{1/\rho_{PPU_{i,j}}-1}$,

where

(4a) $\quad \rho_{SPR} = \dfrac{\sum_{i=1}^{R} P_{SPR_i} a_{CPU_i}}{u_{SPR}}$,

(4b) $\quad \rho_{PPU_{i,j}} = \dfrac{P_{i,j} a_{CPU_i}}{u_{i,j}}$,

(4c) $\quad \rho_{CPU_i} = \dfrac{a_{CPU_i}}{u_{CPU_i}}$, and

(4d) $\quad \rho_i = \dfrac{P_{SPR_i} a_{CPU_i}}{\sum_{r=1}^{R} P_{SPR_r} a_{CPU_r}}$

When an SCS system configuration is a homogeneous network (i.e., all ICSs are identical or balanced), then (3b) can be simplified to the following, for arbitrary i

(5) $\quad J_i = \dfrac{1/R}{1/\rho_{SPR}-1} + \dfrac{1}{1/\rho_{CPU_i}-1} + \sum_{j=2}^{S_i} \dfrac{1}{1/\rho_{PPU_{i,j}}-1}$.

Both (3) and (5) can be efficiently sloved to obtain the unknown a_is by using a bounded binary search; see [8,10] for details. Once the unknown is obtained, then the following performance measures can be computed.

Device mean queue length:

(6) $\quad Q_{i,j} = \dfrac{1}{1/\rho_{i,j}-1}$

Device throughput:

(7) $\quad T_{i,j} = u_{i,j} i,j$

Device wait time:

(8) $\quad W_{i,j} = Q_{i,j}/a_{i,j}$

The remainder of this paper deals only with the homogeneous network configuration of an SCS system (i.e., eqn (5) vs. eqn (3)).

The mean cycle time of a job is the mean time between successive requests to the CPU by the same job. This is the weighted average of the mean time it takes a job to be serviced at each device (8), which includes both waiting in queue and being served.

Mean cycle time:

(9) $\quad W_i = \dfrac{1}{a_{CPU_i}} \left\{ Q_{SPR}/R + Q_{CPU_i} + \sum_{j=2}^{S_i} Q_{PPU_{i,j}} \right\}$

$\qquad = J_i/a_{CPU_i}$.

IV. Analysis of SCS Modular Expansion

Suppose a computer system engineer wishes to modularly expand a given SCS homogeneous network consisting of R ICSs, to one having R' ICSs with R'>R>1. The user community for this network would desire the system performance to be the same after the modular expansion as before it. The computer system engineer, wishing also to satisfy the user community, desires a guideline or analysis tool to determine how system performance can be maintained after the modular expansion. In the following analysis we provide such a tool.

In our analysis it is assumed that system performance can be maintained after a modular expansion by increasing the mean service rate of the SPR. This is based on the fact that each ICS is an independent system and no change has occurred in the ICSs internally. The only change that has occurred is the external effect of adding ICSs, causing an increase in the workload of the SPR resulting in degraded service to each of the ICSs. We express this increase in the SPR mean service rate as a multiplicative factor b times the old (before the modular expansion) SPR service rate. The performance measure we use in our analysis, to judge system performance, is the mean cycle time of a job, which depends on both the SPR mean service rate and the number of ICSs.

Our analysis consists of establishing the desired relation between the mean cycle time before and after modular expansion, and then of solving this relation for the multiplicative factor b. We desire that the mean cycle time of a job after a modular expansion not exceed its mean cycle time before the modular expansion; this can be expressed as

$$W_i(b\, u_{SPR}, R') \leq W_i(u_{SPR}, R) \ .$$

Using (9) to expand the above results in

$$(10) \quad \frac{1}{a'_{CPU_i}} \{Q'_{SPR}/R' + Q_{CPU_i} + \sum_{j=2}^{s_i} Q_{PPU_{i,j}}\} \leq \frac{1}{a_{CPU_i}} \{Q_{SPR}/R + Q_{CPU_i} + \sum_{j=2}^{s_i} Q_{PPU_{i,j}}\} \ .$$

where a'_{CPU_i} is the flow rate into CPU_i and Q'_{SPR} is the mean queue length of the SPR after the modular expansion. Because we assume that the mean service rate of the SPR is increased by a factor b to satisfy the equality of (10). We can then assume that the wait at each device within each ICS remains the same since no internal change has occurred in the ICSs. Thus we can reduce (10) to

$$(11) \quad \frac{1}{a'_{CPU_i}} \{Q'_{SPR}/R'\} \leq \frac{1}{a_{CPU_i}} \{Q_{SPR}/R\} \ .$$

This assumption also implies that the internal flow rate within an ICS does not change. Therefore, $a'_{CPU_i} = a_{CPU_i}$, which further reduces (11) to

$$(12) \quad Q'_{SPR}/R' \leq Q_{SPR}/R \ .$$

Using (1), (4), and (6) to expand (12) results in

$$(13) \quad \frac{1/R'}{(b\, u_{SPR}/R'\, p_{SPR_i}\, a_{CPU_i}\, -1)} \leq \frac{1/R}{(u_{SPR}/R\, p_{SPR_i}\, a_{CPU_i}\, -1)} \ .$$

One solution for (13) can be obtained by forcing equality of the denominators by letting

$$b\, u_{SPR}/R' = u_{SPR}/R \ ,$$

which yields

$$(14) \quad b = R'/R \ .$$

The solution indicated by (14) satisfies the strict inequality of (13), and as a result actually improves the mean cycle time rather than simply maintaining it. The interpretation of this solution implies that if the mean service rate of the SPR is increased in direct proportion to the increase in the number of ICSs, then the mean cycle time is reduced; therefore, system

performance is improved. For example, if the mean service rate of the SPR were doubled after a modular expansion in which the number of ICSs were doubled, the performance would improve.

To determine the value of b required to maintain the mean cycle time, rather than improve it, one must solve (13) for exact <u>equality</u>. We proceed to do this below. Cross multiplying yields

$$R\, (\, u_{SPR}/R\, p_{SPR_i}\, a_{CPU_i}\, -1) = R'\, (b\, u_{SPR}/R'\, p_{SPR_i}\, a_{CPU_i}\, -1) \ .$$

After some algebraic manipulation we obtain

$$(b - 1) = (p_{SPR_i}\, a_{CPU_i} /u_{SPR}) (R'-R) \ .$$

Using the homogeneity assumption that $\rho_{SPR} = R\, p_{SPR_i}\, a_{CPU_i}/u_{SPR}$ and subtituting it into the above yields

$$(b-1) = (\rho_{SPR}/R) (R'-R) \ .$$

Solving for b results in

$$(15) \quad b = 1 + \rho_{SPR}(R'/R\, -1) \ .$$

The interpretation of (15) is that by increasing the mean service rate of the SPR by ρ_{SPR}/R for each additional ICS in the resultant expanded system, the mean cycle time of the unexpanded system is preserved. Using the above example, doubling the number of ICSs (i.e., adding R more) requires the mean service rate of the SPR to increase by a factor of $\rho_{SPR}<1$, to maintain the existing mean cycle time.

The increase in the SPR mean service rate to maintain system performance as indicated by (15) is quite intuitively appealing. Consider the fact ρ_{SPR} represents the current total traffic intensity to the SPR, ρ_{SPR}/R represents the fraction of that traffic intensity generated by a single ICS. Using this perspective of traffic intensity, each ICS added would generate additional traffic also proportional to ρ_{SPR}/R. If the mean service rate of the SPR is increased by that fractional increase in traffic, the mean cycle time will not increase; therefore, system performance will be maintained. These results are consistent with results obtained by Klienrock [7], pp 270-285, for the general case of M/M/m queues.

There is an additional implication to this fractional increase in SPR mean service rate. A system in the class of homogeneous network considered here may undergo one or more modular expansions during its life cycle, possibly encompassing a large increase in the number of ICSs. The extent of expansion will in general be limited technically by the maximum attainable service rate of the SPR, which is for the most part dependent on the existing technology for that type of device. The service rate of applicable devices will generally span several orders of magnitude and may include a number of different technologies. Therefore, depending on a fractional service rate increase, rather than some greater increase, will allow a given technology to support a larger range of expansion. This minimizes, or at least delays, the implementaion and investment risk of changing device technology in a given system. Additionally this fractional service rate increase will also allow for a far greater maximum expansion range, since the overall existing device class limit will be approached at a much slower rate.

V. Examples

Two hypothetical examples of homogeneous networks are presented to illustrate the utility of our analysis. The first example is a complex of multiple minicomputers linked to a common shared secondary memory subsystem by a local area network, typical in engineering and scientific environments. The second example is a point-of-sales (POS) application, typical of grocery and department stores, and to certain office automation environments.

Example 1

Suppose the current processing system of a technical organization consists of 2 minicomputers (ICSs); each having an average multiprogramming level of eight; both ICSs share a common secondary disk storage subsystem. The minicomputers are identical and each has a CPU and the same complement of four peripheral devices (PPU). These PPUs consist of (1) an input card reader (CR), (2) an output line printer (LP), (3) a private local disk (disk), and (4) a set of interactive devices (TTY).

Suppose the interactive devices, as a set, are been characterized as a single device with an exponential service time distribution. The service times required by the jobs at each device are assumed to be exponentially distributed with the following characteristics:

mean service time	normalized service rate	estimated transition probabilities
SPR= 100 msec	u_0= .25	p_0= .25
CPU= 25 msec	u_1= 1.0	p_1= .05
disk= 25 msec	u_2= 1.0	p_2= .45
TTY= 2.5 sec	u_3= .01	p_3= .05
LP = 250 msec	u_4= .10	p_4= .10
CR = 250 msec	u_5= .10	p_5= .05

The organization plans to expand the processing complex by implementing a local area network. Due to existing software investment and staff familarity, the organization wishes to retain the existing two minicomputers and modularly expand by adding identical ones; initially doubling the ICSs to a total of 4, then to 16, and finally to a total of 32.

Suppose the shared common secondary storage subsystem has been very successful, so the retention and expansion of this facility is also planned; however, the current SPR does not have sufficient speed or capacity to handle the planned expansion. The system design engineer must size the new SPR so that current system performance is maintained and must determine if an SPR sized for the 16 ICS system will be able to adequately service a 32 ICS system.

To determine the approximate job flow rate and traffic intensity of the current system we solve (5) using the system parameters listed above. These values are then used to obtain the approximate traffic intensity, ρ_{SPR}=.3508, and mean SPR wait time, W_{SPR}=6.16, by applying (4), (6), and (8). Then using (15) we obtain the b's from which the mean service rate of an SPR required to maintain the original system performance for each configuration is computed. This results in

ICS	b	mean service rate	time
4	1.35	.338	74 msec
16	3.46	.865	29 msec
32	6.26	1.57	16 msec

Service rates for various secondary storage technologies [6,14] indicate that an SPR subsystem using existing rotating disk technology can support a 16 ICS configuration. This same SPR subsystem cannot adequately support a 32 ICS configuration, although a faster SPR subsystem using this same technology can support a 32 ICS configuration.

Example 2

For the second example a POS environment is postulated. We decribe POS as many small independent processors, each processing a single job, and accessing a shared inventory data base subsystem (IDBS). Structurally each POS station consists of a processor and a number of local I/O devices. These I/O devices may include any of the following typical devices; (1) a digital display or two, (2) a printer for a sales receipt, (3) an input scanner, (4) an input alphanumeric keyboard, and (5) an auxiliary input device, for instance a scale.

A normal transaction consists of one or more human interactions to enter data through the I/O devices. The station processor, once it accepts the data, requests service from the IDBS to process this data. This request is serviced on a FCFS basis by the IDBS with an exponentially distributed service time. The processed data is returned to the POS station, which has been idle while waiting, and it is then displayed. The cycle is then repeated. There is no need to model each device within a station separately because there is only a single job at each station and, hence, no contention for devices. It is assumed that all of these devices and the station processor logically can be thought of as a single device with an exponentially distributed service time. A feedback loop to the POS station provides for error conditions that arise, which mainly occur when entering data.

Suppose a system designer wishes to size an IDBS for two possible configurations. The first configuration being considered is a number of distributed installations each supporting 20 POS stations with its own local IDBS. The second configuration is a centralized one with a single IDBS supporting 1000 POS stations. An acceptable

IDBS mean wait time is on the order of .25 sec. The POS mean service time is 1 sec. Therefore, IDBSs which have service rates many times faster than the POS station must be considered.

For this model the mean service times and their estimated transition probabilities are as follows:

mean service time	mean service rate	estimated transition probabilities
0.5 to 200msec	u_{IDBS}=5 to 2000	p_{IDBS}= .90
1 sec	u_{POS}= 1	p_{POS}= .10

To determine the approximate job flow rate of a 20 POS station configuration we solve (5) using the system parameters listed above. This value and the target IDBS mean wait time of W_{IDBS}=.250 are then used to obtain the corresponding approximate traffic intensity by applying (4). This results in ρ_{IDBS}=.6797 and $u_{IDBS}(20)$=12.5, which is equivalent to an IDBS with a mean service time of 80 msec. This is well within the capabilities of existing disk technology. To determine the mean service rate of an IDBS to support a 1000 POS station configuration with a mean wait time of .25 sec, we apply (15). Then using the previously computed value of ρ_{IDBS}=.6797, we obtain b from which the mean service rate of an IDBS to support a 1000 POS station configuration is u_{IDBS}=428.9, which is equivalent to an IDBS with a mean service time of 2.33 msec. This speed exceeds the current capability of disk technology, thus, eliminating this configuration.

VI. Conclusion

An analysis of a modular expansion was performed using an existing approximate model. One of the key design aspects is the effect on performance due to a modular expansion, or conversely, the amount of increased capability required by the shared resource to continue to deliver some threshold amount of performance after a modular expansion has occurred. Analysis of the approximate model yields a useful and intuitively satisfying relation between the addition of ICSs and the incremental increase in SPR mean service rate required to maintain system performance.

It is shown that for each ICS added during a modular expansion of a homogeneous network the required increase in the incremental mean service rate of the shared resource is directly related to the incremental traffic intensity caused by each additional ICS. This implies, for example, that by doubling the number of ICSs, an increase in the shared resource mean service rate of less than two is sufficient to maintain system response time. The relation we derive is useful to designers and analysts when they consider building or augmenting homogeneous networks within this class.

References

[1] Basket, F., Chandy, K., Muntz, R. and Palacios, F. "Open, Closed, and Mixed Networks of Queues with Different Classes of Customers", J. ACM, VOL. 22, No. 5, pp 248-260, Apr. 1975.

[2] Bruell, S. C. and Balbo, G. Computational Algorithms for Closed Queueing Networks, Elsevier North Holland, Inc., Limerick, Ireland, 1980.

[3] Buzen, J. P. "Queueing Network Models of Multiprogramming", Ph.D. Dissertation, Harvard University, 1971.

[4] Buzen, J. P. "Computational Algorithms for Closed Queueing Networks with Exponential Servers", C.ACM, Vol. 16, No. 9, pp 527-531, Sept. 1973.

[5] Coffman, E. G. Jr. and Denning, P. J. Operating Systems Theory, Printice-Hall, Inc., N.J., 1973.

[6] Hoagland, A. S. "Storage Technology: Capabilities and Limitations", IEEE Computer, Vol. 12, No. 5, pp 12-18, May 1979.

[7] Kleinrock, L. Queueing Systems Volume II: Computer Applications, John Wiley and Sons, Inc., N.Y., 1976.

[8] Mink, A. "An Analytic Study of a Shared Device Among Independent Computing Systems", Ph.D. Dissertation, University of Maryland, 1980.

[9] Mink, A. and Silio, C. B. "A Queueing Network Model of a Shared Device Among Independent Computing Systems", Proc. of the 15th Annual Conf. on Information Sciences and Systems, The John Hopkins University, Baltimore, Md., pp 418-423, Mar. 1981.

[10] Mink, A. and Silio, C. B. "An Approximate Queueing Network Model of a Shared Device Among Independent Computing Systems", Proc. of COMPCON Fall 1981, Wash., D.C., pp 156-166, Sept. 1981.

[11] Muntz, R. R. and Wong, J. W. "Efficient Computational Procedures for Closed Queueing Network Models", Proc. of the Seventh Hawaii International Conference on System Sciences, Honolulu, Hawaii, pp 33-36, Jan. 1974.

[12] Shum, A. W. "Queuing Models for Computer Systems with General Service Time Distribution", Ph.D. Dissertation, Harvard Univ., Dec 1976.

[13] Thornton, J. E. "Back-End Network Approaches", IEEE Computer, Vol. 13, No. 2, pp 10-17, Feb. 1980.

[14] Warnar, R. B. J., Calomeris, P. J. and Recicar, S. A. "Computer peripherial Memory Systems Forecast", National Bureau of Standards, Washington, D. C., NBS #SP500-45, Apr. 1979.

[15] Watson, R. W. "Network Architecture Design for Back-End Storage Networks", IEEE Computer, Vol. 13, No. 2, pp 32-48, Feb 1980.

On Updating Buffer Allocation[*]

Ashok K. Thareja, Satish K. Tripathi, Richard A. Upton

System Design and Analysis Group
Department of Computer Science
University of Maryland
College Park, Maryland 20742.

ABSTRACT

Most of the analysis of buffer sharing schemes has been aimed at obtaining
the optimal operational parameters under
stationary load situations. It is well
known that in most operating environments
the traffic load changes. In this paper,
we address the problem of updating buffer
allocation as the traffic load at a network node changes. We investigate the
behavior of a complete partitioning buffer
sharing scheme to gain insight into the
dependency of the throughput upon system
parameters. The summary of the analysis
is presented in the form of a heuristic.
The heuristic is shown to perform reasonably well under two different types of
stress tests.

1. Introduction

Recently, computer communication networks have proliferated, taking a variety
of forms. Despite this diversity, however,
the underlying elements, and in particular
the critical resources comprising computer
networks, remain the same. Clearly, the
most important resource within a network
is link or channel capacity. Without sufficient link capacity a network may not be
able to accommodate the traffic load
intended for it. Given adequate link
capacity, though, the next most critical
resource is buffer space. This resource
affects the ability of a network both to
receive external data and to accommodate
internal data and control information. The
critical nature of buffer space stems from
the fact that it is a finite resource
which is usually shared by multiple, com-
peting users. As a consequence, the sizing
of buffers and their sharing of buffers
among different and contending traffic job
streams must be carefully controlled to
prevent such phenomena as deadlock, lost
information, monopoly of buffers by a
small subset of all users, and other forms
of performance degradation [2].

Buffer sharing policies have received
intermittent attention for some time.
Rich and Schwartz [8] investigated a sharing scheme in which a minimum amount of

---

* This research was supported by the
National Aeronautics and Space Administration, Goddard Space Flight Center, under
grant Nas5-26649.

buffer space is allocated to each stream with any remaining space dynamically allocated in its entirety to one stream at a time. Drukey [1] analyzed a scheme whereby all streams share the available buffer space under the assumption that the ratios of the arrival rates of each stream to their service rates are equal. Irland [3] studied a scheme wherein all streams share the same storage but are constrained not to exceed a certain maximum queue length. Lam [6] also investigated the buffer constraint problem for single nodes and entire networks (the latter using a continuity of flow constraint).

More recently, Irland [4] used a finite capacity queueing model with typed servers to analyze buffer sharing schemes in a single node. Kamoun and Kleinrock [5] and Latouche [7] have formulated and analyzed several other schemes. Finally, Thareja and Agrawala [9] proposed a buffer sharing scheme called the stationary delayed-resolution policy and showed it to be optimal in the context of a finite capacity queueing model with typed servers.

An assumption that prevails in the design and analysis of most buffer sharing schemes (and in all of the cases above) is that the traffic load is stationary. Given the parameters for the traffic load and a particular buffer sharing scheme, all of these analyses determine optimal (equilibrium) operational values for the parameters comprising the sharing scheme.

It is our contention that this assumption represents a major weakness in the latter analyses, since it is well-known that network traffic loads and, in particular, traffic loads at individual nodes may vary significantly with time. The objective of this paper is to begin to analyze the impact that traffic load changes have upon the performance of a small set of buffer sharing schemes for a single node. In particular, we consider a fixed partition buffer sharing scheme (sometimes termed complete partitioning) wherein each stream is assigned its share of buffer space, and there is no interaction between different streams. An optimal (with respect to total nodal throughput) buffer partition can be obtained using a simple search procedure which looks at all possible allocations of the finite buffer storage. Having found such an optimal partition for a given load mix, we then examine the change in system throughput as the traffic load changes but the partition remains fixed. Based on insights provided by this analysis, we describe a heuristic algorithm to determine when an update to the most recent partition is needed. This heuristic takes into account such parameters as the current load for each traffic stream, and the changes in system throughput since the last update.

2. Statement of the Problem

Consider a two class, finite buffer system with typed servers, i.e., the servers are each dedicated to a particular class. Assume that all arrival rates and service rates are exponential, and that the buffer sharing scheme is complete partitioning (see Section 1). Assume further that U_1, U_2, and K are given where U_i is the service rate of the ith class and K is the maximum buffer size for the entire system. Given the values of these parameters and the traffic load at time t (defined by the arrival rates $L_1(t)$ and $L_2(t)$), the objective is to operate the system with an optimal partition. The optimality criterion used in this study is the total system throughput. The problem we are interested in, then, is given the values dR_1 and dR_2, where $R_i(t) = L_i(t) / U_i$ and $dR_i = R_i(t_2) - R_i(t_1)$, how to decide whether or not the buffer partition should be updated. The decision to update the allocation may be made by computing the optimal partition using a search procedure, given the current values for R_1, R_2 and comparing gains in system throughput. In this paper we present an insight into the behavior of complete partitioning buffer sharing scheme so that it may be decided whether or not to update by merely examining the parameters.

Two important concepts are required before proceeding. Define the _resolution_ of a buffer sharing scheme as the minimum values for dR_1 and dR_2 required to change

the buffer allocation. Define the _update gain_ as the system throughput that would be achieved for the current values of R_1, R_2 if an optimal buffer partition were performed minus the system throughput if no change is made to the buffer allocation divided by the former throughput. It is clear that the partition should not be updated if one or both of the following conditions hold:

1) dR_1 and dR_2 are less than the resolution of the complete partitioning scheme

2) a partition update would yield an update gain less than some preselected threshold value.

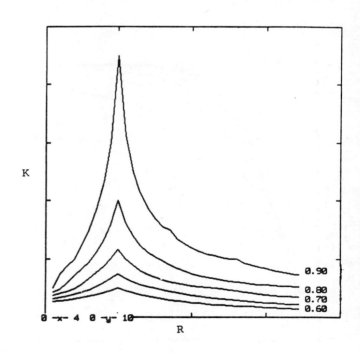

Figure 3.1
Buffer size required to provide a given percentage of maximum througput vs. R.

3. Impact of Buffer Size in a Single Server, Single Class Case

Before proceeding to the problem discussed in Section 2, it is worth looking at the simple case of a single server, single class M/M/1/K system. We would like to examine the impact of the buffer size, K, and the throughput of the system for various loads (i.e., values of R). In Fig. 3.1, the number of buffers vs. R is provided for several levels of required throughput. The number of buffers required to yield a throughput equal to a specific percentage of the maximum possible throughput achievable for the system (i.e., min (L, U)) depends heavily upon the value of L. The value of the minimum number of buffers for a specific percent of the maximum throughput was obtained by allowing the allocation of non-integer valued buffers.

non-integer K is described in the Appendix. As can be seen from Figure 3.1, the number of buffers required increases sharply as R -> 1, with the maximum occurring at R = 1. As R increases from 1 to oo, the number of buffers required decreases monotonically to 1. This is not surprising since, for R >> 1, the probability that an arrival will occur while the server is busy is near 1; therefore, as long as 2 buffers are available a high throughput can be maintained. It is also possible to conclude from the figure that for small values of R (say, R < .25) and large values of R (say, R > 2.0) the buffer size has only a limited impact on system throughput.

A related issue worth examining is the sensitivity of the numbers of buffers

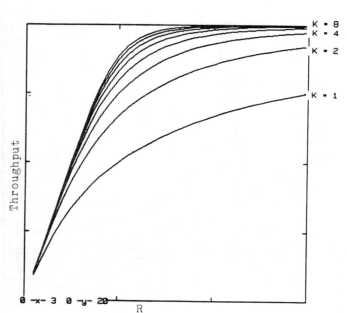

Figure 3.2
Throughput Vs. R for different buffer Siz

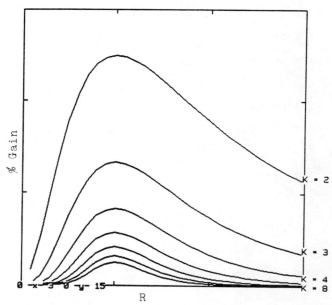

Figure 3.3
Percentage increase in throughput due to one additional buffer Vs. R.

required for a desired throughput with respect to R. For example, if 6 buffers are required to maintain 90% of the maximum throughput for a given R, how much degradation in system throughput would occur if only 5 buffers were available? Figure 3.2 presents throughput vs. R for several values of K. Figure 3.3 illustrates the relative gain in throughput obtained by adding one extra buffer to the original value for K. As is seen, the maximum relative gain always occurs at R = 1. However, note also that the relative gain increases sharply for $0.3 \leq R \leq 1$ and for values of K which are small (i.e., K < 10).

In summary, examination of the simple M/M/1/K queue suggests that if R is less than 0.25 or greater than 2.0, changing the buffer allocation does not significantly affect system throughput. Likewise, for K > 10, the impact upon system throughput of a change in buffer allocation will be minimal. Any heuristic intended to decide whether or not a current buffer allocation should be updated must consider these findings.

4. Buffer Sharing in a Two Class, Two Server Case

In this section, we examine the behavior of a two class two server, finite buffer system under complete partitioning. As described in Section 3, we assume that the servers (denoted S1 and S2) are typed, and that interarrival and service times

associated with each class are exponential. In this discussion, we will be especially interested in determining the sensitivity of the system to variations in R_1, R_2, U_1, U_2, the total buffer space available for both classes, and the number of buffers allocated to each class. The insights acquired will be applied to the development and analysis of the heuristic for deciding when to update the buffer allocation.

4.1. The Case U_1 = U_2 (Equal Speed Servers)

Figure 4.1 illustrates the relationship between R_2 and the update gain for several fixed values of R_1. For this example, it was assumed that the total number of buffers was 8 and that the initial

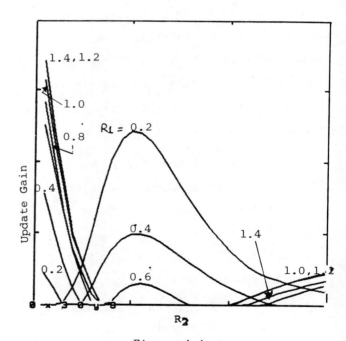

Figure 4.1
Update gain Vs. R_2 for different R_1, with U_1=U_2, K=8, equal allocation.

buffer allocation to each server was 4. An observation obtained from this example (and others in which the total number of buffers was varied) is that the smaller the total buffer space available, the larger the update gain. A more important observation is that, for relatively small values of R_1, as R_2 increases from 0, the update gain increases monotonically, reaching a maximum around $R_2=1$. After this, the update gain decreases monotonically to 0. The intuitive explanation for this is that, since R_1 is assumed to be small, only a minimal buffer allocation is necessary to ensure that S1 is nearly always responsive (i.e., the server will have a high probability of being free whenever an arrival occurs). Likewise, as R_2 approaches 1, its demands for buffer space will increase; however, once R_2 exceeds 1, the probability that the server will be busy approaches 1 regardless of the buffer allocation since an arrival is certain to quickly follow a departure from the server (see Section 3).

For larger values of R_1, the situation just described changes. In fact, for $R_1 \geq 1$, relatively large update gains are observed for small R_2. However, as R_2 approaches 1, the update gain goes to 0 where it remains until R_2 begins to differ sizably from R_1. When this occurs, a slight gain is observed.

Figure 4.2 illustrates the behavior of the system presented earlier except that the total number of buffers is 4 and

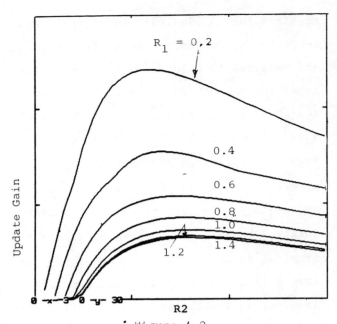

Figure 4.2
Update gain Vs. R_2 for different R_1, with $U_1=U_2$, $K=4$, and 3 and 1 buffers allocated to S1 and S2 respectively.

server S1 has 3 of the 4 buffers allocated to it. Obviously, for small values of R_1 and large values of R_2, the gain is more sizable than with equal allocation since there is a larger imbalance between the initial and optimal allocations. On the other hand, with R_1, R_2 near or greater than 1, the update gain is relatively small and stable. If the initial allocation were to be reversed (i.e, S1 had only 1 buffer allocated to it), it is clear that the curve shown in the figure would be reversed in the sense that the largest gains would be observed for R_2 small and R_1 large, decreasing as R_1 approached 1 and increasing as R_2 surpassed R_1. In fact, although the latter rate of increase in the update gain goes to 0 as R_2 approaches infinity, the update gain itself is never 0.

4.2. The Case $U_1 \neq U_2$ (Unequal Speed Servers)

Figure 4.3 illustrates the situation where the servers in our system have different service rates. In this example, it is assumed that $U_1 = 3 U_2$ and that the total number of buffers, is 4 with 2 buffers allocated to each server. As is seen for small R_1, the gain is significant only when $R_2 \leq R_1$. The gain in negligible for small R_1 and large R_2. For R_1 large, the update gain decreases as R_2 increases, and does not begin to increase again until $R_2 > 1.5$. Thus equal initial allocation in this case produces an imbalance which is in some respects the dual of the imbalance produced by equal servers with unequal initial allocation. One obvious result of this analysis is that if $R_1 \neq R_2$ ($U_1 = U_2$), the faster server should receive a greater number of buffers. To further study such situations consider Figure 4.4, which gives optimal buffer requirements of S1 as a function of the speed ratios of the two servers, i.e. U_1/U_2, assuming $R_1 = R_2$. Note that the buffer requirement changes considerably between ratios 0 and 2. However, for large ratios the requirement is less sensitive, e.g., there is no change between 2 and 8. We have also observed that the curve is not sensitive with respect to the absolute values of U_1 and U_2.

5. Heuristic for Updating Allocation

In the last two sections, we provided some insight into the behavior of the complete partitioning scheme. The observations can probably be best summarized in the form of a heuristic that examines some

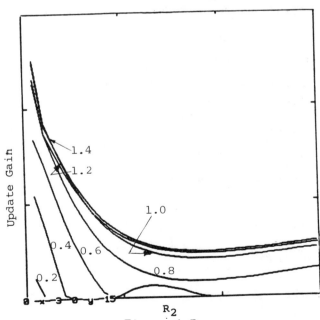

Figure 4.3
Update gain Vs. R_2 for different R_1, with $U_1 = 3U_2$, K=4, and equal allocation.

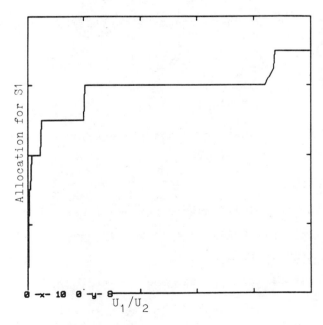

Figure 4.4
Number of buffers allocated to S1 for optimal throughput Vs. speed ratio U_1/U_2.

of the parameters and decides whether or not to update the allocation. Description of one possible heuristic follows.

Let the current allocation to S1 and S2 be b_1 and b_2 respectively; $b_1 + b_2 = K$. We term the allocation <u>even</u> if $0.3 + shift \leq b_1/K \leq 0.7 + shift$, where shift is zero whenever the servers are of equal speeds. When the servers are not of equal speeds, shift is assigned a value proportional to the speed ratio. The value assigned is positive if the ratio $U_1/U_2 > 1$ and is negative otherwise.

<u>Heuristic</u>: Significant update gains will result and therefore the allocation should be updated in the following situations.

Case 1: The current allocation is even

   a) For $(R_1 < 0.4)$ and $(0.8 < R_2 < 2.0)$

   b) For $(R_2 < 0.4)$ and $(0.8 < R_1 < 2.0)$

Case 2: The current allocation is <u>not</u> even

   a) For $(U_1/U_2 > b_1/b_2)$ and $(R_1 > 0.6)$

   b) For $(U_2/U_1 > b_2/b_1)$ and $(R_2 > 0.6)$

We test whether or not the heuristic makes the right decisions by subjecting it to the following two experiments.

In the first experiment, we choose <u>all</u> the parameters of the system randomly from uniform distributions. Namely, the parameters are the speed ratio U_1/U_2, the buffer size K, the values of R_1 and R_2 at the previous allocation, and the current values of the R_1 and R_2. The actual updated gain is computed and, if the gain is greater than 5%, the allocation is considered worth updating. This decision to update is compared against the one made by the heuristic. The result of this experiment is as follows.

  Total Trials: 10,000

  Correct Guesses by the Heuristic: 82.2%

  Number of Times Decided to Update: 7.68%
   (i.e., gain > 5.0)

  Avg. Gain Due to Updates: 16.93
   (departures/unit time)

  Heuristic Estimates:

  No. of times Gain Over-estimated: 15.74%

  No.of times Gain Under-estimated: 2.04%

  Avg. Gain Loss by Under-estimates: 13.61
   (departures/unit time)

In the second experiment we consider a more realistic situation. The speed ratio, and the buffer size are assigned fixed values. Initial values are chosen for R_1 and R_2 to decide an optimal allocation. For each successive trial a new pair of values of R_1 and R_2 are chosen from uniform distributions. With these new values and the prior allocation, the updating decisions using computation and the heuristic are compared. The result of the experiment are summarized in Table 1. The table contains all of the statistics given for the first experiment, for different buffer sizes and speed ratios of the two servers.

From the results of the two experiments, it seems that the heuristic performs reasonably well over a wide range of parameters. The heuristic can be fine tuned by adjusting the values of various thresholds. Besides the fine tuning, other heuristics can also be invented to exploit the tradeoff between the cost of heuristic over- and under- estimates. Whenever the heuristic under-estimates, the system incurs a loss of throughput. An over-estimate costs in terms of the overhead in implementing the update. In most environments, the over-estimate cost would be less significant than an under-estimate cost. However, this may not always be the case.

6. Conclusion

Most of the analysis of buffer sharing schemes has been aimed at obtaining the optimal operational parameters under stationary load situations. In this paper, we addressed the problem of updating the buffer allocation as the traffic load at a network node changes. We investigated the behavior of complete partitioning buffer sharing scheme to gain insights into the dependency of the throughput upon the system parameters. The summary of the analysis was presented in form of a heuristic. It was shown that the heuristic is reasonable by subjecting it to two types of stress tests.

We note that the methodology used in this paper can also be used for other buffer sharing schemes as well as for some of the flow control and routing procedures. One of the basic problems that needs attention is that of enforcing the updated allocation. There are several alternatives, e.g., immediate enforcement, gradual enforcement. We believe that more analyses of the kind presented in this paper will be needed to derive an operational policy for updating the buffer allocation.

APPENDIX

An M/M/1/K system where K = n + a, with $0 \leq a < 1.0$ and n an integer, can be interpreted as follows. An arrival to the queue with n jobs waiting, will be accepted with the probability a. In such a system, the throughput is given as follows.

Throughput = $(1 - P_0)$ U

where P_0, the probability that there is no job waiting, is given by

$$P_0 = \begin{cases} \dfrac{1}{n + a + 1} & \text{if } L/U = 1 \\[2ex] \dfrac{1 - R}{1 - R^{n+1} + (1-R) a R^{n+1}} & \text{Otherwise} \end{cases}$$

Note that the above solution reduces to those for the special cases of M/M/1/n and /M/M/1/n+1, for a = 0 and 1, respectively.

REFERENCES

[1] Drukey, D. L., Finite buffers for purists, TRW,Inc. Redondo Beach, CA. TRW Systems Group Rep. 75.6400-10-97, 1975..

[2] Gerla, M. and L. Kleinrock, Flow control: A Comparative Survey, IEEE Trans. on Communication COM-28, pp. 553-574, April 1980.

[3] Irland, M., Queueing Analysis of a Buffer Allocation Scheme for a Packet Switch, Proceedings of National Telecommunications Conference, p. 24, 1975.

[4] Irland, M., Buffer Management in Packet Switch, IEEE Transactions on Communication COM-26, pp. 328-337, March 1978.

[5] Kamoun, F. and L. Kleinrock, Analysis of Shared Finite Storage in Computer Network Node Environment under General Traffic Conditions, IEEE Transactions on Communication COM-28, 7, pp. 992-1003, July 1980.

[6] Lam, S. S., Store-and-Forward Buffer Requirements in a Packet Switching Network, IEEE Transactions on Communications COM-24, 4, pp. 394-403, April 1976.

[7] Latouche, G., Exponential Servers Sharing a Finite Storage: Comparison of Space Allocation Policies, IEEE Transactions on Communication COM-23, 6, pp. 910-915., June 1980.

[8] Rich, M. A. and M. Schwartz, Buffer Sharing in Computer Communication Network Nodes, Proceedings ICC, Sanfransisco Cal., pp. 33-17 - 33-20, June 1957.

[9] Thareja, A. K. and A. K. Agrawala, On the Design of Optimal Policy for Sharing Finite Buffers, University of Maryland, Computer Science Dept. Tech. Rep. TR-1081, July 1981. Also Submitted to IEEE Trans. on Communications.

Table 1.

Speed Ratio	Buffer Size	Correct Guesses (%)	Updated Actual (%)	Over-Estimated (%)	Under Estimated	Average Gain	Avg.Gain Lost
						(departures/unit time)	
1.5	4	87.4	12.23	9.02	3.81	12.50	10.66
1.5	8	90.8	6.81	7.62	1.80	9.53	7.14
1.5	15	88.98	2.81	10.61	0.80	9.95	7.14
1.0	4	93.99	16.83	3.41	3.01	11.83	11.11
1.0	8	90.58	6.01	8.42	1.40	12.35	12.10
1.0	15	88.98	3.41	10.42	1.00	8.77	6.98
0.5	4	84.97	14.43	11.22	4.21	13.36	11.86
0.5	8	90.98	6.61	7.41	2.00	10.83	9.26
0.5	15	88.38	2.61	11.22	0.80	7.33	6.56

SESSION 6: LOCAL NETWORKS

Chair: David L. Mills
COMSAT Laboratory
Washington, DC

An Analysis of a Time Window Multiaccess Protocol with Collision Size Feedback (WCSF)*

M. Y. Elsanadidi** and Wesley W. Chu

**Computer Science Department
University of California at Los Angeles
Los Angeles, California 90024**

Abstract

We analyze the performance of a window multiaccess protocol with collision size feedback. We obtain bounds on the throughput and the expected packet delay, and assess the sensitivity of the performance to collision recognition time and packet transmission time. An approximate optimal window reduction factor to minimize packet isolation time is $r^a = \dfrac{1}{n\sqrt{R/2}}$, where n is the collision size and R the collision recognition time (in units of packet propagation delay). The WCSF protocol, which requires more information than CSMA-CD, is shown to have at least 30 % more capacity than CSMA-CD for high bandwidth channels; that is, when packet transmission time is comparable to propagation delay. The capacity gain of the WCSF protocol decreases as the propagation delay decreases and the collision recognition time increases. Our study also reveals the inherent stability of WCSF. When the input load increases beyond saturation, The throughput remains at its maximum value.

1. Introduction.

Since the development of ALOHANET [1] at the University of Hawaii, there has been an ever increasing interest in broadcast mode communication where nodes share a common broadcast channel bandwidth, and transmissions can be received at many (possibly all) nodes of the networks. The nodes coordinate their use of the channel, according to some access protocol, such that the *total* channel bandwidth is allocated to one of the nodes ready to use the channel. Given the existence of an efficient channel access protocol, such multiplexing of the total channel bandwidth among the nodes should result in high system performance, especially in terms of transmission times and therefore delay . Broadcast mode communication was shown to be highly effective, even when the traffic required is point-to-point [2,3,4].

Random access protocols allow nodes to randomly access the channel with the possibility of destructive interference when more than one transmission overlap in time. If such interference occurs, all transmissions involved are assumed lost and must be repeated at a later time according to some retransmission policy. The nodes must have the knowledge of whether their attempt was successful so that they can decide on their next action.

If the nodes cannot monitor their transmission, they must rely on some acknowledgment scheme to determine whether their transmissions were successful. The effects of acknowledgment traffic on broadcast networks performance was reported in [5,6,7]. If the nodes are able to continuously listen to the channel and if all nodes operate in the same environment, no acknowledgments are needed; the nodes can determine success or failure on their own. Further, by monitoring the channel events, the nodes can deduce information that help them coordinate their transmission and adapt to the instantaneous channel load.

Here, we consider the case where nodes are able to detect success or failure on their own and therefore need no acknowledgments. A delay is incurred during which the nodes detect the result of the attempt made at using the channel.

A new class of channel access and collision resolution protocols have appeared recently in the literature. In [8] a method for collision resolution is suggested to avoid random retransmission delays and therefore reduce system instability. Rather than retransmitting after a random delay, a subset of the nodes involved in a collision have the right to retransmit in the next attempt. The subset is determined based on the nodes IDs. If the subset contains exactly one node, a successful transmission of one of the messages involved in the collision occurs. Otherwise, the retransmission attempt results in a collision to be resolved in the same way as the original collision. During the collision resolution process, nodes with new packet arrivals are not allowed to transmit. After the successful transmission of packets involved in an original collision, all nodes with new packet arrivals have access rights in the next attempt. Instability due to variation in channel load can occur in such a scheme due to correlation between a collision resolution time and the offered load immediately following that collision resolution. Thus, a dynamic control procedure is required for maintaining stable channel performance.

A window scheme where transmission rights depend on packet arrival times at the nodes rather than the node IDs is proposed in [9]. This protocol provides first come first serve (FCFS) service according to packet arrival at the nodes, and is free from stability problems [8,10,11]. An adaptive window scheme which considers the number of packets involved in a collision is studied in [12]. The throughput of this protocol is obtained numerically for two values of collision recognition time. The corresponding delay is obtained via simulation.

*This research was supported in part by ONR Contract Number N 000-14-79-C-0866.

**This author is now with the Department of Computer Science, University of Maryland, College Park, Md. 20742.

In this paper, we describe WCSF, a protocol based on the time window scheme, in which window reduction depends upon collision size feedback. Using an analytical model we obtain bounds on both throughput and delay performance of the protocol for arbitrary collision recognition time. The analysis reveals the impact of feedback delays, and the network performance sensitivity to various system parameters.

2. The WCSF Protocol.

We assume that the nodes can continuously listen to the channel and can detect idle periods, successful transmissions, and collisions. Further, in case of collisions, the nodes can estimate accurately the number involved in the collision, or 'collision size'. We assume a slotted time axis with a slot length equal to a packet propagation time. The nodes are synchronized such that all transmissions start at slot boundaries.

A common time window is maintained by all nodes at all times. The nodes update the location and the width of the window after each transmission attempt. Nodes whose packets had arrived during the window currently considered have access right for the next transmission attempt. If no node requires transmission, the window is shifted forward in time and its length is set to an agreed upon initial window length. If exactly one node had a packet that arrived during the current window, its transmission would be successful. Subsequently, the window is shifted forward and its length is reset to the initial length. Finally, if two or more nodes have had packet arrivals during the current window, a collision occurs and the window length is reduced in order to 'isolate' one of the packets involved in the collision.

To illustrate the operation of the protocol, we constructed an example as shown in Figure 1. For simplicity, windows are identified by a single variable which indicates both the location and the width of the window. The protocol execution consists of a series of transmission attempts. In each attempt, packets that arrived during some window are allowed to transmit. Let τ_i be the set of windows considered by the protocol. From the outcome of each attempt the nodes learn about the number of arrivals in some interval of the initial window. In Figure 1, these intervals are denoted by ν_i. The information is stored in a stack in each node. A stack element includes the time interval and the number of arrivals in it. Elements of the stack are processed in last come first served order (LCFS).

In the example, the initial window τ_o is positioned on a time interval containing four arrivals. After the initial attempt, the nodes recognize a collision of size four. This information is stored as the pair $\nu_o,4$ on the stack in each node. Because they detected a collision, the nodes compute the length of the reduced window τ_1. During the next step, nodes whose packets had arrived during τ_1 have transmission rights. Since only one node had a packet arrival during the new window, it would be successful in transmitting its packet. All nodes recognize this success and update their stack information to $\nu_1,3$. This process continues until all arrivals in the initial window τ_o are transmitted successfully.

The sequence of collisions, successes, and idle periods that constitute the service period of the arrivals in the initial window is shown in Figure 2. For convenience, we let the propagation time equal one time unit. Since it takes one propagation time for a node to determine that no transmission has begun in the current attempt,

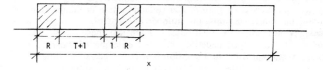

Figure 2.

the detection of an idle period takes one slot. Let T be the packet transmission time in slots or time units. A successful transmission takes $T+1$ time slots on the channel since we need to add the packet propagation delay to its transmission time. Let R be the 'collision recognition' time; that is, the time required to detect a collision and to estimate the collision size. Let x be the total time used to serve (arrivals in) the initial window. For the example above, the service period contained two collisions, four packet transmissions, and one idle period, thus

$$x = 2R + 4(T+1) + 1$$

In general x depends on the number and instants of arrivals during the window, and the windows processed during the successive steps of the protocol execution.

3. Throughput Analysis.

We view the service period of arrivals during a window as a set of 'isolation processes' and a set of successful transmissions. An isolation process starts when the window to be considered is known to have more than one packet arrival, and the process terminates when a packet is isolated. The isolation process may contain several idle and collision intervals. In the following we will study the length of the isolated process.

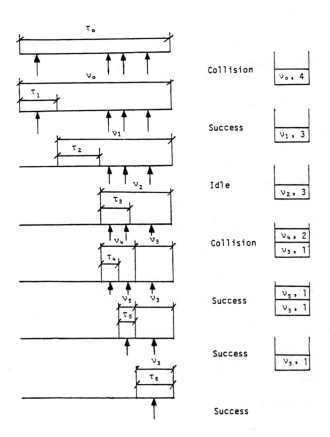

Figure 1.

3.1 The Packet Isolation Process.

Assume that the arrival process is Poisson with rate λ. Let r be the reduction factor by which the nodes reduce the window size when they recognize a collision. Intuitively, the optimal reduction factor depends on the collision size n and the collision recognition time R. When R is large, the cost of a collision is large relative to the cost of an idle period. The reduction factor should be higher in such a case, thus favoring idle periods over collisions. However, as we will see, some collisions are considered successes in terms of isolation due to new information gained concerning the colliding packets distribution in a window. Therefore, while it appears that the reduction factor should be higher in systems with higher collision recognition time, it is interesting to study the characteristics of this dependency since, as we mentioned, some collisions constitute success as far as isolation is concerned.

Assume that a window of length τ is known to contain n packet arrivals. In this case, only $n-1$ isolations must be carried out, since the nth packet will be transmitted successfully without uncertainty. Let u_m be the probability that the reduced window of length $r\tau$ contains m packet arrivals. Since the arrivals are Poisson, this probability is

$$u_m = \binom{n}{m} r^m (1-r)^{n-m} \qquad (1)$$

A reduction step is successful in isolating a packet if $0 < m < n$. This is because the new reduced window containing m packets needs only $m-1$ isolations, and the mth packet will be successfully transmitted without uncertainty. If $m=0$ or $m=n$, the reduction step is a failure since we are left with a window with the same number of packets n. Although the new window has a shorter length, this is irrelevant to the isolation process progress as can be seen from the independence of u_m from τ. Since the success or failure of a reduction step is independent of previous reduction steps, the number of steps of an isolation process is geometrically distributed. Each of these steps take a different time which depends upon the outcome of the reduction step. A step resulting in a collision ($m > 1$) takes R time units, while a step resulting in an idle period takes one time unit. If the reduction step results in a successful transmission ($m=1$), the time contribution of the successful step to the isolation process time is 0.

Let p_i be the probability that an isolation process takes i steps. Since the number of steps is geometrically distributed, we have

$$p_i = (1 - u_o - u_n)(u_o + u_n)^{i-1} \qquad (2)$$

Let N be the expected number of steps of an isolation process. Clearly, $N = \dfrac{1}{1 - u_o - u_n}$. The expected time of the first $N-1$ steps is

$$\bar{t_1} = (N-1)\ \frac{u_o + R\,u_n}{u_o + u_n} \qquad (3)$$

and the expected time of the last step is

$$\bar{t_2} = \frac{R\,(1 - u_0 - u_n - u_1)}{1 - u_o - u_n} \qquad (4)$$

Substituting (1) into (3) and (4) and adding them we obtain the following expression for the expected time of an isolation process $\bar{t}$

$$\bar{t} = \frac{(1-r)^n + R\,(1 - (1-r)^n - nr(1-r)^{n-1})}{1 - r^n - (1-r)^n} \qquad (5)$$

Differentiating with respect to r yields no closed form solution for the optimal value of the reduction factor r. We therefore use numerical techniques to find the best r value that minimize the expected isolation time. These results are portrayed in Figure 3 which illustrate the relationship of the minimum expected isolation

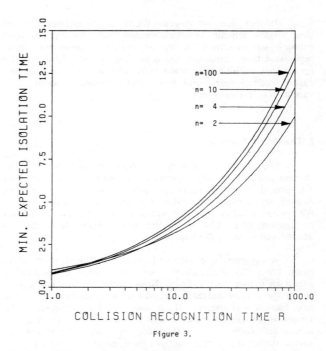

COLLISION RECOGNITION TIME R

Figure 3.

time to collision recognition time R. Note that t' is almost insensitive to n, except when R is high.

Intuitively, the optimal reduction factor r^o should be proportional to the inverse of the collision size n. Let us assume that r^o is a function of n, R of the form

$$r^o = \frac{\rho}{n} \qquad (6)$$

where ρ is some function of R that needs to be determined. Differentiating (5) with respect to r, substituting (6) into that expression, and then taking the limit as $n \to \infty$, we get

$$\rho + e^{-\rho} = \frac{R+1}{R}$$

Using the first three terms of the series expansion of $e^{-\rho}$, we get the following approximation

$$\rho = \sqrt{\frac{2}{R}} \qquad (7)$$

$$r^o = \frac{1}{n\ \sqrt{R/2}} \qquad (8)$$

Comparing the above approximation results with the numerical results, we found that the error introduced by the approximation is very small (Figure 4). For $R > 1$ the relative error is negligible. Since using (8) yielded longer t', the approximate reduction factor in (8) yields pessimistic results.

Assume that the limiting optimal isolation time when n is large holds for all n. Using the reduction factor in the form given in (6) and considering the case ($n \to \infty$), equation (5) reduces to

$$\bar{t} = \frac{e^{-\rho} + R\,(1 - e^{-\rho} - \rho e^{-\rho})}{1 - e^{-\rho}} \qquad (9)$$

Such an approximation is clearly pessimistic and thus $\bar{t}$ should be interpreted as an upper bound on the minimum expected isolation time.

3.2 Expected Window Service Time.

Let the service time of a window be the time spent in the isolation and transmission of all packets that arrived during the win-

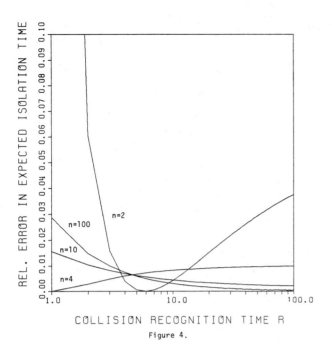

COLLISION RECOGNITION TIME R

Figure 4.

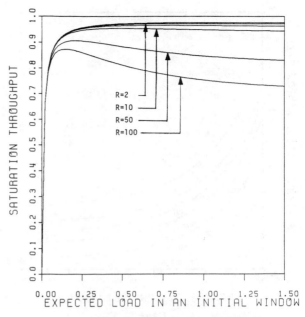

Figure 5. The Effect of Collision Recognition Time on Saturation Throughput.

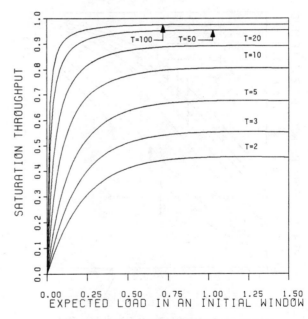

Figure 6. The Effect of Packet Transmission Time on Saturation Throughput.

dow. In the following we determine the expected service time of a window with length τ_o. Given that n arrivals occurred during a window, the conditional expected service time is

$$E[x \mid n] = \begin{cases} 1 & \text{if } n=0 \\ 1+T & \text{if } n=1 \\ R + (n-1) \bar{t} + n (1+T) & \text{if } n>1 \end{cases} \quad (10)$$

Let $P(n)$ be the probability that a window has n packet arrivals, and let γ be the expected number of arrivals. For an initial window of length τ_o, assuming that the arrivals follow a Poisson distribution with rate λ packets per unit time. Thus, $\gamma = \lambda \tau_o$ and $P(n) = e^{-\gamma} \gamma^n / n!$. Let $\bar{x}$ be the unconditional expected service time of a window,

$$\bar{x} = \sum_{n=0}^{\infty} E[x \mid n] \ P(n) \quad (11)$$

Substituting from equation (10) into (11) we obtain

$$\bar{x} = e^{-\gamma} + (1+T) \ \gamma \ e^{-\gamma} + \sum_{n=2}^{\infty} [R + (n-1) \ \bar{t} + n (1+T)] \ e^{-\gamma} \frac{\gamma^n}{n!}$$

After some algebraic simplification, we have

$$\bar{x} = e^{-\gamma} + (1+T) \ \gamma + R \ (1-e^{-\gamma}-\gamma e^{-\gamma}) + \bar{t} \ (\gamma - 1 + e^{-\gamma}) \quad (12)$$

When $\bar{x} = \tau_o$, the expected packet interarrival time equals the expected service time of a packet. The system reaches saturation, and the expected packet delay becomes infinite.

Before reaching saturation, the protocol throughput is equal to the offered traffic rate λ. We find numerically the saturation throughput from the equation $\bar{x} = \tau_o$. The saturation throughput is a function of R, T, r, τ_o. The analysis of the isolation process has yielded r^o, the optimal window reduction factor. The effect of the collision recognition time R and the packet transmission time T on saturation throughput is shown in Figures 5 and 6. These plots reveal that the packet transmission time has more effect on the saturation throughput than that of the collision recognition time.

The capacity of the network is obtained by finding the optimal initial window length that maximizes the saturation throughput. In Figure 7 we show the optimal initial window length

in units of packet transmission times for selected values of R. Note that the optimal initial window size reduces to less than a packet transmission time for high values of R and T. Since small initial windows yield less collisions, we need to use a small window size for large values of R and T.

Figure 8 presents the capacity of the WCSF protocol as a function of packet transmission time for selected values of R. Note the effect of small packet transmission time. In comparison to CSMA-CD [13] we find that the WCSF protocol provides higher capacity, particularly as the propagation delay increases, and the collision recognition time decreases (Figure 9). This is because the WCSF protocol utilizes more collision detection information (the size of the collision) in the retransmission of collided packets.

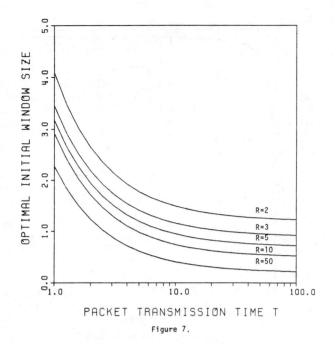

Figure 7.

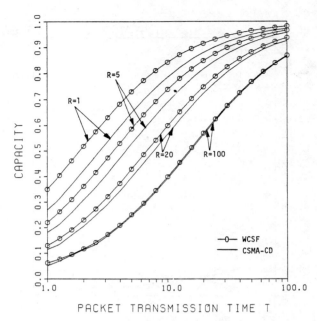

Figure 9. Capacity Comparison between CSMA-CD and WCSF.

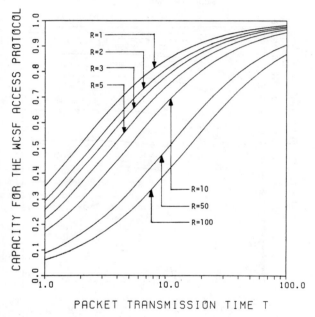

Figure 8. Capacity vs. Packet Transmission Time, for
Selected Collision Recognition Times R.

Our study shows that the gain in capacity of WCSF over CSMA-CD is at least 30 % when T=1 and R=2. However, for high packet transmission times, and for high collision recognition time, the difference in capacity between the two protocols is less pronounced.

4. The Expected Packet Delay.

The packet delay is defined as the time from its arrival at a node until its last bit is successfully transmitted on the channel. In the WCSF protocol, packets are considered for transmission only when the initial time window in which they arrived is processed by the protocol. Thus, the packet delay includes the time its window waits until it is processed by the protocol. Once its window is being processed, the packet will be successfully transmitted, possibly after

additional delays depending on the isolation processes and the packet position in its initial window. Because of the window mechanism used in WCSF, the system can be regarded as a D/G/1 queue. The fixed interarrival time is the initial window length τ_o, and the service time is the time spent in isolation and transmission of packets that arrived during a window. The expected service time is $\bar{x}$ as given by equation (12). The 'customer' is assumed to arrive at the end of a window of length τ_o and his service time depends on packet arrivals during the window. In the following we derive a bound on the expected waiting time of a window using Kingman's formula [14].

4.1 A bound on the expected wait of a window.

Let D_w be the expected wait of a window. From Kingman's bound

$$D_w \leqslant \frac{\overline{x^2} - \bar{x}^2}{2\,\tau_o\,(1 - \bar{x}\,/\,\tau_o)} \tag{13}$$

In order to calculate such a bound we need to derive $\overline{x^2}$, the second moment of the service time distribution. Let the isolation time of the ith packet in a window be a random variable denoted as t_i. The second moment of the service time conditioned on the number of arrivals n can be expressed as

$$E[x^2 \mid n] = \begin{cases} 1 & \text{if } n=0 \\ (1+T)^2 & \text{if } n=1 \\ E[\,(\,R + \sum_1^{n-1} t_i + n(1+T)\,)^2\,] & \text{if } n>1 \end{cases} \tag{14}$$

The unconditional second moment $\overline{x^2}$ is obtained from

$$\overline{x^2} = \sum_{n=0}^{\infty} E[x^2 \mid n]\ P(n) \tag{15}$$

Substituting (14) into (15), we get

$$\overline{x^2} = P(0) + (1+T)^2\,P(1)$$

$$+ \sum_{n=2}^{\infty} P(n)\ \left[E[(\sum_{i=1}^{n-1} t_i)^2] + (R+n(1+T))^2 \right.$$

$$+ 2(R + n(1+T)) \; E[\sum_{i=1}^{n-1} t_i] \Bigg] \qquad (16)$$

Since the t_i are independent identically distributed random variables, we have

$$E\left[\sum_{1}^{n-1} t_i\right] = (n-1)\,\bar{t} \qquad (17)$$

and,

$$E\left[\left(\sum_{1}^{n-1} t_i\right)^2\right] = E\left[\sum_{1}^{n-1} t_i^2 + \sum_{i \neq j}\prod_{i \neq j} t_i\, t_j\right]$$

$$= \sum_{1}^{n-1} E[t_i^2] + \sum_{i \neq j} E[t_i]\, E[t_j]$$

$$= (n-1)\,\overline{t^2} + (n-1)\,(n-2)\,\bar{t}^2 \qquad (18)$$

Substituting (17) and (18) into (16) and after some algebraic simplification, we obtain

$$E[x^2] = (1 - e^{-\gamma} - \gamma\, e^{-\gamma}) \; (R^2 - \overline{t^2} - 2R\bar{t} + 2\,\bar{t}^2)$$

$$+ \gamma (1 - e^{-\gamma})(\overline{t^2} + (1+T)^2 + 2R(1+T+\bar{t}) - 2\bar{t}^2)$$

$$+ \gamma^2 (1+T+\bar{t})^2 + \gamma\, e^{-\gamma} (1+T)^2 + e^{-\gamma} \qquad (19)$$

Of all the terms of the expression above, only $\overline{t^2}$ is yet to be derived. To derive $\overline{t^2}$, we shall first derive the distribution of the isolation time process.

Recall that for analytic tractability we assumed that the collision size n is large. As $n \to \infty$, from equation (1), we have $u_n \to 0$, $u_1 \to \rho\, e^{-\rho}$, $u_o \to e^{-\rho}$. Note that the limiting forms are reached rather quickly. For example, for $R = 8$, $u_n < .00025$ at $n = 4$.

Observe that $u_n \to 0$ implies that no reductions will result in $m = n$ and thus, all failing steps of the isolation process are 'idle' steps. The successful step can be a collision of size $m < n$ or a successful transmission. Recall that a collision takes R time units, but the successful transmission is not part of the isolation process and therefore its contribution to the isolation process time is 0.

Let q_t be the probability mass function of the isolation time. For $t < R$, the isolation process must have had t idle failures, and a last step that resulted in a successful packet transmission. Thus

$$q_t = u_o^t\, u_1 \qquad \text{for } t < R$$

For $t \geqslant R$ the isolation process either ended by a collision, in which case it had $t - R$ idle failures; or the process ended with a successful transmission in which case it had t idle failures. Thus

$$q_t = u_o^{t-R}(1 - u_o - u_1) + u_o^t\, u_1 \qquad \text{for } t \geqslant R$$

Let $G(z)$ be the Z-Transform of the isolation time probability function.

$$G(z) = \frac{\rho e^{-\rho} + z^R (1 - e^{-\rho} - \rho e^{-\rho})}{1 - z\, e^{-\rho}}$$

The second moment of the isolation time can be obtained from the Z-transform as follows:

$$\overline{t^2} = \frac{\partial^2 G(z)}{\partial z^2}\Big|_{z=1} + \bar{t}$$

Carrying out the above operation we obtain

$$\overline{t^2} = \frac{R^2 + e^{-\rho}(1 + 2\,\bar{t} - R^2 \rho)}{1 - e^{-\rho}} \qquad (20)$$

It is easy to verify from the Z-Transform that the first moment of the isolation time has the expression given in equation (9). Substituting (9) and (20) into (12) and (19), we can calculate the service time moments and thus can calculate the upper bound on the expected waiting time of a window as given in (13).

4.2 The total expected packet delay.

A bound on the expected wait of a window D_w was derived in the preceding section. The waiting time of an initial window is the time interval starting from the window right boundary until the window is processed by the protocol. Since the packet arrival process is Poisson, on the average, a packet arrives to the system $\tau_o / 2$ time units before the right boundary of its initial window. Thus, on the average, a packet waits $\frac{1}{2}\tau_o + D_w$ before its initial window enters service.

After its initial window enters service, a packet could be further delayed by isolations and transmissions of packets which arrived in the same initial window. Given that $n > 0$ arrivals occurred in the window, a packet, on the average, arrives after $n - 1/2$ packets; thus, it will be delayed $\frac{(n-1)}{2}(1+T)$ time units due to transmissions of those packets that arrived before it. The number of isolation processes that precede a packet transmission is difficult to predict. Therefore we assume that *all* isolations precede *all* packet transmissions and obtain the following bound on the delay due to isolation and transmission of other packets.

let D_s be the expected delay of a packet due to isolations and transmissions of other packets in its window. Recall that arrivals in a window follow a Poisson process with parameter γ. Thus,

$$D_s \leqslant \sum_{n=2}^{\infty}\left[R + (n-1)\bar{t} + \frac{n-1}{2}(1+T)\right]\frac{e^{-\gamma}}{1 - e^{-\gamma}}\frac{\gamma^n}{n!} \qquad (21)$$

Note that in computing the delay of a packet the case $n = 0$ is excluded by dividing by the probability of no Poisson arrivals in a window which is $1 - e^{-\gamma}$; if $n = 1$ the packet suffers no delay due to other packet isolation or transmission. After some algebraic simplification, the bound in (21) reduces to

$$D_s \leqslant R\left[1 - \frac{\gamma e^{-\gamma}}{1 - e^{-\gamma}}\right] + \left(\bar{t} + \frac{1}{2}(1+T)\right)\left(\gamma - 1 + \frac{\gamma e^{-\gamma}}{1 - e^{-\gamma}}\right) \qquad (22)$$

A bound on the total packet delay D can be expressed as

$$D \leqslant \frac{1}{2}\tau_o + D_w + D_s + 1 + T$$

where the bounds on D_w and D_s are given by (13) and (22), and $1+T$ is the time required to transmit a packet to its destination.

The delay results are presented in Figure 10. Each curve is for a selected collision recognition time and packet transmission time. In each case the window width is set to its value that maximizes the saturation throughput. The curves reveal the inherent stability of the protocol. At high throughput, the delay increases to infinity, but the saturation throughput remains at its maximum level.

The stability of the protocol is due to the uncorrelated service time of successive initial windows. Thus, if at any particular initial window the system finds a burst of arrivals, these will be served with no interference from new arrivals which belong to other windows. In addition, the next window load is independent from the service time of the heavily loaded window since we use fixed size initial windows. Finally, the collision resolution process, consisting of window reductions within an initial window, leads to nonincreasing collision sizes.

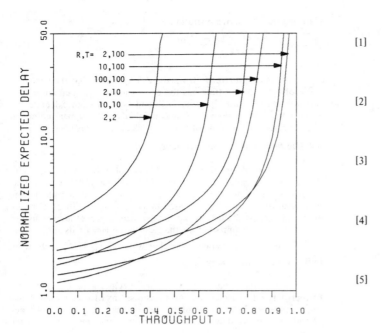

Figure 10. Throughput-Delay Performance of the WCSF.

5. Conclusion.

We have analyzed the performance of a window multiaccess protocol with collision size feedback (WCSF). The protocol utilizes the collision size as feedback information, and based on this information, the nodes adapt to the instantaneous channel load. Collision sizes could be obtained by using a reservation channel or signal energy information. Such implementation issues need further study.

The throughput-delay performance of the protocol is better than that of other protocols in many respects. For high speed communication channels, the packet transmission time and propagation delays become comparable. Under this environment and when collision recognition time is small, the WCSF protocol capacity exceeds that of CSMA-CD by at least 30 % . The gain reduces as the propagation delay decreases and the collision recognition time increases. In addition to its high capacity, the delay analysis showed that the saturation throughput retains its maximum value as the channel load increases, confirming the protocol inherent stability. In addition, the protocol execution orders the packet transmissions in FCFS order according to packet arrival times at the nodes which is a desirable feature. The serialization of service in FCFS order to a distributed set of customers is a general problem that may have such applications as synchronization in distributed data bases and distributed processing systems.

Acknowledgment.

The authors wish to thank Kin-Kwong Leung for his programming assistance during the writing of this paper.

References

[1] R. Binder, N. Abramson, F. F. Kuo, A. Okinaka, and D. Wax, "ALOHA Packet Broadcasting — A Retrospective," *AFIPS Conference Proceedings, NCC* **44**, pp.203-215 (1975).

[2] L. G. Roberts, "Dynamic Allocation of Satellite Capacity through Packet Reservation," *AFIPS Conference Proceedings, NCC* **42**, pp.711-716 (June 1973).

[3] R. E. Kahn, S. A. Gronemeyer, J. Burchfiel, and R. C. Kunzelman, "Advances in Packet Radio Technology," *Proceedings of the IEEE* **66**, pp.1468-1496 (November 1978).

[4] R. M. Metcalfe and D. R. Boggs, "Ethernet: Distributed Packet Switching for Local Computer Networks," *Communications of the ACM* **19**(7) (July 1976).

[5] F. A. Tobagi and L. Kleinrock, "The Effect of Acknowledgement Traffic on the Capacity of Packet Switched Radio Channels," *IEEE Transactions on Communications* **COM 26**, pp.815-826 (June 1978).

[6] M. Y. Elsanadidi, *Analysis of Broadcast Communication Systems with Acknowledgment Considerations,* Computer Science Department, University of California, Los Angeles (1982). Ph.D. Thesis.

[7] M. Y. Elsanadidi and W. W. Chu, *Study of Acknowledgment Schemes in a Star Multi-Access Network,* Submitted for publication.

[8] J. I. Capetanakis, "Generalized TDMA: The Multi-Accessing Tree Protocol," *IEEE Transactions on Communications* **COM-27**, pp.1476-1484 (October 1979).

[9] R. G. Gallager, "Conflict Resolution in Random Access Broadcast Networks," *Proceedings of the AFOSR Workshop in Communication Theory and Applications,* pp.74-76 (Sept. 17-20, 1978).

[10] S. S. Lam and L. Kleinrock, "Packet Switching in a Multiaccess Broadcast Channel: Dynamic Control Procedures," *IEEE Transactions on Communications* **COM-23**, pp.891-904 (September 1975).

[11] F. A. Tobagi and L. Kleinrock, "Packet Switching in Radio Channels: Part IV — Stability Considerations and Dynamic Control in Carrier Sense Multiple Access," *IEEE Transactions on Communications* **COM-25**, pp.1103-1119 (October 1977).

[12] D.Towsley and G.Venkatesh, *Window Random Access Protocols for Local Computer Networks.* to appear in IEEE Transactions on Computers.

[13] F. A. Tobagi and V. B. Hunt, "Performance Analysis of Carrier Sense Multiple Access with Collision Detection," *Proceedings of the Local Area Communication Network Symposium* (May 1979). also in Computer Networks, November 1980.

[14] L. Kleinrock, *Queueing Systems, Vol II., Computer Applications,* Wiley-Interscience, New York (1976).

PERFORMANCE ANALYSIS OF LOCAL COMMUNICATION LOOPS

Kuno M. Roehr and Horst Sadlowski, IBM Germany.

ABSTRACT.

The communication loops analyzed here
provide an economic way of attaching many
different terminals which may be some
kilometers away from a host processor. Main
potential bottlenecks were found to be the
loop transmission speed, the loop adapter
processing rate, and the buffering capability, all of which are analyzed in detail.
The buffer overrun probabilities are found
by convolving individual buffer usage
densities and by summing over the tail-end
of the obtained overall density function.
Examples of analysis results are given.

1. INTRODUCTION

Local networks are obtaining more and more
attention as a solution to the data processing requirements of single establish-
ments (Ref. 1). The discussed loop system
has basically the wiring hardware of a ring
structure. But, instead of using the
any-to-any transmission philosophy, the
loop satisfies the one-to-many and
many-to-one data transfer requirement. All
traffic passes through the single loop
master station, causing potential
contention problems. This will be analyzed
in later sections.

After a short description of the external
loop characteristics in section 2, protocol
overhead is derived in section 3. In
section 4 the loop adapter hardware and
firmware are described from a performance
point of view. Based on the data presented
in sections 3 and 4, the main performance
analysis is carried out in three steps:
analysis of loop contention (section 5.1),
of processing contention (section 5.2) and
of buffer space contention in the loop
adapter processor (section 5.3).

Analysis procedures are given in sufficient
detail to allow straight forward implementation as interactive computer programs.
An experimental version of such a program
was used to analyze many potential applications of interest. The results of such an
evaluation are given as an example.

2. EXTERNAL PERFORMANCE CHARACTERISTICS.

The investigated loops connect to IBM 4331
model 1 or model 2 processors and allow the
attachment of a variety of DP and Industry
terminals suitable, for production planning
and control, inventory administration,
shipment and order entry. (Ref. 1)

In comparison to star wiring of attachments, the loop provides better wiring
efficiency and has found wide-spread
acceptance throughout the industry. In
comparison to standard I/O channels, the
loop can span much larger distances, 3.2 km
being the maximum length with one lobe. A
second lobe of 3.2 km per loop attachment
can be used to efficiently double the loop
length or to provide backup for the first
lobe in case of loop failures. One process-
or allows the attachment of two local
loops. To bridge larger distances, two
teleprocessing ports are provided for the
attachment of two additional remote loops,
each able to transmit or receive at a rate
of 9.6 kbit/s (compare Fig. 1).

The total number of nodes that can be
connected via loops is presently limited to
80. The loop transmission speeds are 9.6
kbit/s or 38.4 kbit/s depending upon the
type of devices attached to the loop.

Transmissions on localy and remotely
attached loops use the basic System Network
Architecture protocol (SNA) together with a
special loop operating procedure to be
described in the section 3 (Refs. 2,3).
This design provides all the benefits of
the basic System Network Architecture like

- standard line procedures
- standard node interfaces
- common TP access methods
- advanced diagnostics and error control

This implies that all node devices and
controllers are basically identical to

FIG. 1: LOOP ATTACHMENT POSSIBILITIES

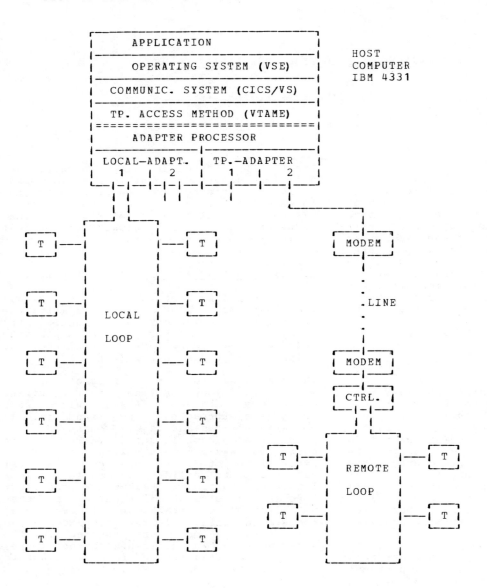

previously existing and proven SNA devices, and require a special adapter logic for transmission over the loop.

The loop wiring hardware was designed to withstand severe environmental conditions. Different grade cables and the associated connectors and bypass relays allow easy installation and maintenance. During regular, short intervals the primary loop station tests operational status of all secondary stations. An eventual line failure can be identified and localized if it persists even after several retransmissions of the the faulty message. The defective lobe segment will be automatically switched off, while maintainig partial communication with the remaining

part of the loop. By these means a high degree of reliability and availability was achieved for the loop.

3. ANALYSIS OF PROTOCOL OVERHEAD

The chosen protocol and its associated control information will have a definite influence on the performance of the loop. An introduction to the Synchronous Data Link Control (SDLC) and the loop protocol can be found in Ref.2. Here only a short overview of the loop architecture will be given as a base for the performance analysis in sections 4 and 5 of this paper.

In the SDLC line protocol two types of

stations are used during communications: primary stations and secondary stations. A primary station has the responsibility for controlling a data link; it issues commands. Secondary stations receive commands and return responses. In a loop, a one-way communication channel originates at the transmitting part of the primary station, connects one or more secondary stations in a serial fashion, and then terminates back at the receive port of the primary station. (see Fig. 2)

The loop configuration is logically operated as a half-duplex link, only one station transmits at any one time, the primary station or a secondary station. The difference between a loop and a regular half - duplex link is that, in a loop, all the transmissions travel the same direction on the communication channel. The secondary stations transmit sequentially, as required, as determined by their physical order on the link. To further clarify the loop operation, two modes of operation, primary station transmitting and secondary station transmitting, are described in detail in the Appendix.

The loop operation described in the Appendix is concerned with forward transmission of data from or to a node on a loop. To account for the total amount of control information on the loop, it is important to consider also the bytes needed for the acknowledgement of SDLC loop transmission frames and for the acknowledgement of SNA messages.

In the considered cases each SNA request unit is being acknowledged by a 3 byte SNA Response Unit. For transmission a 3 byte Request Header and a 6 byte Transmission Header is added. The total SNA acknowledgement information thus consists of 12 bytes which have to be transmitted on the loop by one SDLC transmission frame.

Similarly, on a lower level of the protocol, each SDLC transmission frame received by a primary or secondary station has to be acknowledged by the receiver with a 6 byte SDLC confirmation frame. The information field of this frame is empty and the control field indicates confirmation of a received frame.

The number of bytes that have to be transferred on the loop for a user message Request Unit of NU bytes requiring NF SDLC frames are then:

    NU - Number of user bytes (RU)
     3 - Request Header bytes (RH)
    6 NF - Transm. Header for user frames
    6 NF - SDLC confirmation of user frames
     6 - SNA ackn. data bytes (RH + RU)
     6 - Transm. Header for SNA ackn.
     6 - SDLC confirmation of SNA ackn.

The total number of bytes on the loop are then per message NU + 12NF + 21. The

number of SDLC frames NF required can be computed from NF = NU / 256 where NF has to be rounded to the next higher integer.

To limit the buffer space required at the terminals, the maximum SNA user Request Unit was limited to 1536 bytes for all traffic on the loop. This maximum size of Request Units is in most cases sufficient to completely handle one input or output transaction from loop attached devices.

4. LOOP ADAPTER TIMINGS

In Fig. 4 the hardware components are shown which are used to attach the loop to the processor.

Four hardware loop adapters are able to drive a maximum total of two independent local loops and up to eight remote loops. Four remote loops each can be attached via two 9.6 Kbit/sec remote data links. One loop adapter can operate one local loop, which may consist of two mechanically and electrically independent lobes each driven by a seperate loop station adapter. Remote loops are attached to the loop adapter via a EIA/CCITT interface card, two modems to drive the TP line, and a remote loop control station.

All four loop adapters are connected to the loop adapter microprocessor via a 2 byte, so called programmed I/O (PIO) bus. One byte of the PIO bus carries data to the microprocessor, the other byte transfers data from the microprocessor. The transfer always occurs in burst mode- stealing cycles from the loop adapter microprocessor.

The data flow from the loop adapter microprocessor to the main memory occurs via the PIO bus, the Bus-to-Bus adapter (BBA), the Adapter Common Card (ACC), and the Integrated Channel (IC) bus. The IC-bus is an internal 4 byte wide bus connecting several I/O attachments to a common, random access main memory. The maximum rate at which data transfers on the IC-bus can occur is 5 Mbyte per sec. The Adapter Common Card converts the 4 byte IC-bus data flow into one byte, one way data flow to the Bus-to-Bus adapter and vice versa. It handles the complete IC-bus protocol including signaling, addressing, and data format conversion.

The Bus-to-Bus adapter's main function is to match the IC-bus operation with the operation of the PIO bus. It synchronizes a planned data transfer from the main memory with the operation of loop adapter microprocessors and vice versa. As soon as both sides are ready, the burst data transfer can procede via the BBA at a maximum rate of 414 KB/sec.

The main characteristics of the loop adapter microprocessor are as given in

FIG. 2 : SDLC LOOP EXCHANGE
        (SECONDARY STATIONS B,C,E,F TRANSMITTING)

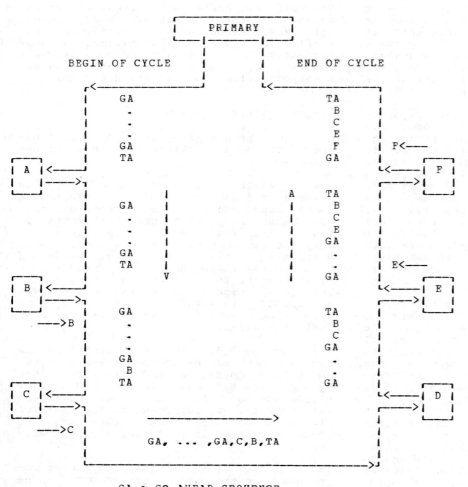

GA : GO AHEAD SEQUENCE
TA : TURNAROUND SEQUENCE

TABLE 1 : CHARACTERISTICS OF LOOP ADAPTER MICROPROCESSOR

— cycle time	.4 microsec.
— ALU data flow	2 Byte
— Instruction format	1 or 2 Byte
— Time per instruction	1.6 ... 7.2 microsec.
— Main memory	96 KByte
— Register space (in memory)	1 KByte
— Interrupt levels	8

FIG. 4 LOOP ATTACHMENT HARDWARE

MAIN MEMORY

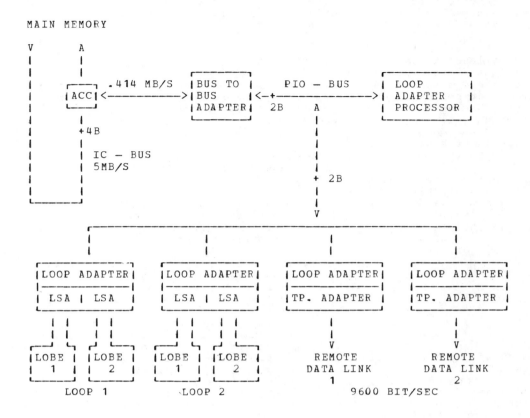

Table 1. The loop attachment hardware is fast and causes little delay. The main delays are due to the microcode controlled adapter processor while it is handling the more logically involved functions. These functions are listed below together with the typical number of microprocessor instructions in brackets ( ) needed per function for inbound messages, where NB is the number of the 56 Byte buffers to be used within the microprocessor:

- Host interface code, handles communications between channel operations in main processors and control unit functions in the microprocessor (803 + 309 NB)
- Host transfer preparation, prepares data transfer to and from host (778)
- Terminal dependent code for SNA devices (130 + 17 NB)
- Loop transfer buffer handling (100 NB)
- Loop adapter control code (1206 + 5 NU, if NU<258) where NU are the number of user bytes as discussed in section 3.

For every command executed together with a loop attached device the above instruction counts and counts associated with outbound

messages can be used to generate loop adapter processor service timings. For a typical display station these timings are :

Read : 18.0 + .03 N milliseconds
Write : 21.8 + .05 N milliseconds

where N is the number of characters transfered.

These numbers represent a straight line approximation to a stair case function, where the steps occur when buffer and frame sizes are exceeded. These numbers are valid for up to 30 terminals. For the write operation, additional .6 msec have to be added for every additional 10 terminals supported. An exhaustive and validated listing of timing for all attachable devices can be found in Ref. 5. These timings have been validated by selective firmware monitoring and were found to be within +20% of measured values.

5. CONTENTION ANALYSIS

A look at the data flow from the loop to the main memory in Fig. 3 shows that internal busses operate at relatively high

123

speeds if compared with the loop transmission rates. In the following section 5.1 it will then first be described how the loop utilization can be computed by considering the overhead bytes derived in section 3.

A second potential "bottleneck" is the processing capability of the loop adapter processor. The processor timings needed for the various device dependent commands have been derived in section 3 from microcode pathlengths. These timings will be used together with polling load to compute the utilization of the loop adapter processor in section 5.2.

A third area of concern is the loop adapter memory space available for buffering data transferered from and to the adapter processor. In section 5.3 buffer overrun probabilities will be computed as a function the number and types of terminals, the message rates, and the size of the buffer pool.

5.1 LOOP UTILIZATION

The procedure to obtain a loop utilization Ul is as follows:

1. Find the total number of characters per message transferred
2. Add the number of overhead bytes, including acknowledgement frames, as described in section 3.
3. Multiply the number of bytes per message by the aggregate message rate resulting from all terminals sending or receiving the same message.
4. Repeat steps 1 to 3 for all message types and add up the resulting byte rates.
5. Devide the total aggregate byte rate on the loop by 8 times the specified loop transmission rate, in bits/sec.

The result of these calculations is the effective loop utilization Ul. If more than one loop is installed, the calculations have to be repeated for every loop.

From the single server queueing formula for exponential interarrival times and exponential service times a first estimate on the loop access delay Tql can be obtained as

$$Tql = Tsl \times Ul / (1-Ul) \qquad (1)$$

where Tsl is the average time messages occupy the loop. Neglecting the distance dependent propagation delay (maximum ca. 10 msec), the average message delay Tsl is obtained by dividing the average message length by the line speed. For an average message length of 250 bytes, and a loop rate of 9600 bit/sec, e.g.,

$$Tsl = 250 \times 8 / 9600 = .208 \text{ sec.}$$

Using this value of Tsl = .208 sec and an assumed line utilization of 50% yields an additional queueing delay of Tql = Tsl = .208 sec. The total loop induced message delay is therefore in this case equal to 2 Tsl = .416 sec.

5.2 UTILIZATION OF LOOP ADAPTER PROCESSOR

The utilization of the loop adapter processor, Ua, consists basically of two parts: the processor utilization due to message handling, Um, and the processor utilization due to loop polling, Up.

To obtain the processor utilization Um due to message handling for one loop procede as follows:

1. Obtain the adapter processor service times for each intended termial operation (see section 4) from the appropriate reference manual, e.g., ref. 4.
2. The second part of these service times has to be multiplied by the average number of bytes transferred by the intended operation. (compare section 3)
3. Multiply these operation and message length specific service times by the frequency of their occurence on the loop. (Number of terminals times message rate per terminal.)
4. Repeat steps 1 to 3 for all operation types to be performed and add up all resulting processor service times per second to obtain the total adapter processor utilization due to message handling from one loop Um.

The adapter processor utilization due to polling alone on a loop is dependent on the selected polling rate Rp, in polls per sec, and the total number of terminals on the loop Nt, and is given as:

$$Up = .001 (.5 + .06 Nt) Rp$$

Loop polling will only occur if the loop is not busy transferring messages. This implies that the actual processor utilization due to polling is equal to Up (1- Ul), where Ul was derived in section 5.1.

The adapter processor utilization from one loop is then

$$Ua = Um + (1 - Ul) Up \qquad (2)$$

If more than one loop is installed, the above calculations have to be repeated for every loop, and the resulting Ua's have to be added.

This calculation was carried out for a number of typical loop applications. In all cases the adapter processor utilization Ua was lower than the loop utilization Ul. In other words, the real system bottleneck found was not the adapter processor, but the transmission loop itself. By doubling the loop transmission delay a safe upper bound for the total loop system delay is obtained. For many practical cases a factor of 1.5 will suffice. The method of calculation as descibed in sections 5.1 and 5.2 was incorporated into a general communication system analysis tool using the APL language, which is available for interactive use on an IBM internal network.

5.3 BUFFER OVERRUN ANALYSIS

Within the loop adapter processor, sufficient data buffering capability has to be provided to match the data transfer speed of internal busses to the relatively low speed of the loops and the terminals attached to it.

During a terminal write operation, e.g., a full message is sent from main memory to the memory of the loop adapter processor. Then, one SDLC loop frame of 271 bytes after the other is sent via the loop to the terminal. After a frame has been sent out, the transmission of the next frame has to be delayed until the terminal has acknowledged the receipt of the last frame and is ready to accept a new frame.

The goal of the analysis was to determine if the remaining available memory space is sufficient to support the simultaneous data transfer from and to many terminals on the loop, without causing additional delays due to buffer space contention. The analysis proceeds as follows:

1. Determine available buffer space (5.3.1)
2. Determine the probability density of buffer space usage per terminal. (5.3.2)
3. Determine the total probability of buffer overruns. (5.3.3)

Since, the buffer space requirements are influenced by the number and types of loops and terminals, and on the message length and rates, the analysis has to be repeated for each configuration of interest.

5.3.1 AVAILABLE BUFFER SPACE

A large portion of the adapter processor storage space is needed for data that has to be permanently resident during the entire operation of a loop. A storage map example for the case of 2 loops, 40 display stations, and 4 different industry terminals may show , e.g., the numbers of byte counts given in Table 2. The space remaining for buffering purposes is in this case
98 304 - 82 304 = 16 000 bytes.

To simplify buffer space management the remaining buffer space is always subdivided into individual buffers of 64 bytes, 56 of which are available for data storage. Buffer space is always allocated and released in mulitiplies of 56 data bytes.

In the example given above the total remaining buffer pool, available for terminal traffic, consists thus of 16000 / 64 = 250 buffers.

5.3.2 BUFFER SPACE USAGE

As an example, the time dependent buffer requirements during writing 18 buffers to a terminal are given in Fig. 5. Before start of the transmission, at time 0, 18 buffers are filled with the complete SNA data frame ready for transmission from the loop adapter processor to the terminal. After T1 seconds the terminal has acknowledged the receipt of the first loop frame of data and the corresponding first 4 buffers can now be released. After an additional T2 seconds the terminal has serviced the first frame of data, and has requested and received the second frame. The second group of 4 buffers can now be released. This continues until the last buffers have been sent to the terminal.

The actual values for T1 and T2 depend on the type of terminal, the loop transmission rate, and the utilizations of loop and loop adapter. In particular the follow elements contribute to T1 and T2:

T1 : Loop adapter initial processing, wait for loop access, loop transmission of data, primary polling, transmission of acknowledgement frame.
T2 : Terminal service time, wait for loop access, transmission of terminal response frame, wait for loop access, loop transmission of data, primary polling, transmission of acknowledgement frame.

To find the overall buffer space needed, first every terminal in the system has to be analyzed as described above. The next step is to derive the probability density function $P_i(N_b)$ for the number of buffers N_b in use by the terminal. This function $P_i(N_b)$ can be obtained from $N_b(t)$ in Fig. 4 by evaluation of the relative frequency $P_i(N_b)$ with which N_b buffers are in use for maximum message rate.(compare Fig. 5)

If the time interval between messages is T_m and maximum buffer occupancy time for one message is T_O (in Fig.4 $T_O = T1+4T2$), $P_i(N_b=0)$ has to be assigned the value $P_i(0) = (T_m-T_O)/T_m$ and all other density values $P_i(N_b=0)$ have to be multiplied by $1-P_i(0) = T_O/T_m$. This way it is assured that the sum over all P_i's is equal to one, which is a necessary condition for P_i to qualify as a probability density function.

This procedure for generating the probability density function $P_i(N_b)$ has to be repeated for all n terminals in the system, i = 1...n.

5.3.3 PROBABILITY OF OVERRUN

With the probability density functions

TABLE 2: STORAGE SPACE REQUIREMENTS IN BYTES

```
44 230  - Microcode base, invariant of configuration
20 700  - Microcode dependent on type of terminals
 2 100  - Data associated with microcode base
 2 108  - Data dependent on loop ports
 4 720  - Data dependent on types of terminals
 8 446  - Data dependent on numbers of terminals
-------------------------------------------------------
82 304  - Total permanently needed storage space
```

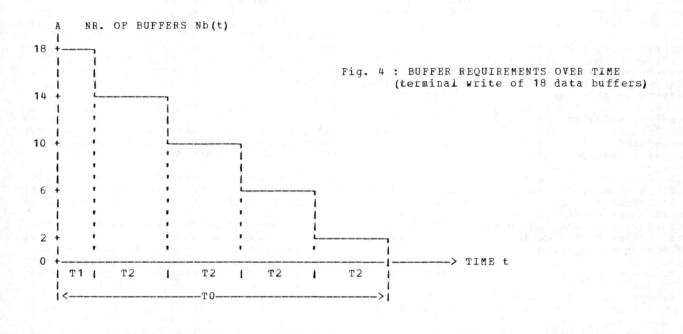

Fig. 4 : BUFFER REQUIREMENTS OVER TIME
(terminal write of 18 data buffers)

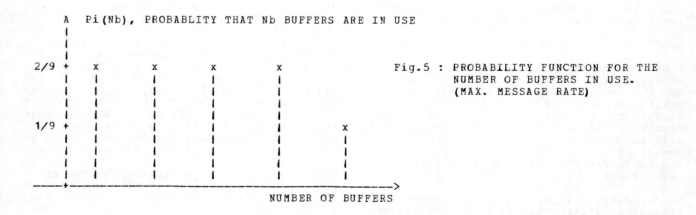

Fig.5 : PROBABILITY FUNCTION FOR THE
NUMBER OF BUFFERS IN USE.
(MAX. MESSAGE RATE)

126

Pi(Nb), derived in section 5.3.2 for each individual terminal i, the overall density function for simultaneous, independent buffer usage by n terminals can be obtained as

P(NB) = P1(NB) * P2(NB) * ... * Pn(NB)

where the star '*' represents the convolution operator (compare, e.g., ref. 6, p. 317).

From the overall density function P(Nb) the average buffer usage can be obtained by building the weighted sum over all discrete probability values, or

Av. [NB] = E[NB] = SUM [(Nb) x p(Nb)]

where the sum extends over all possible number of buffers Nb and the associated usage probabilities p(NB). This average does not answer the question of overrun, but gives preliminary, first pass information on buffer usage.

The probability of overrun Po(Nbmax) for a given maximum number of buffers in the pool, Nbmax, is obtained from the overall density function P(Nb) by adding all probability values for Nb larger than Nbmax, or

Po(Nbmax) = SUM [P(Nb)] ; Nb > Nbmax.

A sample evaluation of a 9.6 Kbit/sec loop with 60 display stations, each displaying .5 messages per minute produced the results shown in Table 3. In this case, 160 buffers of 64 bits each are sufficient to guarantee that overruns occur with a frequency of less than 1 in 1000. The peak buffer requirement is about 4 times larger than the average buffer requirement. It is also of interest to note that the utilization of the Loop adapter processor in this case is at most 5.9%, and thus more than seven times lower than the utilization of the loop.

Calculations like the ones above have been done for many larger configurations of interest. In all investigated cases, enough buffer space was left over to reduce the probability of overruns to below 1/1000. In addition Loop adapter processor utilizations were always factors below the limiting loop utilizations.

6. SUMMARY

The main points of mutual contention were found to be the loops themselves and not the Loop adapter.

Loop and network protocol overhead was evaluated in section 4 , and terminal dependent adapter processing times were used together with polling loads to generate adapter processor utilizations in section 5.2. In addition, total, probabalistic buffer space usage was derived from individual, terminal and time dependent buffer space requirements. Based on this useage, probabilities of overruns were derived as a function of available buffer space in section 5.3.

The method of buffer overrun analysis derived in section 5.3 seems to be sufficiently general to be applicable to many other buffer assignment problems in the design of computer networks.

TABLE 3: PROBABILITY OF OVERRUNS VERSUS MESSAGE LENGTH

Message Length	400	600	800	1000
Loop-Ut	18%	27.6%	36.8%	45%
Loop Adapter-Ut	3.2%	4.1%	5%	5.9%
Average Buffers used	4.7	13.5	22.7	40.5
Probability to exeed				
60 buffers	.0056	.0115	.1824	.2725
80 buffers	.0002	.0008	.0529	.1092
100 buffers	.0000	.0000	.0116	.0355
120 buffers	.0000	.0000	.0019	.0096
130 buffers	.0000	.0000	.0003	.0051
140 buffers	.0000	.0000	.0000	.0022
160 buffers	.0000	.0000	.0000	.0004

ACKNOWLEDGEMENTS

The authors want to thank especially Mr.
A. Fratezi and Mr. S. Sutter from the
engineering department for the many
important discussions on loop operation
and implementation. Acknowledgements are
also due to Dr. W. Kraemer who contrib-
uted an APL program for performing the
convolution operation of section 5.3.3.

REFERENCES

1. Clark, D.D., et al, "An Introduction
   to Local Area Networks", Proc. IEEE,
   Vol. 66, No 11, Nov. 1978
2. IBM 4331 Processor Functional Charac-
   teristics and Processor Complex
   Configurator, Doc. Nr. GA33-1526 and
   Technical Newsletter GN 33/1733,
   Sept. 15, 1980.
3. IBM Synchronous Data Link Control,
   General Information Doc. Nr.
   GA27-3093, Third Edition, March 1979.
4. IBM Systems Network Architecture
   Introduction Doc. Nr. GA27-3116.
5. IBM 4331 Processor Model Group 2
   Channel Characteristics, Doc. Nr.
   GA33-1535, First Edition, October
   1980.
6. Parzen, Emanuel, "Modern Probability
   Theory and its Application", Wiley
   1960.
7. IBM 4331 Processor Multiuse Communications Loop, Functional Characteristics, Doc. Nr. GA33-1534.

APPENDIX : FORWARD TRANSMISSION ON LOOP.

PRIMARY STATION TRANSMITTING:

The primary station sends command frames
that are addressed to any or all the
secondary stations on the loop. Each
frame transmitted by the primary carries
the address of the secondary station or
stations to which the frame is directed.

Every secondary station on the loop
decodes the address field of each frame
transmitted by the primary station and
serves as a repeater for all primary
transmissions to the down-loop stations.
When a secondary detects a frame with
its address, it accepts this frame from
the loop for processing. This frame is
also passed to down-loop stations.

When the primary has finished transmitting frames, it follows the last flag
with a minimum of eight consecutive 0's
(a flag followed by eight 0's is a
turnaround sequence). It then transmits
continuous 1's which create a go-ahead
sequence (01111111). In this way, the
primary totally controls all loop
communications. The primary, while
Due to buffer space limitations in the
attached terminals, the maximum size of
the present loop transmission frame was

continuing to transmit 1's, goes into
receive mode.

SECONDARY STATIONS TRANSMITTING:

In this mode the primary station has
completed transmission of data, has
placed itself in receive mode, and is
transmitting continious 1's (go-ahead
sequence).

Before transmitting on the loop, a
secondary station must have received a
poll command, calling either for an
optional response or a mandatory
response.

The first down-loop secondary detects
the go-ahead sequence. If the secondary
has a response to send, it changes the
seventh 1-bit to a 0-bit, thereby
creating a flag. It follows the flag
with a response frame or frames that
contain it's individual adress. Following it's last frame, it then again
becomes a repeater, forwarding the
continuous 1-bits. This procedure
continues until the last down-loop
secondary to transmit completes it's
transmission.(See Fig. 2)

When the primary station finally
receives the go-ahead signal, ending
zero bit of the final flag followed by
at least seven 1's, it knows that all
secondary stations have been polled.

The SDLC transmission frame on the loop
consists basically of six parts: (compare Fig. 6)

- A beginning flag (F), 01111110, that
  indicates the beginning of a frame
- An 8 bit address field (A) that
  identifies the secondary station that
  is sending (or is to receive) the
  frame
- An 8 bit control field (C) that
  specifies the purpose of the particular frame (e.g., initialization,
  error reporting, confirmation), or
  contains send and receive counts.
- An optional, variable length information field (I) that contains information data in multiple of 8 bits
- A 16 bit frame check sequence (FCS)
  that enables the receiving station to
  check the correctnes of address,
  control and information fields.
- An ending flag (F), 01111110, that
  signals the end of the frame.

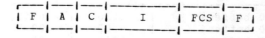

Fig. 6: SDLC Transmission Frame

limited to 271 bytes or 8 x 271 = 2168
bits. The maximum size for the information field (I) within the SDLC trans-

mission frame is then 271 - 6 = 265 bytes, where the 6 bytes are needed for 2 flags (F), the adress field (A), the control field (C), and the 2 byte frame check sequence (FCS).

Within an SNA system environment one or several information fields (I) contain the basic user Request Unit (RU) to be transferred in addition to SNA control information, like the Request Header (RH = 3B) or the Transmission Header (TH = 6B) (compare ref. 3). For an SNA message sent or received by a terminal on the loop, this additional control information amounts then to 9 bytes (RH + TH) of additional data within the first SDLC transmission frame, and 6 bytes TH for each additional frame of the message.

Distributed Virtual Hosts and Networks:
Measurement and Control

R. H. Sherman

Ford Aerospace and Communications Corporation

M. G. Gable
A. W. Chung

Ford Motor Company

Abstract

Diverse network application requirements bring about local networks of various size, degree of complexity and architecture. The purpose of this paper is to present a network protocol layer which is used to provide a homogeneous operating environment and to ensure the availability of network resources. The network layer process probes the underlying local network to discover its properties and then adapts to changing network conditions. The principle contribution of this paper is to generalize properties of diverse local networks which can be measured. This is important when considering maintenance and service of various communication links. Three type of links are point-to-point links, multi-drop, loop or switched links and multi-access contention data buses. A prototype network is used to show a complexity improvement in the number of measurement probes required using a multi-access contention bus. Examples of measurement techniques and network adaption are presented.

Introduction

A prototype network has been developed for use in experimenting with designs suitable for in plant and between plant applications. These applications require a diverse set of local networks because of demands for communication efficiency, reliability, connectivity and cost effectiveness. Application programs, on the other hand, would like to view computer processes on more abstract terms for support of high level languages, end user functions and isolation from network changes. A problem that arises is how to effectively maintain and service these diverse network technologies during network operation.

The principle contribution of this paper is to show how practical steps can be taken to simplify design and operation of diverse local networks. The overall network is designed to adapt to various local network performance, provide a virtual space of hosts and networks for application programs and to permit network instruments which reveal actual performance and allow reconfiguration. This design is based on defining a few network performance

properties which can be used in local network state measurement. Controls can then be applied to reconfigure around fault conditions and to adjust data flow for present operating conditions.

The prototype network contains a multiaccess contention bus called LNA[1,3,4] and a local network called DCNet[2] containing point-to-point links. The combined local network uses the Department of Defense standard IP/TCP[5] protocol for a common network and transport service. User level protocols consist of file transfer, mail transfer, virtual terminal and services for names, cross network booting, etc.

The plan for the paper is to first present a number of design guidelines for a network layer of protocol. A categorization is made of various local networks based on the procedures required to make state measurements. Implementation techniques which deal with time, names, addresses and routes are given. Finally, network instruments are defined with an example of there use in a typical maintenance scenario.

Network Layer Design Concepts

The network layer is designed to provide adaptability and simple operation. Network components such as network interfaces and computers can be installed as easily as modems, without the need of specialists. Just as some modems can learn the speed and modulation type of a dialed computer, the network layer learns the properties of an attached local network. These properties include host connectivity, round trip link delays, data throughput rates and network absolute time. Property values are derived from regular test probes and are stored as a collection of state vectors called the host table.

Different communication facilities can appear to have the same properties under one load (data flow) and quite different properties for another load. For example, a 2400 baud link can have the same delay property as a 1 Mbit/sec satellite channel. The difference in the facilities is the maximum throughput provided which only shows up on an incremental basis as applications approach saturated load conditions.

Another distinction in local networks is the delay properties in reaching a number of hosts through the network interface. A network broadcast is used to provide this delay measurement. The procedure for broadcast depends on the type of local network which are categorized as follows:

1. Point-to-point data links

2. Multidrop and switched data links

3. Multiaccess contention bus

Figure 1 shows the network architecture with the three types of local network interfaces at the lowest level and the DoD standard protocol corresponding to higher ISO layers.

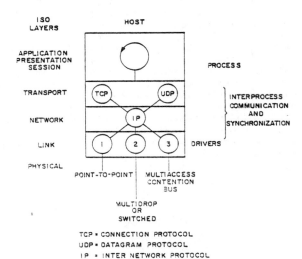

TCP = CONNECTION PROTOCOL
UDP = DATAGRAM PROTOCOL
IP = INTER NETWORK PROTOCOL

Figure 1. Network Architecture

The design principles expand upon other inter-networking approaches[6] in the virtual concepts employed as listed below:

A. Separation of Function The network layer functions are modular and include measurement and control as follows:

M1. Round trip packet delay to each host

M2. Network wide absolute time maintenance

M3. Host and network connectivity

M4. Network interface transfer rate

C1. Route selection

C2. Network time synchronization

C3. Computer control broadcasts (worms)

C4. Congestion control

Hosts derive information for routing, clock synchronization and addressing on a dynamic basis. Independent information is used for each function. Delay information is used for routing, absolute time information is used for synchronization and rate information is used for flow control. The independence of these functions provides for separate operation, for example, the clock may not by synchronized but delay values are still valid. Routing is determined by measuring link delays, not queuing delays. The buffer dynamics are minimized by a rate based flow control mechanism[7]. Measuring link and interface speeds is a more general approach to

routing than special routing designs[8] which take account of preconfigured link and interface speeds.

B. Network Broadcast

Network broadcasts are used to determine the round trip delay to each host, the hosts reachable on each link, the optimal route to a host and to synchronize a network clock. Delay measurement is useful in detecting changes in links and link interface speeds. As a separate function absolute time synchronization can be used for network instrumentation and to maintain a total ordering of transactions on a higher layer distributed data base.

C. Host Autonomy

Hosts are autonomous and may connect to the network only on a temporary basis. A host comes up on the network without any configuration information accept for its own resources. The host informs the network of its existence by sending a "hello" broadcast with its own address. The hello is a data probe that is sent to each link on the host. The network configuration is then derived from responses received. This procedure works on all type links because the hello message is encapsulated in each specific link level protocol. Hosts which receive hello messages, but do not implement this protocol, simply return messages to the originator. For example, a host can go down and the same host can be brought up somewhere else on the network in a different computer.

D. Reaching Agreement about Disturbances

Broadcast packets may be lost, therefore, several broadcasts may be attempted before an agreement is reached. The broadcast packets are passed on by hosts until all network hosts have received the information. Faulty processors are assumed not to pass on any bad information. This assumption is made because of two design factors:

1. The broadcast uses the same table lookup mechanism as the data packets. Failures in forwarding data packets can be sensed as broadcast failures.

2. Individual broadcast packets are often responses to earlier broadcasts from an originator. The feedback of state information on broadcasts can be used to check consistency and to protect against the propagation of bad information.

E. Virtual Host/Network Partitioning

Processes are grouped into hosts, local networks and networks based on the autonomous control desired and performance objectives. The particular hardware assignment of processes may be temporary for the maintenance of service during some disturbance.

The network broadcast delay determines how quickly fault information propagates throughout the network. The broadcast delay is defined as the largest roundtrip delay in the local network.

If we reduce the broadcast delay by reducing the number of hosts, then the number of alternative data paths are reduced for reconfiguration alternatives. Multiaccess contention buses provide an opportunity for improved broadcast speed.

Delay Measurement

Time measurements can be performed to measure relative delay or absolute time[10] in a local network. The specific procedures are sensitive to the type of local network. Eventhough LNA is a high bandwidth network, the delay between hosts accessing the LNA is non-zero for several reasons. First, the transfer rate of a packet between the host and the LNI is dependent on the baud rate for serial access, and the host operating system performance for asynchronous parallel access. Secondly, the transfer rate between the source and destination LNI's may experience a contention delay depending on LNA utilization. Finally, the transfer into the destination host depends on the interface rate. The result is that LNA represents more delay than a point-to-point link with corresponding throughput.

A broadcast method depends on the link type, not on the actual communication facility used. Each host contains a real-time clock which it uses to measure round trip delay. The hello interaction on a point-to-point link is shown in Figure 2.

The time stamp sent from B to A is t0(A)+t1(B)-t0(B) which becomes t1(A)-t0(A)+ t1(B)-t0(B) as the round trip delay at host A. For multidrop, loop or switched links, ie., type 2, this procedure is repeated for each host directly reachable on the link.

For a multiple access contention bus the procedure is to measure the delay of the link port and sum this delay with the delay each host has on the link port. This separation of delay as the sum of two different host delays is possible because the same contention resolution exists at each host. A broadcast hello is sent with a time stamp to the link port. All hosts including the originating host receives the hello packet. When the hello is returned, the calculation of round trip local network delay is made. This delay value includes the contention delay of the local network. Other hosts send hellos with their link port delay. The round trip delay is the sum of the originator link delay and the other link port delays. Figure 3 shows a similar interaction with a time history of the broadcast events given next.

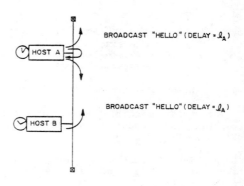

BROADCAST "HELLO" (DELAY = ℓ_A)

BROADCAST "HELLO" (DELAY = ℓ_A)

Figure 3. Time Measurement: Multiple Access Contention Bus

The time, t0, is the start of the broadcast, the time, t0´, is the link return of the broadcast and the time, t1, is the host return of the broadcast. LA and LB are measured link port delays for hosts A and B, respectively.

Host A	Local Net	Host B
t0(A)	--->	
t0´(A)	<-----	
	------>	t0(B)
	<-----	t1(B)
t1(A)		

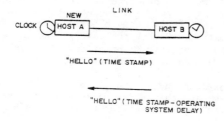

LINK

CLOCK HOST A   HOST B

"HELLO" (TIME STAMP)

"HELLO" (TIME STAMP – OPERATING SYSTEM DELAY)

Figure 2. Time Measurement: Point-to-Point

Host A sends a hello containing a time stamp to host B. Host B returns the hello with the original time stamp value plus the time delay in the operating system. Host A computes the round trip delay by subtracting the time received minus the packet time stamp. The time history is shown in the following diagram:

Host A	Local Net	Host B
t0(A)	----->	
		t0(B)
	<------	t1(B)
t1(A)		

A further reduction in overhead occurs by reducing the rate of sending hello packets by hosts with only one link. A bridge host is defined as a host with more than one link. Non-bridge hosts receive broadcasts from bridge hosts to keep network status rapidly updated. When a non-bridge host comes up, a hello is sent to measure the local port delay and to inform the other hosts of the event.

Time Synchronization

Time synchronization is achieved by comparing the absolute clock times. The interaction of hello packets is used to continually feedback absolute clock values. The convergence to zero offset is particularly fast on a contention network because the same hello packet is received by all hosts within microseconds. The time offset can be driven to zero by slewing the absolute times until all offsets are gone. The offset is calculated for all links as follows:

$$Offset = t1(a)-t1(B) + Delay/2$$

The real time clock, RTC, is slewed proportional to the offset value as follows:

$$D\ RTC/Dt = Offset* \ Constant$$

D/Dt is the time derivative. The slewing is implemented by keeping a virtual clock and incrementing the amount of the real clock plus slew rate. Process times are given by the normal real time clock.

Network Implementation

An example local network is shown in Figure 4 for use in discussing the implementation.

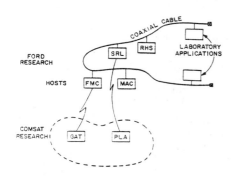

Figure 4. Network Configuration
Two bridge hosts, FMC and SRL, use point-to-point links to connect the Ford LNA with the Comsat DCNet.

Name Space

A name space exists for use in referencing local networks, hosts, processes and data objects such as files and records. A name process resides on several hosts and is used to translate symbolic names to addresses. The name table search is hierarchical with the host being searched for the name first. When a name is not found in the local context, the global context is used to find the

name. When multiple addresses exist for the same name, other qualifiers must be used to designate a unique name.

Internetwork addresses are composed of four bytes referred to as Net, Subnet, Host and Subhost. Example host names and addresses are given below:

Name	Net	Sub	Host	Sub
RHS	35	0	15	2
FMC	35	0	12	2
	35	1	12	2

Process names are identified with generic service port numbers known throughout the network, and specific local port numbers. Data objects are found by using service processes associated with the data object.

Address Map

The LNA behaves like an associative lookup table when an LNA destination address locates the particular LNI or group of LNIs. The address mapping is shown in Figure 5.

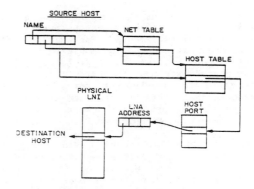

Figure 5. Address Mapping
The NetId byte is used to locate the network, the Subnet byte is used to locate the subnetwork and the HostId byte is used to locate the host. A host port entry defines the route to a logical host. For local network access from a logical port, the Host Table leader entry is used to form an LNA address.

For addresses derived from the network, an inverse address map is possible. When a hello arrives at a host port, entries in the mapping tables are made. The logical port of the hello is saved in the host table, and the leader entry is derived from the hello source IP address.

Routing

Routing is accomplished with the use of logical host address tables. The host table contains several host names, the port number, the round trip delay to that host, a status of when the last update was received and an update time stamp. As an example, the host table shown below is from SRL since there is a zero delay to itself.

Host	GAT	SRL
PortID	6	6
Delay	down	0
Offset	-2	-14
Status	119	110
Leader	40513	40517
Update	19:43:07	19:43:08

The delay to GAT is over 30 seconds indicating "down" and the route is through the local network, Port 6, by means of FMC, local leader 13. The host identification is 13 and the segment identification is an ASCII ´A´ in the upper half word (405 in octal). The following table shows GAT "up" after about 2 minutes and a new route is found over the lease line, portid 12, local leader 17.

Host	GAT	SRL
PortID	12	6
Delay	2100	0
Offset	10	-12
Status	92	119
Leader	40513	40517
Update	19:43:49	19:44:45

Routing is direct on the LNA network. LNI and link interface faults, however, can be bypassed with the use of delay measurements. For example, if two local network hosts cannot communicate because of attenuation problems, but a host in between the two hosts can communicate to both hosts, then a path is established. Unfortunely, the store and forward host also hears collisions that are undetected by other hosts and the contention scheme losses performance, however, everything works.

Broadcasts are implemented using a reverse path forwarding technique[9]. A host forwards the broadcast packet on each port except the incoming port. When a broadcast packet is sent to the local network, a broadcast destination address is used. The following procedure describes the broadcast mechanism:

```
IF Pkt.Dest = all network host

THEN BEGIN

   IF incoming_port =
      Routing_Table(Pkt.Source)

   THEN BEGIN

   FOR ALL ports DO
      IF port = MAC Network THEN
      LNA destination=
         selective broadcast

      forward along port

      END

   ELSE discard

ELSE  BEGIN

      normal routing

END
```

The selective broadcast is implemented by an address filter function in the LNI. The LNA destination address contains the HDLC all parties broadcast address which is represented by ´@´. The address filter is used to discriminate on address bytes port, segment and user. The LNI port address represents the LNI on the shared medium. The segment address byte is used to designate the particular virtual network or network application. User address bytes are used as virtual circuit channel numbers or as a wildcard for the case of datagrams. The address filter is given as a procedure with the "my" data structure for the resident address values and "Pkt" the incoming packet address data structure.

```
IF ( Pkt.Port =
   My.Port OR Pkt.Port = ´@´ )

   AND ( Pkt.Segment =
      My.Segment OR Pkt.Segment = ´?´)

   AND ( Pkt.User =
      My.User OR Pkt.User = ´?´ )

THEN "accept packet"

ELSE "discard packet"

END
```

Instrumentation

Convenient network instrumentation tools are desirable when measuring performance and tracking component problems. These network instruments are particularly important at Ford since computers must operate in a vast manufacturing complex. Special purpose instruments (oscilliscopes, data analyzers, and time domain reflectometers) do exist for specific diagnostic purposes, but these have not as yet been integrated into a more general setting.

Since the virtual terminal service (TELNET)
can be used to remotely obtain access to the host,
the delay measurements can be easily viewed at a
site remote from the local network. When pursuing
a problem as sensed by an increase in delay between
a host and the local network, statistics on the
host local network driver can be displayed. Host
interface hardware errors as well as software overrun conditions can be identified. The host local
network driver program collects statistics gathered
by the LNI on its operation. The LNI gathered
statistics include hardware errors, overrun conditions and a packet retry histogram as measured over
the last 100 packets sent. The example table 1
below shows no hardware errors existing and only
2% of the LNA packets were retried. These
retransmissions are most likely due to LNI congestion during adapting to host interface speed
differences.

Input packets:	9261
leader only:	2
bad format:	0
bad checksum:	5
misrouted:	0
returned:	0
HELLO messages:	7648
Output packets:	1334
No buffer:	0
Hardware errors:	13
LNA Statistics:	
Input:	
errors/100:	0
no buffer:	4
Output:	
errors/100:	2
lengths:	95
packets+acks:	3210
sample:	149
% Retry:	
0:	98
1:	2
2:	0
3:	0
4:	0
5:	0
6:	0

Table 1: Host driver statistics display

For collecting network statistics, there are
several experiments that can be performed. Figure
6 shows the various data probe loops used in measurement. The following is a list of controlled
data loops that can be examined:

1. Internal loop back within one host computer.

2. A host can send data to its attached LNI to have
   it looped back internally within the LNI and
   returned to the host.

3. A host can send data to its attached LNI to have
   it looped back externally through the shared
   medium.

4. A host on a local network can send data to a
   remote LNI on the local network and have the data
   looped back through the remote LNI without dis-
   turbing data flow to the remote host attached.

5. A host can loop data back from a remote host.

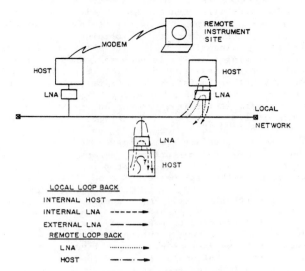

Figure 6. Loop Back Options

As corrective tools, resets can be performed
on the hosts or the LNIs. In fact, any loopback
described above can also be used to execute commands. This means that low level displays/alters
of memory and device registers, for example, can be
performed on remote LNIs and hosts.

Data delay statistics can be collected and
displayed as a histogram of delay versus frequency
by using the PING program, see table 2 below. Any
packet loss is used to stop the data loop back. A
typical delay histogram on a local network host-
to-host loopback, item 5, contains frequency peaks
corresponding to LNA retransmissions. When Hellos
are being processed, another characteristic delay
occurs because of the multiplexing of packets
through one host port.

Samples: 567 mean: 131 min: 100 max: 450

Value	Count	
100	550	|************************
150	10	|*****
200	4	|**
250	0	|
300	1	|*
350	1	|*
400	0	|
450	1	|*

Table 2: Delay Histogram

An interesting property of the LNA network Hello is
that the looping back takes priority over incoming
packets, thus delays measured by local hellos are
not disturbed by packet traffic. This loopback, #3
above, occurs simply by defining the destination
address equal to the source address in LNA packets.
The remote LNI loopback over the shared medium, #4
above, is performed using an LNA echo command.

As an example of using network instruments to isolate problems consider a user on MAC who complains about file transfer speeds with PLA. A service person using RHS starts to examin possible causes. First, the route is obtained by virtual terminal connecting to MAC and obtaining the host table showing that PLA is accessed through portid 6 and local leader 15 which represents SRL. Secondly, the statistics on MACs network interface, portid 6, is displayed in a form shown in Table 1. Then a virtual terminal connection to SRL showing both portid 6, the LNA interface, and portid 12, the lease line interface can be made. Finally, a display of interface statistics on PLA can be made. When no excessive hardware errors have been detected it may be noticed that a loss of buffer is occuring on the link between SRL and PLA.

The detailed data flow properties of this link can be found by running the Ping program from either the RHS or SRL host. A histogram as in Table 2 could reveal multiple peaks representing packet retransmissions by higher layer protocols. The source of buffer losses could then be traced to congestion in going from high speed to low speed data links.

Conclusion

Network instrumentation has been found quite useful and a minimal burden. These instruments can provide the raw data for more advanced strategies of logging and alarming significant network events. One lesson we have learned is the utility of alternative data paths for the design and operation of local networks.

The LNA design has fit remarkably well into an internetworking system primarily because of dynamic, hierarchical addresses. Disturbances to computer and communication facilities are accommodated with a host network layer protocol. The network layer complexity is improved by the LNAs ability to allow broadcast packets to measure round trip delay.

Acknowledgements

We gratefully acknowledge the continued help and encouragement of Dave Mills at Comsat.

References

1. R.H. Sherman, M.G. Gable, and G.MCClure," Concepts and Strategies in Local networks", Data Communication, July, 1978.

2. D.L. Mills,"An Overview of a Distributed Computer Network", AFIPS Conf. Proc. 1976, pp523-532.

3. M.G. Gable and R.H. Sherman,"Feedback Carrier Sense Multiple Access Contention", Local Network Conference , May, 1981, London, England.

4. M.F. Alvarez and M.G. Gable, "Local area contention network physical level design", National Telecommunication Conference, Dec. 1980.

5. Cerf,V. and Kahn,R.,"A Protocol for Packet Network Intercommunication", IEEE Trans. on Communications, Vol Com-22, No. 5, pp 637-648, May 1974.

6. Boggs, D.R. , Shoch, J.F., Taft, E.A. and Metcalfe, R.M.,"Pup: An Internetwork Architecture", IEEE Trans. on Communications, Vol Com-28, No 4,pp 612-621, April 1980.

7. Pouzin,"Rate versus Window Flow Control", AFIPS Conf. Proc. 1979.

8. McQuillan, J.M, Richer, I., and Rosen, E.C.,"The New Routing Algorithm for the ARPANET", IEEE Trans. on Communications, pp 711-719, Vol. Com-28, No 5, May, 1980.

9. Dalal,Y.K.,"Broadcast Protocols in Packet Switched Computer Networks", PhD Thesis, Stanford Univ., April, 1977.

10. D.L. Mills,"Time Synchronization in DCNET Hosts", internet note 173, Feb. 23,1981.

SESSION 7: SIMULATION AND MEASUREMENT TOOLS

Chair: Jeffrey Mayersohn
Bolt Beranek and Newman Inc.
Cambridge, MA

A Network Performance Analyst's Workbench
by

Richard Brice

William Alexander

Los Alamos National Laboratory

ABSTRACT

Performance measurement and analysis of the behavior of a computer network usually requires the application of multiple software and hardware tools. The location, functionality, data requirements, and other properties of the tools often reflect the distribution of equipment in the network. We describe how we have attempted to organize a collection of tools into a single system that spans a broad subset of the measurement and analysis activities that occur in a complex network of heterogenous computers. The tools are implemented on a pair of dedicated midicomputers. A database management system is used to couple the data collection and analysis tools into a system highly insulated from evolutionary changes in the composition and topology of the network.

1. INTRODUCTION

A growing number of computer installations are faced with managing complex networks of heterogeneous computers and their interconnecting mechanisms. The Integrated Computing Network (ICN) at Los Alamos (Fig. 1) includes 12 large computers called workers (the center column of the figure), several other computers that perform specialized services, called hosts (the extreme left column of the figure), and over 24 computers called switches that provide message switching/concentration, security, and related functions. These computers come from five vendors. The Computing Division currently supports eight different operating systems to run these various types of computers. The number of computers and operating systems are expected to increase. Other computers, called distributed processors, are located at sites physically remote from the ICN and connect to it through the gateway switches called XNET. Distributed processors are not considered in this paper.

This proliferation of computing equipment and operating systems at Los Alamos causes serious problems for those of us responsible for performance measurement and analysis (PMA) of the network and each of its components. A common approach to providing PMA tools is to implement or acquire them as each new type of computer is added to a pool of computing equipment. In our case, this has resulted in a growing collection of tools that must be understood and maintained by a staff that changes over time.

Acquisition and maintenance of PMA tools is only a part of the problem. Performance data must be organized into numerous different input sets suitable for each tool. Output from the tools must be merged somehow into a consistent form to provide information about all components in the computer network. As new types of data are collected, the problems inherent in merging the new data with the old must be solved.

Another class of problems arises from the difficulty in collecting data that are related by time or function from numerous different computers distributed throughout the ICN. It is desirable to relate network traffic to the user or system program that caused the traffic, that is, to relate measurements taken from switches to measurements taken on workers. In our case, the problems of data collection are made more difficult by Department of Energy (DOE) rules governing management of classified data.

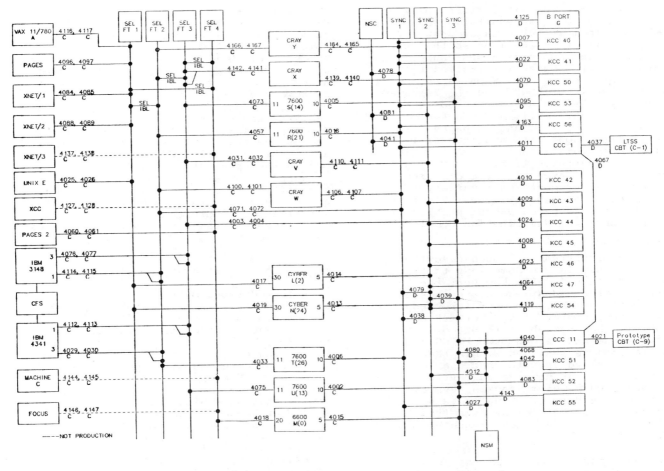

Fig. 1. Los Alamos Integrated Computer Network.

A special node is now being added to the ICN called the Facility for Operator Control and Utilization Statistics (FOCUS) that is intended to solve many of these problems as well as some of those faced by operators, administrators, and users in dealing with the complexity and diversity of the ICN. FOCUS has three major functions: gathering and analyzing performance measurements, providing status and load information to users and operators, and controlling and tracking production jobs submitted by users. In this paper we concentrate on the performance measurement and analysis component.

On FOCUS we have tried to create a network performance analyst's workbench: a set of PMA tools that will support all facets of the PMA work to be done and that are all implemented on a single "trusted" computer (a VAX 11/780) that is allowed to communicate with any other element in the ICN. All PMA tools on this computer are coupled through a general-purpose database management system (DBMS) that is capable of insulating the PMA tools (as much as possible) from the changes in computing environment that are bound to occur.

2. RELATED WORK

The ARPA network Network Control Center (NCC) [1,2] overlaps in functionality with FOCUS to some extent. Both FOCUS and NCC are implemented on standalone machines that are not required for continued operation of the networks, both interrogate network components to collect workload and network status information, and both maintain historic databases for generating reports.

There are significant differences between NCC and FOCUS. Specifically, NCC has the responsibility for maintenance of code that runs in IMPs and for downloading system changes (or program reloads when the system crashes) whereas FOCUS does not. Another important difference lies in emphasis on how performance data is to be used. FOCUS makes this information available to any user logged on to any worker in the network. Further, our basic purpose is not to charge for services, but rather to parameterize models of the network components and to observe workload trends.

There are also similarities between FOCUS and CSIRONET in Australia [3]. We both want to make our data or answers available in an online mode so that users, operators, and administrators can get any status or performance information that they find interesting. Significant differences in CSIRONET and the ICN stem from geography and network composition. CSIRONET is physically distributed throughout Australia and is based on a single large host with numerous similar switches for distribution of data. The ICN is concentrated within a few thousand square meters (excepting the distributed processors) but contains a variety of worker computers and switches. It is the variety that complicates our problem whereas physical distribution complicates theirs.

The sidestream approach described in Ref. 4 is similar in some ways to FOCUS, NCC, and the CSIRONET; however, the basic thrust of the sidestream approach seems to be making available to operators and users the current status of the network and problems that have been reported to the network administrators. On FOCUS, this information is included within the function called operator and user information. We have no current plans for the detailed problem tracking system described in Ref. 4. Finally, a natural consequence of collecting data from the network will produce measurements such as those in Ref. 5.

Our approach to FOCUS was shaped in part by the concept of a programmer's workbench as described by Ivie [6]. This idea is expanded in Sec. 3.3.

3. OBJECTIVES

A vast amount of measurement and analysis must be done on a network as large and heterogeneous as ours, and results must be directed to a wide variety of people for a wide variety of reasons. A significant amount of automation is necessary to accomplish it at all.

3.1. PMA Work to be Done on Individual Machines

Some of the PMA work on the individual workers is independent of the fact that they happen to be embedded in a network. Workload must be characterized and utilizations analyzed to determine needs and trends and to find bottlenecks. Data must be prepared as input to models, and the models must be run to evaluate alternate hardware and software configurations. The workload and utilization measurement, at least, should be done more or less continuously. In this way, trends of both short and long duration can be spotted, and local extrema will not be taken as typical. This is especially true if measurements from different machines of the same class and running the same operating system can be combined. The collection and routine analysis of such large amounts of data will be done only if it can be completely automated. Further, the total amount of such work can be reduced if the data are collected and sent to a central place and analyzed there. We would also like to develop definitions of resource capacities and usages that have the same meanings for all machines in the ICN, that is, a machine-independent definition of resources and their usage. We recognize the difficulty of this [7], but it is a necessary step in achieving our goal of a set of analysis programs that are independent of the way data are collected and stored.

3.2. PMA Activities Unique to the Nework

In addition, many PMA activities are unique to networks. As a base we need information about the message traffic between each pair of nodes, such as the frequency, distribution of sizes, transit times, and number of retrys, all in the context of date and time and level of other network activity. With this information we can detect workload trends, ensure that switching nodes and lines have sufficent capacity, do bottleneck analysis, and parameterize models with which to investigate alternate network hardware and topology. As is true for individual network components, this traffic data should be recorded frequently and collected in one place for analysis. Security, economic, and reliability considerations dictate that this one place not be an ordinary worker node in the network.

Beyond a taxonomy of the traffic through the lines and switches, we want another type of information about our network. The fact that the worker computers are embedded in a network determines the workload put on them as well as the way users see them; the topology of the network and the services it offers influence what users do. But these influences are likely to be too subtle for us to guess accurately. We need to find out not only what the traffic is, but why it is, by determining what processes at the various nodes are generating it. We need to know what proportion of the network traffic is being generated by interprocess communication, by file shipping to specialized nodes, and by terminal interactions. Only with this information can we ensure that the network will continue to meet the evolving needs of the users [8]. The causes of traffic can only be determined from time-correlated measurements on the workers and other nodes, and this in turn requires as global a measuring instrument as possible.

Similarly, the network affects the user by, for example, its response time. Poor response may be caused by a number of network elements and by different elements at different times. Such dynamic system behavior can only be observed with time-correlated measurements.

3.3 Workbench Concept

Before discussing the ideal performance analyst's workbench, let us list some typical analyst's activities as they are done without FOCUS. We write and install changes in various host operating systems that count and measure events of interest. We start up programs, which we have written, that sample system tables or process system record files. The output of these programs is our primary data, and we spend time simply scanning through it, building up a picture in our mind of the behavior of the system. If the period we have looked at seems representative or interestingly anomalous, we may save a printed listing of the output and refer back to it. (There is no DBMS that we can get to from all nodes of the network.) Next, we convert this output into input for numerous models (we have modelling packages that run on three different types of workers). We also summarize it in various ways for presentations and reports. Both of these activities are mostly manual. The reports are prepared on a node with good word processing capabilities, making a total of four computers with four operating systems that we commonly use to process measurements taken on any node. All this is not to say we lack adequate resources or support to do our job; we have them, but their arrangement is not ideal, partly because we are analyzing a network rather than a single system and partly because we are just starting our workbench.

What then do we want? We want a single, integrated system containing all of our tools in one place. The system that serves as our workbench must, of course, be interactive; in fact, because we will always be developing new analysis packages and models on it, it should have all of the characteristics of the programmer's workbench. In addition, we need word processing capabilities and graphics software and hardware for presenting results. Perhaps most important, we need a good DBMS with a rich query language to facilitate exploratory questions about relations among measured quantities. The machine on which the workbench is implemented must be integrated into the network in such a way that from it we can address and query any other node in the network and initiate processes on them. In Sec. 4 we describe in more detail our implementation of some of these features on the FOCUS system.

In describing the programmer's workbench, Ivie listed several anticipated advantages, some of which we believe apply to FOCUS also. Storing all the measurements on a separate machine should encourage common and machine-independent representations of performance and workload parameters. By developing analysis and presentation tools only once, better software can be developed for less cost in time and money. The software and the procedures for using them need be documented only once. An ongoing PMA effort at any installation inevitably means facing personnel additions and turnover; training and learning time can be minimized if new analysts can do most of their work on only one system. Some possible disadvantages include adding still another node to an already complex network, slowing down response to certain user status requests because more than one machine will be involved, and converting character sets and number representations.

4. DESIGN AND IMPLEMENTATION OF THE FOCUS ANALYST'S WORKBENCH

FOCUS is implemented on two VAX 11/780s. One VAX will be online at all times, and the other will serve simultaneously as backup and as a system development machine. This arrangement requires that both machines be configured identically and that all tools be resident on both.

The kinds of PMA tools that we need to provide the services desired by operators, administrators, users, and analysts can be divided into four areas:

1. data collection,
2. data management,
3. data analysis, and
4. information reporting.

In the following subsections we describe tools from each of these categories and show how we have merged them into a single unified system on the FOCUS machine.

4.1. Data Collection Tools

Implementation of data collection tools can occur at several levels in a system. Data collection at the user, accounting, and system levels are supported by numerous tools on all of our worker computers. Unfortunately, the types of data collected are not the same on all workers. None of the tools collect all of the data that are needed by the analysis programs. This appears to be a common failing [9].

Instead of describing in detail all collected data, we indicate the breadth of the data by noting that most workers allow read access to all system tables. From this we extract utilization and access counts for most resources. Some of our systems collect and establish relations among more detailed measures, for example, CPU burst length as a function of a job's memory size. The sets of collection tools and collected data are both constantly growing.

4.1.1. Data Collection from Workers

The ICN supports two features that have proven very useful: user processes can initiate other processes on the same or different workers, and a protocol supported with convenient library routines provides intermachine process-to-process communication. We use these two features to collect performance data from any worker in the ICN. A user-level job is defined (offline) that will run on a particular class of worker machine. The job definition is stored in the FOCUS database. When data are needed at the FOCUS machine the job definitions are sent to the required workers where they are scheduled like ordinary user jobs. When the data collection job runs on a worker, it communicates data to its counterpart process running on the FOCUS machine. Response time for this kind of job is usually very short. If necessary, these jobs can be initiated at a high enough priority to guarantee short response times. The data collected in this manner can be routed to the program or user that requested them, or the data can be stored in the FOCUS database, or both.

4.1.2. Data Collection from Switches

Data collection from the switches is less general. The switches have no secondary storage; as a result, most of the performance data collected by them is in the form of histograms. They will send these data to FOCUS on demand. Some circular tables of trace data are possible, but FOCUS must ask for them frequently to avoid overflow. More detailed data can be collected from many of the switches by hardware monitors or through the operator's console on the switch. However, this data must be manually collected, encoded, and entered into the FOCUS database, and this violates one of the basic reasons for having a FOCUS machine.

4.1.3 Data Collection Common to All Systems

In the next section on data management, we discuss another, implicit, form of data collection where the collected data are not typically observed by operating systems. These data lie in the gray area between performance data and analysis results. One of our goals is to define a set of such data that is common to all our computer systems, or at least common across a set of computer systems

with common function, for example, switches. Further, we want to base as many of our analysis programs as possible on these data so that the analysis programs can be insulated from additions or deletions of equipment from the ICN. We recognize that some PMA results will probably always be based on data peculiar to a particular piece of equipment. We wish to minimize these instances.

4.2 Data Management Tools

Data management is often the weakest link in a set of PMA tools. Typically, data are gathered into one or more files, and any change in file structure is likely to cause serious disruption to existing analysis programs. The dynamic aspect of our hardware acquisition and system instrumentation programs requires constant change to any global definition of collected performance data.

The data management tool we have chosen to implement is the glue that binds all other features into a complete package. It allows both interactive users and batch analysis programs to access all collected data in a way that is highly independent of the manner in which the data are actually stored in the database. Reorganization of the database should be transparent to all users.

The FOCUS data base management system (DBMS) supports the relational data model [10]. We maintain a growing set of relations into which all collected data will be mapped. The DBMS allows new relations to be dynamically created either through explicit definition or, implicitly, by combining existing relations through execution of the DBMS commands JOIN, PROJECT, INTERSECT, and SUBTRACT. (For a complete description of the database management system see Ref. 11.) The relations defined in Figs. 2-5 are examples of those included in the database. As data samples are collected from the network nodes, records (rows) are added to the appropriate relation instances.

Note that these are only examples and do not imply that Relations 1-4 are the best way to structure the data in the database.

We provide two different types of interface to the database, one for FOCUS implementors and analysts, and one intended for users. The first requires detailed knowledge of the relations in the database; the second does not.

The first type of interface simply consists of the commands provided by the DBMS. (In the DBMS command examples that follow, we have taken some liberties with syntax and command function to simplify the presentation. We distinguish key

Machine	Time-date	Number jobs in memory	Number jobs in CPU queue	Number jobs in memory queue

Fig. 2. Relation-1: Job and CPU loading per machine.

Machine	Time-date	Job id	Job size	Mean cpu burst	Std dev burst

Fig. 3. Relation-2: User job CPU and memory data.

Machine	Time-date	Messages line 1	. . .	Messages line n

Fig. 4. Relation-3: Line by line message traffic.

Machine	Time-date	Job id	User think time	Priority	Mean response time

Fig. 5. Relation-4: Priority and response times.

words from relation or attribute names by completely capitalizing key words and by naming each relation in the form Relation-n where n is some integer. Attributes, domains, in a relation have their first letter capitalized.)

Any authorized user who knows the form of Relation-1 can retrieve actual historical instances of job and CPU loading using as keys some subset of the fields contained in the relation definition, for example,

SELECT ALL FROM Relation-1 WHERE Machine
EQ 4 AND Time .GT. 0800 AND Time .LT.
1200 AND Date EQ 8/4/81

Execution of the above SELECT command retrieves all records from Relation-1 that contain data for Machine 4 on the morning of August 4, 1981. The user or analysis application can process the records as desired. Other commands exist for automatically performing arithmetic operations on fields in the records, for example,

COMPUTE AVE Attribute FROM Relation-1
WHERE ...

This command can be used to average the number of jobs in memory on Machine 4 on the morning of August 4 if the same WHERE qualifiers are used as in the SELECT command above and "attribute" is "Number_jobs_in_memory."

JOIN allows a user to combine two relations to produce a third, for example,

JOIN Relation-1 USING Machine WITH
Relation-2 USING Machine FORMING
Relation-5

In this case, a relation having nine domains (fields) would be produced. The resultant Relation-5 could then be queried using the other commands.

Users can query the database to obtain instances of data from any existing relation. However, most users will not (be allowed to) know much about the logical structure of the database because the structure may change. Instead, a second type of interface to the DBMS is provided that insulates users from changes in the underlying structure. We refer to this interface as the "performance parameter" interface. A performance parameter is a unit of information defined as a sequence of operations on existing or temporary relations. An extensible set of these exists to answer common user questions. For example, we can create a performance parameter called "high priority response time" that is defined as the average response time (during some interval) for small jobs with priority greater than some value. The user command

RETRIEVE High_priority_response WHERE
Priority .GT. 3 and Time .GT. 0800
AND Time .LT. 0900 AND Job_size .LT.
20000

would trigger a performance-parameter definition function that would execute the following sequence of commands.

143

```
SELECT ALL FROM Relation-4 FORMING
Relation-6 WHERE Priority .GT. 3
AND Time .GT. 0800 and Time .LT. 0900

JOIN Relation-6 USING Job_id WITH
Relation-2 FORMING Relation-7

COMPUTE AVE Mean_response_time FROM
Relation-7 WHERE
Job_size .LT. 20000
```

This sequence of three commands includes much more knowledge of the underlying structure of the database than was required by the original RETRIEVE command. The users are insulated from changes in database structure through the performance-parameter definition approach. Any change in the underlying structure will be mediated through changes to the performance-parameter definition that implements the RETRIEVE command.

The notion of performance parameters permits a crude mapping from a user view or external schema to the underlying conceptual schema as represented by the relations in the database. Of course, the mapping from external to conceptual schema must be maintained and updated whenever definitions change. Such changes are expected to be very minor, especially in comparison with changes to code that might be necessary if external views of the data are explicitly coded into the analysis programs that use the data.

The set of performance parameters has been made easily extendable. The extension mechanism in its simplest form involves only definition of a set of database commands to be applied to existing relations and inclusion of the definition in the performance-parameter dictionary. In some cases, it may be necessary to define new relations; in the worst case, additional data collection tools may be required.

The performance-parameter mechanism is our approach to providing the machine-independent definitions of resource capacities and usages that we stated as a goal in Sec. 3.1.

4.3. Data Analysis Tools

By analysis tools, we generally mean one of two classes of tools: (1) analytic or simulation models and the languages that support their implementation as computer programs, and (2) statistical analysis tools, such as regression analysis or curve fitting programs. However, we also include graphics programs because we often look at this kind of output when we are trying to understand some phenomenon.

In our implementation, we have tried to include both commercially available general-support tools and locally developed ones. Our current set of commercial products includes CADS, a queueing network analysis system [12]; ASPOL, a discrete system-simulation language system [13]; PAWS, a discrete system-simulation language system (and eventually also a queueing network analysis system) [14]; and SIMPL, a discrete system-simulation language [15]. All our analysis tools except those implemented in ASPOL can run on either the FOCUS machine or one of the other more powerful worker machines. Also, there are a number of tools that we have not chosen to use, such as SIMULA, GPSS, and SPSS; these are available at Los Alamos but not on our VAX/VMS system.

In addition to the commercial packages, we have a growing library of analysis application programs that have been developed at Los Alamos. Many of these programs are models of ICN components implemented in either CADS, ASPOL, or PAWS. We currently have validated models of the Cray-1 running the CTSS operating system, the Cray-1S I/O subsystem, and subsets of the ICN.

The FOCUS implementation automates the process of data collection, organization, and analysis. All data analysis programs are directly coupled to the FOCUS DBMS. We are trying to automate execution of the simulation and analysis programs, triggered by, for example, interesting circumstances detected by the data collection programs. Further, we would like to automate a procedure in which a manually validated model is run periodically with workload data, and the model output compared with measured output for the same period. In theory, the model and actual sets of performance data should agree to within some confidence interval; when they do not, this data set would be flagged for further manual analysis as indicating a possible shift in workload characteristics or system performance. We realize that this is very ambitious.

4.4. Information Reporting

The PMA information generated by FOCUS will be of interest to four broad and overlapping groups: the operations staff, administrators, users of the computing facility, and performance analysts.

The operations staff are concerned with immediate, short-term problems, for example, status of machines and interconnecting links. In some cases, operators may want historical data to evaluate the effectiveness of operations procedures. Administrators tend to be more concerned with long-term trends, for example, how the workload is changing and how well the users' needs are being serviced. Users are able to access numerous similar computers and are interested in knowing the current operational status and workload on each machine. They are also interested in following the progress of their job. Performance analysts are (by definition) interested in all aspects of a system's behavior.

Operators and administrators are similar in that the information they want is somewhat predictable, so the process of supplying it can be largely automated. Also, both groups want graphical output on a regular basis; operators need frequently refreshed diagrams of the network annotated with status information, and administrators will presumably be interested in bar graphs showing system up-times and utilizations.

Users present a more interesting problem because we do not know in advance all the information they will want nor the forms in which it will be most useful. In addition, because users will initiate the information presentation, utilities with friendly interfaces must be designed. So far we have implemented user utilities for ascertaining status and load at any worker or host and for job tracking. Users will undoubtedly ask for more.

As for the performance analysts, we feel like kids in a candy store. We believe that we will be able to get more information with less effort than ever before.

5. CONCLUDING REMARKS

Computer systems are usually developed with insufficient thought for performance measurement. This makes PMA work on an individual system difficult and time consuming. When this difficulty is multiplied by the number of different systems comprising a large heterogeneous network, such as the one at Los Alamos, and when overall network performance, which is a complicated function of individual system performances, must also be measured and analyzed, then the task becomes effectively impossible using single-system techniques. We had to create a better way.

We believe that we are developing this better way on FOCUS. Considerable progress has been made in this development. The DBMS that provides data to the analysis and simulation programs, the analysis programs, compilers for the queueing analysis and some simulation languages, some of the simulation models, and the general program development tools (editors, compilers, etc.) are all resident on the two dedicated VAX 11/780 machines on which FOCUS is implemented. The data collection probes, some of which

are embedded in the operating systems of the computers in the network, cannot be located on the FOCUS machine. Also, we frequently execute some of our analysis or simulation models on other, more powerful computers to obtain faster completion times.

Much work still needs to be done, but we believe that the system we are developing will enable us to do a task that is otherwise impossible. We hope that eventually it will also free us from vast amounts of routine and let us spend more time on the PMA tasks we find most interesting, such as implementing new measurements, and building and experimenting with models.

The tools and working conditions that we are trying to implement on the FOCUS machine should improve our ability to produce useful results, but the increased automation that we also want to include in the project carries a potential danger that we cannot as yet evaluate: PMA has traditionally included a large element of serendipity; the chance observation of a measure larger or smaller than expected often leads to new insights into the behavior or performance of the system being investigated. Each increment of automation may decrease our chance to enjoy these fortuitous benefits.

REFERENCES

[1] McKenzie, A. A., B. P. Cosell, J. M. McQuillan, and M. J. Thorpe, "The Network Control Center for the ARPA Network," Proc. International Conference on Computer Communication (1972) pp. 185-190.

[2] Santos, P. J., B. Chalstrom, John Linn, and J. G. Herman, "Architecture of a Network Monitoring, Control and Management System," Beranek and Newman, Inc. internal report (1980).

[3] Lance, G. N. and A. C. Edington, "Network Usage Statistics," Computer Networks 1 (1977) pp. 295-305.

[4] Leach, J. R. and R. D. Campenni, "A Sidestream Approach Using A Small Procesor as a Tool for Managing Communications Systems," IBM SYS Journal, Vol. 19, No. 1 (1980) pp. 120-138.

[5] Abrams, M. D., I. W. Cotton, S. W. Watkins, R. Rosenthal, and D. Rippy, "The NBS Network Measurement System," IEEE Transactions on Communications, Vol. 25, No. 10, (October 1977), pp. 1189-1198.

[6] Ivie, E. L. , "The Programmer's Workbench-A Machine for Software Development," Communications of the ACM, Vol. 20, No. 10 (October 1977) pp. 746-760.

[7]   Schwetman, H. D., "Workload
Characterization: Why? What? How?",
Computer Performance Evaluation, Online
Conferences Limited (Uxbridge, England,
1976) pp. 457-471.

[8]   Alexander, W. and R. Brice, "Long
Range Prediction of Network Traffic,"
Proc. CPEUG81, (San Antonio, Texas,
November 1981).

[9]   Rose, C. A. "Modeling Requirements
for Measurement Devices,"
Proc. 1977 SIGMETRICS Conference on Computer
Performance, (December 1977) pp. 21-17.

[10] Codd, E. F., "A Relational Model of
Data for Large Shared Data Bases,"
Communications of the ACM, 13, 6 (June
1970).

[11] Relational Information Management
Users Guide, Boeing Commercial Airplane
Co. manual D6-IPAD-70045-M, (Seattle,
Washington, 1981).

[12] Computer Analysis and Design System
Users Manual, Information Research
Associates (Austin, Texas, 1975).

[13] ASPOL Reference Manual, Pub. No.
17314200-B, Control Data Corporation
(Minneapolis, Minnesota, 1975).

[14] The Performance Analyst's Workbench
System Users Manual, Information Research
Associates (Austin, Texas 1981).

[15] "SMPL- A Simple Portable Simulation
Language," Amdahl Corporation Pub. No.
820377-700A (Sunnyvale, California, 1980).

A HIERARCHICAL MODELING SYSTEM
FOR COMPUTER NETWORKS

Donald F. DuBois
General Electric Company
M&DSO-Western Systems

ABSTRACT

This paper describes the Hierarchical Modeling System (HMS). HMS is a tool - a unified and expandable system - which supports the development of analytic and simulator models of computer networks. The same system and workload descriptions can be interpreted as analytic queueing models with optimization techniques or as discrete event simulation models. The rationale behind the development of HMS is that high level analyses incorporating analytic techniques may be used in the early design phase for networks when many options are considered while detailed simulation studies of fewer design alternatives are appropriate during the later stages.

Key Words and Phrases
Computer networks, performance evaluation, simulation, analytic models, hierarchical models.

SECTION 1
INTRODUCTION

It has long been recognized that analytic and simulation models are useful tools for the design of computer systems and networks. Each tool has its distinct advantages and costs. Analytic methods, such as those based on queueing models, have the advantage of relatively low computational requirements. This permits the models to be used interactively which can greatly reduce the time needed to study the behavior of a particular system. When design constraints are quantified analytic models can sometimes be optimized with respect to certain parameters such as response time and throughput. By simplifying the system structure analytic models can also provide insight and clarify the effect that individual components have on the overall behavior of the system. However, analytic models are sometimes not tractable and when they are essential details of the system may be missing; This has the effect of limiting the usefulness of the models to only a small range of values for the input parameters. On the other hand much more detail may be incorporated into simulation models without making special assumptions about the behavior of the system. Often the computational and developmental costs of simulators are much greater and the corresponding increase in output sometimes difficult to evaluate. They are difficult to optimize and frequently their complexity can mask the important controlling parameters of the system. However, analytic and simulation models can be used in a complementary way during the design stages for computer systems or networks. It is frequently the case that at the beginning of a design study a relatively larger number of options is available for different components of the proposed system. As the choice is narrowed a more detailed look at the final candidates for system components is desirable. This suggests that analytic techniques may be used as an efficient means of narrowing the larger set of options while the cost for simulation studies should be limited to the final stages of the design process. Also, in practical situations detailed data on the system workload is frequently not available. It is usually developed on an iterative basis between the designers and the prospective users. Therefore in the early stages it is unwise to build detailed simulations which require more reliable input data than is available - irrespective of any cost or time constraints for the design process.

Hierarchical models of computer systems which can be used for the purpose of incorporating different levels of detail as the design process evolves have been developed [1, 2, 3, 4]. In each of these cases decomposition techniques are used to reduce the complexity of analytic models and permit efficient solution of the overall system model. The theory of analytic model decomposition has been well developed by Courtois [5]. This paper concentrates on expanding the applicability of hierarchical models by incorporating simulation tools to form a hybrid modeling system.

Hybrid modeling tools are not new. Some practitioners have used simulation for modeling the long-term behavior of systems while using analytic methods to describe the macroscopic behavior [6, 7, 8, 9]. These techniques assume that sub-system behavior can be modeled independently, with the resulting analysis used as input to parameterize the higher level models. The models in these papers are tailored to particular systems and require methods that are not easily applicable to a range of systems or networks. HMS is a tool - a unified and expandable system - which supports the development of analytic and simulator models of computer networks. It differs from the extended queueing network model approach in RESQ2 [10, 11] in that a full simulation capability is provided. For example, under HMS inter-process communication - a key element in the design of distributed systems - may be simulated. The analytic sub-system of HMS is more restricted but it does have an optimizing capability.

In this paper we describe the Hierarchical Modeling System (HMS). Its goal is to present the network designer with the best of both worlds: an interactive modeling system (IMS) incorporating analytic techniques for gross level analysis and a Distributed System Simulator (DSS) for detailed simulation modeling of computer networks. An interface between these two sub-systems facilitates their interaction. The IMS/DSS interface is a key element of HMS which makes possible the <u>routine</u> application of the hierarchical method in modeling computer networks. The rest of this paper is divided into 4 sections. Section 2 gives an overview of HMS, it's capabilities and uses. Section 3 is a brief description of DSS; Section 4 presents the major portions of IMS and a summary is contained in Section 5.

SECTION 2
AN OVERVIEW OF HMS

The Hierarchical Modeling System is a single software package that provides a simulation and analytic modeling capability for computer networks. There are two major sub-systems within HMS, the Interactive Modeling System and the Distributed System Simulator (Figure 1). IMS is used to produce high level models of computer networks. Since it relys on analytic modeling techniques it has the advantage of producing model results interactively. In addition there is an optimizing capability which allows the user to relax the values of some model parameters in order to estimate device characteristics necessary to achieve certain performance goals such as device utilization factors and message delay times. DSS is a modeling tool especially designed to simulate computer networks. It has high level constructs that facilitate the development of simulators for a wide variety of networks at any level of detail. Trace facilities and a broad range of output reports aid in the debugging and validation phases for simulators.

The user interfaces for IMS and DSS have been made as compatible as possible. This minimizes the time needed to become familiar with the system. Files are created which describe the system to be modeled along with its operating characteristics and workload. In the case of IMS these input files are translated into analytic model formulas which describe on a gross level the

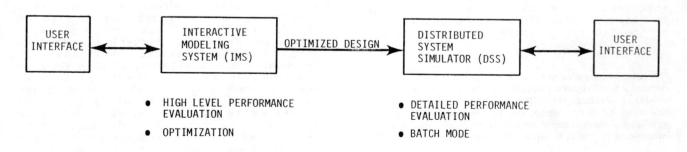

SECTION 5
AN OVERVIEW OF HMS

- HIGH LEVEL PERFORMANCE EVALUATION
- OPTIMIZATION

- DETAILED PERFORMANCE EVALUATION
- BATCH MODE

behavior of the system. On the other hand DSS interprets the input files as components of a discrete event simulation model which is then run in batch mode.

As stated before IMS can produce estimates for device characteristics that would be required for the modeled systems to meet specified performance criteria. The DSS simulator has access to these device estimates through the IMS/DSS interface connecting the two sub-systems. In this way a simulation model can provide a detailed analysis of a system which uses as part of its input the optimized parameters from the IMS model. This interface provides an easy way of passing device characteristics from IMS to DSS. As will be described below the implementation of this interface is only possible because every DSS simulator has the property of being structually valid [12]. The IMS/DSS Interface provides a bridge between the analytic and simulation sub-systems which makes possible the routine application of the hierarchical modeling technique a practical reality. Without this property of DSS and IMS models there would be no automatic way of providing optimized parameters to DSS simulators. Most simulators are not structually valid because the simulation languages in which they are implemented do not support the development of this type of model. Besides giving the network designer an easy way of going from IMS to DSS this interface provides an almost automatic method for verifying the analytic model through simulation.

We can also go in the opposite direction, from a model in DSS to one in IMS. A detailed model of certain parts of a network can produce results which are then summarized and used for input parameters to the IMS model. For example, a simulator could be designed which models only the contention for resources in a host site which is intended to be at a later stage a site within a computer network. Part of the output from this simulator might be the number of resource requests over a period of time that can not be satisfied at the host site. These unsatisfied requests could be considered as the job input rate to the communication sub-network in the high level IMS model. In this way a detailed simulation model has helped to parameterize the IMS model. Since there are no standard means of summarizing detailed output from a simulator so that it may be factored into a high level model, HMS does not provide an automatic interface for this purpose.

In the next two sections we describe in greater detail the two major sub-systems of HMS.

SECTION 3
THE DISTRIBUTED SYSTEM SIMULATOR

DSS has been developed as a modeling tool for the performance analysis of computer networks through simulation. This section gives a brief overview of DSS (for a more detailed description see [13]). DSS is a precompiler which has as a subset ECSS (Extendable Computer System Simulator) [14], a language specially designed for simulating single and multiple processing systems. The output of DSS is an ECSS program which is translated into Simscript II.5 [15], compiled and run [Figure 3].

Every ECSS program has three main sections which correspond to the three major components of most computer systems. The first major component is the finite set of hardware resources and their interconnections. This component of real systems is modeled by the System Description section of an ECSS program. SPECIFY statements with Characteristic Clauses define hardware devices and their attributes. For instance, the statement

SPECIFY 2 PROCESSORS, EACH
EXECUTES 50000 INSTRUCTIONS/SEC

declares that the modeled system has two processors; the characteristic clause defines the instruction execution rate. Storage capacity and transmission rate for devices may also be defined by using characteristic clauses in SPECIFY statements:

SPECIFY 2 DISKS, EACH
TRANSMITS 150000 BYTES/SEC
HAS CAPACITY OF 2000000 BYTES

SPECIFY 3 CHANNELS, EACH
TRANSMITS 150000 BYTES/SEC.

There are five basic types of devices in ECSS, each with its own set of attributes. These types include private devices, storage devices, job store devices, processor devices and I/O devices.

The interconnections between devices are defined in the System Description Section by means of PATH statements with the general form:

PATH Name CONNECTS
Device Name 1 TO
Device Name 2 TO
:

Device Name N

For example, the DISKS and CHANNELS defined above may be interconnected by the following PATH statement:

```
PATH IO CONNECTS
CHANNELS TO
DISKS
```

The second major component of real systems that must be modeled is the set of tasks to be processed. The Workload Description Section of an ECSS program defines the computer jobs that run on the system. These jobs are simulation processes [16] that describe sequences of resource demands. Jobs are STARTED on processors with the statement:

```
START A  Job Name  ON  Processor Name
```

There are two main ECSS statements which simulate resource requests of computer jobs:

```
EXECUTE N INSTRUCTIONS
```
and
```
SEND N DATA.UNITS VIA PATH NAME
```

The EXECUTE statement holds a processing device for an amount of time which is a function of the instruction rate of the processor and the number of instructions in the statement. The processor the job is running on was declared in the START statement at activation time. The SEND statement causes a set of IO devices to be held for a simulated time. This set is specified by the 'PATH NAME' which had previously been defined in the System Description section and which logically connects a string of devices such as channels and disks. The length of the simulated time depends on the transmission rate of the devices in the PATH set and the number of DATA.UNITS in the SEND statement.

It is the operating system in real computers which determines the allocation policies for the system resources. This third major component of computer systems is modeled in ECSS simulators by Simscript routines called resource managers. Whenever an ECSS job requires one of the devices declared in the System Description section an ECSS resource manager is called. For example, if an ECSS job EXECUTEs a given number of instructions on a processor the ECSS Exection Manager is invoked. This manager determines the order in which jobs will have access to a particular processor - for instance, round robin or priority driven.

Every processor in the simulator may have its own Execution Manager or they may share managers. New resource managers may be created and assigned to particular devices in the System Description section of an ECSS program. For example, this statement in the System Description section

THE CPU EXECUTION-MANAGER IS CALLED EXCOM declares 'EXCOM' as the new Execution Manager for the device called 'CPU'. Besides Execution Managers there are managers for the four other basic types of devices; these include Transmission, Storage, Allocation (for private devices) and Job Flow Managers (for job store devices such as main memory).

An ECSS simulator is structurally valid in the sense that its three main sections - System Description, Workload Description and resource managers - divide the modeling task into components that in a natural way correspond to the major components of actual systems. This adds to the flexibility of ECSS simulators. For instance, resource managers may be changed in a simulator without altering any other code. Different System Descriptions may be run with the same Workload Description. This feature is quite valuable when performing simulation experiments for computer design alternatives. The amount of simulator code to be written and debugged is greatly reduced.

Because ECSS contains Simscript II.5 as a subset the increased specialization of ECSS has not reduced its flexibility - any level of detail in a computer system may be simulated. ECSS contains a macro facility and extensive statistics gathering and trace options [17].

DSS has extended ECSS to make it more readily applicable to simulating computer networks. A computer network may be viewed as a set of interconnected nodes (Figure 2) each one with a unique ID number. (In this paper we describe packet switched networks. In the general case a "node" to DSS is simply a collection of computer resources that communicate with the rest of the networks over some transmission medium. For example, in local areanetworks work stations may be considered nodes in DSS which communicate over a shared bus). In a packet switched network jobs that are to be processed by the system, such as data base updates and file transfers, orginate at some of the nodes called host sites. At each of these sites reside the processing, storage and I/O devices normally associated with computer facilities. The communication network consists of nodes called switching computers which connect the host sites. Their primary responsibility is to relay messages between host sites as quickly and reliably as possible. Each node in the network may be viewed as a separate entity which communicates with other nodes via a set of data communication channels. The actual medium of communication may be satellite links, transmission lines and so on.

DSS had to address two broad problems in providing a tool for the simulation of computer networks. The first is the wide range of networks, architectures and protocols that actually exist or have been proposed including message (store and forward) and circuit switched networks. It is desirable to provide a tool which does not limit the types of networks that may modeled. The second major problem addressed by DSS is the fact that building simulators of complex systems can be a time consuming and costly exercise.

The concept of a DSS model has evolved to meet these problems. A DSS model is basically a generalized ECSS program with its own System Description, Workload Description and resource managers. As such there is no limit to the level of detail that may be simulated in a DSS model. It also has all of the trace and statistics gathering routines of any ECSS program. Each node in a computer network is associated with a DSS model. Different nodes may be associated with the same model if they share basically the same characteristics. For example, all of the host sites in a packet switched network might be identified with one DSS model while switching nodes may share another model. In this way only two model descriptions need be written and debugged. A DSS model is a prototype model that may be duplicated any numer of times depending on how many nodes share the same prototype. A DSS program is simply a set of DSS models. A user created set called M.FILE associates each unique nodal ID number with a particular DSS model. DSS simulators extend the notion of structural validity. Not only is each DSS model structually valid but there is a one - one correspondence between nodes in a network and DSS models. Therefore the entire DSS simulator (multiple copies of DSS models) is structually valid. This factor plays a key role in the implementation of the IMS/DSS interface.

DSS has a communication facility [10] which allows for a standard way of simulating message transmission between nodes. Messages may be of arbitrary length and contain information (such as header information in a message switched network) that is needed for simulating routing algorithms, error control, etc.

The network topology is described in a file called TP.FILE. This file is created by the user and lists for each node in the network the nodal ID numbers of neighboring nodes. DSS uses the TP.FILE to write ECSS PATH statements that connect one model for a node with another. The DSS communication facility uses these paths to simulate the transmission of messages between nodes.

All the information needed by DSS to create an ECSS program of a computer network is contained in the DSS model library as well as the two input files TP.FILE and M.FILE. By having a separate file for the network topology we can evaluate through simulation different topological organizations by changing only the TP.FILE. No ECSS or Simscript need be written because the building blocks for DSS simulators, the DSS models, do not have to change. A library of DSS models is being developed which will aid in the analysis of specific problem areas in the design of computer networks. Among these problems are routing algorithms, flow control procedures, network access techniques and distributed data base design. New models may be added to the library by a DSS user. In this way DSS is an extendable modeling tool for the evaluation of computer networks.

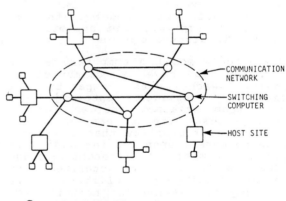

1110

Figure 2 High Level Representation

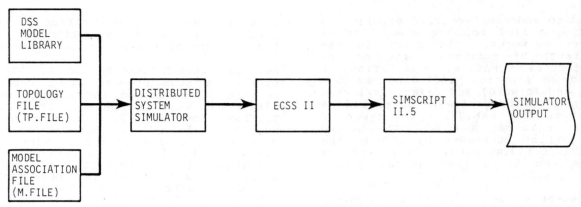

Figure 3

SECTION 4
INTERACTIVE MODELING SYSTEM

The Interactive Modeling System (IMS) is the second major sub-system of HMS. It is designed to support a variety of analytic modeling approaches for computer networks. For our first implementation of IMS we are using Kleinrock's open queueing model for computer networks [13, 14]. A description of this model with its underlying assumptions and optimization techniques is discussed below.

In Kleinrock's model a computer network is assumed to have M communication channels, each with capacity C_i (bits/sec). Messages entering the network from external sources form a Poisson process with a mean of γ_i for node i. The probability that a message will go to node i upon leaving node j is $r_{j\ i}$. Any number of different message classes may be characterized by different routing probabilities. The probability of leaving the network from node j is simply $1 - \sum_{i=1}^{m} r_{j\ i}$.

The throughput for node i, λ_i, may be defined as

(1) $$\lambda_i = \gamma_i + \sum_{j=1}^{m} \lambda_j\ r_{j\ i}$$

and the throughput for the entire network is

(2) $$\gamma = \sum_{i=1}^{m} \gamma_i$$

The average message delay at node i is T_i while the average message delay for the entire network is a weighted sum of these individual delays:

(3) $$T = \sum_{i=1}^{m} \frac{\lambda_i}{\gamma}\ T_i .$$

These equations assume ergodicity $(\lambda_i / \gamma_i < 1)$.

The problem of finding the overall message delay is reduced by the above equation to finding each of the delays at the separate nodes. The message rates from external sources are characterized by Poisson processes and the overall average message length is chosen independently from an exponential distribution with mean $1/\mu$. The Poisson assumption has been validated through several empirical studies [20,21]. simulation results have shown that the independence assumption for message lengths is a good approximation for networks with nodes having more than one input and output channel [19].

Under these assumptions we may derive the following performance measures at node i:

(4) $T_i = \dfrac{1}{\mu\ C_i - \lambda_i}$ expected time delay

(5) $\rho = \lambda_i / \mu C_i$ utilization

(6) $W_i = \dfrac{\rho_i / \mu C_i}{1 - \rho_i}$ average queueing time

(7) $N_i = \lambda_i\ T_i$ average number of messages

In IMS we concentrate on the network design problem of choosing channel capacities (C_i) that will achieve certain stated performance measures. Since the optimization procedures that IMS uses treat channel capacities as continuous variables the network designer will be required to choose the next highest capacity (as a conservative estimate) from the finite set of options that is actually available. Very often one of the constraints for a new system design is that resource utilization will have a fixed maximum to insure excess capacity for anticipated workload increases. For a given set of arrival rates equation (5) can be used to solve for channel capacities that will provide for utilization factors no greater than a stipulated maximum. Another important criteria that must be meet by system designers is the average time delay for messages. In certain situations we would like to estimate the channel capacities necessary to achieve a given time delay, say T_O, for messages traversing a path of M nodes from source node i to node j. We can arbitrarily stipulate that the contribution of each node to the total delay will be T_O/M. Then equation (4) may be used to solve for the C_i for each of the nodes in the path which guarantees that the time delay will be no greater than this quantity. And hence the average delay constraint will be met for any given path in the network.

A third form of optimization for channel capacities is to minimize the average message delay, T, given the nodal input rates, λ_i, i=1, ..., M and the network topology subject to a cost constraint of D dollars. We assume linear capacity costs, that is, $d_i(C_i) = d_iC_i$ where d_i is the cost of channel i and varies linearly with the capacity of C_i. Since D dollars is the constraint we must have

$$(8) \quad D \geq \sum_{i=1}^{m} d_i C_i$$

Kleinrock [14] has solved for the optimal solutions:

$$(9) \quad C_i = \frac{\lambda_i}{\mu} + \left(\frac{D_e}{d_i}\right) \frac{\sqrt{\lambda_i d_i}}{\sum_{j=1}^{m} \sqrt{\lambda_j d_j}}$$

where D_e is defined to be

$$(10) \quad De = D - \sum_{i=1}^{m} \frac{\lambda_i d_i}{\mu}$$

These then are the optimization procedures incorporated into IMS for this model.

The user interface for IMS is constructed along the lines of DSS. Each node of the network is associated with a previously defined DSS model. Each model has the System Description and Workload Description sections as well as resource managers. In keeping with Kleinrock's model the System Description section declares channels with specified transmission rates as the only device for each node. The Workload Desription section defines ECSS jobs as arrival processes for incoming tasks to the nodes. Any number of jobs may be defined for different classes of jobs. The general format of a job is simply:

```
    JOB NAME.A
'START' CREATE MESSAGE
    LET LENGTH (MESSAGE) EQUAL N BITS
    WAIT      FOR      EXP.F    (MEAN
INTERARRIVAL.TIME)
    GO TO START
    END "JOB NAME.A
```

This job describes an incoming stream of tasks with a given bit length and mean interarrival time. The routing probabilities for messages between nodes are defined in a user created file called RT.FILE. For a particular node with ID number K in the network there is a line in this data file with format:

K, J_1, P_1; J_2, P_2; ...; J_n, P .

P_i is the probability a message will go to node J_i after leaving node K. Each node will have the same resource manager - designated 'MS' for message (packet) switched network.

IMS is designed in a modular way so that other resource managers may be added in order to represent a variety of network architectures. For example, different random access techniques (e.g., ALOHA) may be incorporated into IMS by specifying alternate resource managers in the System Description section. This is analogous to the method in DSS where a variety of operating systems may be simulated by changing the resource managers while the System Description and Workload sections remain the same.

IMS/DSS Interface
As previously described the optimization procedures for IMS allow us to estimate channel transmission rates under various constraints. These new rates along with the nodal ID numbers are written to a file called OPT.FILE. By setting a control variable within a DSS simulator the OPT.FILE is read and the channel capacities that are contained in the System Description section are changed to the new optimized values. The simulator may then be run using these new values. No recoding of the simulator has to be done for this procedure to work. In this way we have automated the transition from a high level analytic model to a detailed simulation model.

This is possible only because a DSS simulator is structurally valid. For every node there is a separate DSS model - one of the prototype DSS models which has been duplicated for a particular node. There is a one -one correspondence between nodes in a network and DSS models in the DSS simulator. Since the OPT.FILE contains nodal numbers the names of devices in the IMS model can be mapped to specific

DSS models in the simulator. And since each DSS model is structurally valid in its own right (every DSS model is an ECSS program and every ECSS program is structurally valid) we can determine which variables name devices in the System Description Section. In this way the mapping from the device names in an IMS model to those in the DSS model is complete.

We will give a brief example of the use of this procedure. We assume a given network topology with a specified set of host sites and switching nodes. Using IMS we may estimate the channel capacities of the switching nodes which would be required to achieve a given average message delay between host sites. If we are interested in modeling a store and forward network message buffers at the switching nodes can become a bottleneck. There are no general analytic techniques that handle this problem without some very special knowledge about the network [22]. A more detailed DSS simulator can explicitly model buffer size. The IMS user can specify that the average number of packets at each of the nodes in the IMS model will be the buffer size required at each node in the DSS simulator model. By writing average queue size and the associated nodal numbers to the OPT.FILE the DSS simulator can read this data and change the buffer sizes at each of the nodes in the simulator. This procedure would be costly and time consuming of if the DSS simulator was not structurally valid. The IMS/DSS interface allows this communication between analytic and simulation models to be carried out routinely.

This procedure is not limited to buffer sizes. For instance, through the OPT.FILE, the DSS simulator can have access to first approximations for the channel capacities when buffer size is not a limiting factor. By having initial estimates for channel capacities fewer costly and time consumming simulation runs are required to meet particular network design criteria.

SECTION 5
SUMMARY

The Hierarchical Modeling System has been designed to exploit the advantages of analytic and simulation modeling techniques. The major subsystems, IMS and DSS, can be used as stand alone modeling tools or in a symbiotic relationship through the IMS/DSS interface. Both subsystems are expandable. With IMS resource managers can be added which increase the number of analytic techniques for performance

evaluation. In DSS new models can be developed and added to a library of models. High level requirements analysis is being performed to determine models that are most useful for computer network designers.

Acknowledgements
The author would like to thank Prof. Walter Kohler for his helpful suggestions and Duane Ball of FEDSIM for his simulation expertise. This work is supported by the Rome Air Development Center under Air Force Contract No. F30602-80-C-0267.

REFERENCES

1. Bhandarkar, D.P. "A hierarchy of analytical models for complex computer systems." The European Comp. Conf. Comptr. Syst. Evaluation Sept. 1976

2. Browne, J.C., et al. "Hierarchical techniques for the development of realistic models of complex computer systems." Proc. IEEE, Vol. 63, June 1975, pp. 966-975

3. Sekino, A. "Performance evaluation of multiprogrammed time-shared computer systems." Tech. Rep. 103, MIT, Cambridge, Mass., Sept. 1971

4. Brown, R.M., et al. "Memory management and response time" CACM, Vol. 20, No. 3, March 1977

5. Courtois, P.J., Decomposability - Queueing and Computer System Applications. Academic Press, N.Y., 1977

6. Kimbleton, S. "A heuristic approach to computer systems performance improvement - a fast performance prediction tool". Proc. 1975 NCC, Vol. 44, AFIPS Press, Arlington, Va. pp. 839-846

7. Lasser, D. "Productivity of multiprogrammed computers - progress in developing an analytic prediction method" CACM, Dec. 1969

8. Schwetman, H.D. "Hybrid simulation models of computer systems." CACM Sept. 1978

9. Chiu, W.W., Chow W.M., "A performance model of MVS." IBM Jour. Resc. and Dcv. Vol. 17 No. 4 1978

10. Sauer, C.H., MacNair, E.A., Queueing Network Software for Systems Modelling. Software Practice & Experience Vol. 9, 369-380 (1979)

11. Sauer, C.H., ManNai, E.A. Salza Silvio, A Language for Extended Queueing Network Models, J. Resc. Devel. Vol. 24, 747-755 (Nov. 1980)

12. Zeigler, B.P., <u>Theory of Modelling and Simulation,</u> Wiley – Interscience, New York, 1976

13. DuBois, D. Distributed Systems Simulator for Computer Networks, Modeling and Simulation Conference, Univ. Pittsburgh, Pittsburgh, PA, April 30- May 1, 1981

14. Kosy, D.W., <u>The ECSS II Language for Simulating Computer Systems,</u> Rand Corporation, Santa Monica, Calif.

15. Kiviat, P.J. et. al. <u>Simscript II .5 Programming Language</u> CACI, Arlington, VA. 1973

16. Franta, W.R. <u>The Process View of Simulation</u> Elsevie North Holland, 1977

17. Federal Computer Performance Evaluation and Simulation Center (FEDSIM), Washington, D.C. 20330 <u>ECSS II Extended Statistics and Trace Features</u>

18. Kleinrock, L; <u>Communication Nets: Stochastic Message Flow and Delay.</u> (New York: McGraw Hill, 1964, out of print. (Reprinted by Dover Publications, 1972)

19. Kleinrock, L., <u>Queueing Systems, Volume II: Computer Applications.</u> New York: Willy Interscience, 1976

20. Fuchs, E., Jackson, P.E., "Estimates of distribution of random variables for certain computer communications traffic models", in Proc. ACM Symp. Optimization of Data Communications Systems, Oct. 1969

21. Lewis, P.A., Yue, P.C., "Statistical analysis of series of events in computer systems" in <u>Statistical Computer Performance Evaluation,</u> W. Freiberger, Ed., Academic Press, N.Y. 1972

22. Labetoulle, J., Pujolle, G., "Modeling of packet switching communication networks with finite buffer size at each node", IFIP Conf. Comp. Sys. Modeling, Yorktown Heights, Aug. 16-18, 1977

NETWORK PERFORMANCE
REPORTING

Dr. K. Terplan
Project Manager
Computer Sciences
Int'l, Munich-Germany

ABSTRACT

Managing networks using Network Administration Centers is increasingly considered. After introducing the information demand for operational, tactical and strategic network management the paper is dealing with the investigation of the applicability of tools and techniques for these areas. Network monitors and software problem determination tools are investigated in greater detail. Also implementation details for a multihost-multinode network including software and hardware tools combined by SAS are discussed.

1. NETWORK ADMINISTRATION CENTER (NAC)

The number of national and worldwide networks is continuously increasing. Network processing is increasingly becoming an integral part of the total operation of the organization. Network administration must therefore ensure that the network is operating efficiently at all times, so as not to cause any problems in the day-to-day operation of the organization.

Networks are differently designed and implemented. Figure 1 shows a multihost-multinode network using two common methods of data transmission; line and packet switching. Also leased lines are included. In order to facilitate network administration the Network Administration Center (NAC) is established and attached to a centrally located host computer.

For successful network management performance related data should be continuously collected in all principal network components. This fundamental information is preprocessed and will be used for different purposes in operational, tactical and strategic network management.

2.   ACTIVITIES

Networks management involves three fundamental types of management decisions: [9]

    A.   Operational   (immediate decisions)
    B.   Tactical   (short term decisions)
    C.   Strategic   (long range decisions)

In order to support these decision making processes three activity areas are of prime importance:

    A.   Network control for supporting operational decisions
    B.   Network administration for supporting tactical decisions and
    C.   Network design for supporting strategic decisions.

2.1   NETWORK CONTROL

Network Control is a collection of activities required to dynamically maintain the network service level. These activities ensure high availability by quickly recognizing problems and performance degradation, and by initiating controlling functions when necessary. The most important functions include: [2]

    -    Data collection - this function deals with analyzing and comparing actual service level with preset standards. If significant deviations are recognized, controlling actions are invoked.

    -    Problem determination - once the nonavailability of the network, or parts of it is recognized, this activity will be invoked. The major goals are:

        °   minimizing effects,
        °   reducing time until restoration.

        To accomplish this, continuous information on network status is required.

    -    Network recovery - this is becoming a very expensive activity unless procedures for rapid network restoration are prepared. Because of the significant number of expected failures, restoring components should be done dynamically. Design of powerful backup procedures requires data on usage frequency and failure profiles.

    -    Network tests - are necessary to dynamically verify correct network operation. These tests should include individual components and links. The tests should be executed concurrently to productive operation, but they must not impair the productive operation in any way. Tests are controlled by the NAC operator.

    -    Configuraton control - to maintaining the proper service level, the utilization of resources by application groups should be controlled. Activities included are:

        °   load balancing,
        °   alternating priorities and
        °   alternate routing
        °   mailing
        °   component bypassing.

        Similarly to tests, the production must not be influenced in any way.

2.2   NETWORK ADMINISTRATION

Administration is the set of short range activities for evaluating the network service level. Information on response time, network availability, utilization profiles and traffic profiles are of prime interest. In this category are the following functions:

    -    Evaluation of the service level
        °   by reducing measurement data
        °   by reporting on network performance
        °   by determining user satisfaction

-   Network accounting

-   Evaluation of problem files

-   Inventory control
    °   installed equipment
    °   vendor contacts
    °   maintenance contacts.

2.3   NETWORK DESIGN

Network design is a typical capacity planning function. Based upon processed measurement data on network performance, traffic flow and resource utilization, the optimal network structure can be constructed. Typical activities include:

-   predicting future workload
-   estimating growth of presently operating applications
-   optimazing network layout and
-   determining the right computing power for each of the nodes.

Figure 2 summarizes in table format the information demand for each of the three areas discussed previously.

3.   TOOLS

Several tools can be used to support the information demand of operational, tactical and strategic management decisions. Fig. 3 gives an overview of tools likely to be implemented.

3.1   CLASSIFICATION OF TOOLS

According to Fig. 3 there are three major groups of tools: [6]

-   data acquisition devices
-   test drivers and
-   driver-monitor-hybrid devices.

3.1.1   DATA ACQUISITION

Hardware monitoring [2] is based on the fact that the performance characteristics of computer systems can be measured by detecting signal voltage transitions in the digital circuitry of the hardware. Using Tesdata-AMS [5] and TITN-DPMS [4] any hardware of any manufacturer can be measured. Not only the central parts of computers, but also lines, concentrators, storage devices, TP-processors, etc. can be measured.

Software monitors (accounting packages) [2] constitute a class of programs for measuring hardware, system and application software. They are resident in store and can be activated or deactivated by the user. Software monitors can measure one part of the response time only, normally the elapsed time between entering the input queue and leaving the output queue.

Network monitors [1] may be employed to collect special data about service and utilization oriented measures. They are connected to the communication interface. Since these interfaces are designed to connect to communication equipment, such connection is easy and unlikely to disturb the equipment to which connection is made.

3.1.2   TEST DRIVERS

As an alternative to the measurement of uncontrolled usage, users at terminals may be employed to generate workload. However, since terminal operators' performance is unrepeatable, error prone, and introduces undesirable variability into the time spent in the user state, operators should not be employed for this purpose unless other more desirable alternatives are infeasible or

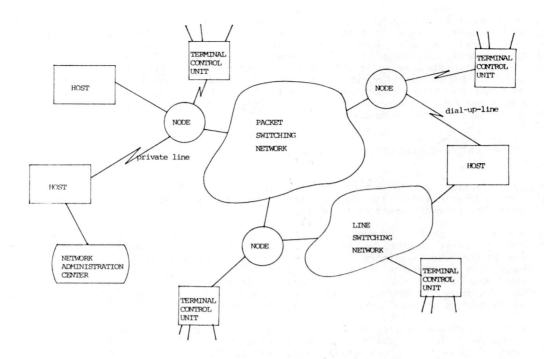

Fig. 1: Multihost-multinode communication network

Time scale / Parameters	CONTROL	ADMINISTRATION	DESIGN
Availability	X	X	X
Response time	X		
Processing			
Host			X
Node			X
Transmission			X
Line			X
Modem			X
Interactive throughput time			X
Transaction rate	X		X
Error rate	X	X	
Location		X	X
Kind of error		X	X
Message analysis			
Byte count		X	X
Net data		X	X
Control characters			X
Number segments			X
Think time			X
Utilization			
Node computer	X	X	X
Control unit		X	X
Line	X	X	X
Terminal		X	x
Configuration			
Number connections		X	
Number applications		X	
Gen. Par.		X	

Figure 2: Information demand of network
management activities

unavailable. Instead of employing users alone Automatic-Send-Receive (ASR) terminals can be used for representing user workload. This technique is very attractive and relatively simple. The operator input is stored on some medium such as paper or magnetic tape or some other memory associated with the terminal, depending on how the terminal is equipped. The terminal is operated with the stored input to produce communications traffic equivalent to that which would have been produced by a user. Barring malfunction, this input is controllable and repeatable. Unless the terminal has been modified to produce automatic data collection, interactions involving ASR terminals are best timed with respect to turnaround time either manually or by obtaining the time from the computer system as part of the interaction.

3.1.3   DRIVER-MONITOR-COMBINATION

Some of the limitations on the use of ASR terminals may be eliminated by the use of intelligent terminals. While theoretically attractive, this approach has not been given much application. The Remote Terminal Emulator discussed below embodies this concept.

Although the use of a driver internal to a computer is not recommended for evaluation and selection of network service provided in part by that computer, it may be useful for such purposes as: a) comparison of the computer system (host computer) components of network service, which are completely homogeneous in hardware and software, b) testing for compliance with standards (such as language and communications protocol), c) tuning of the computer, and d) detecting the effect of change in host hardware, software, or utilization. The use of an internal driver is less expensive and complicated than an external driver since only one computer is required.

When an external computer is used to provide the workload on an interactive computer network service, the computer performing the testing is known as a Remote Terminal Emulator (RTE) and the entire network being tested is the Service Under Test (SUT). The capacity of RTE's can range from one terminal to the maximum number the service can support [4]. An RTE may be an appropriate test tool when there is a specified number of access ports which the service must provide.

While the statistical treatment of data is important in all measurement and evaluation endeavors, the volume of data which may be collected by an RTE makes necessary the complete specification of what data is to be recorded, how the data analysis and report generation is to occur, and how the correctness of the data reduction software is to be established.

Fig. 4 gives a short summary of the applicability of tools for the different decision areas. The network performance reporting field will be well supported by network monitors and partially well supported by software monitors.

3.2   NETWORK MONITORS

The purpose of network monitors is the continuous measurement and analysis of the most important control parameters in a network. Network monitors can simultaneously collect performance related data on over thousand lines and many thousands of terminals. As a data collecton interface the RS-232 (V.24 later X.21) seems to be the one best suited.

Designing network monitors the following criteria are of prime interest [10]:

- total picture on network performance
- modular design
- flexible monitor configuration
- systems independency
- flexibility towards selecting the location of the RS-232-interface (local and/or remote)
- powerful alarming
- ease of use.

Fig. 5 shows a general picture of a network monitor.

The modules for data collection are microcomputers (e.g. ZILOG, MOTOROLA, INTEL, etc.) include all the elements of any computer system; namely control logic, internal memory and input/output capability. The function of the data collection modul is to monitor multiple communication lines for the purpose of determining the status of the system by interpreting the traffic. The number of lines for simultaneous monitoring is determined by the bandwidth of the modules. Practical values are presently between 30 and 60 KBIT/s. The programs for traffic interpretation are stored in PROM. These programs are protocol-dependent. The data collection modules are usually attached to the Central Processing Unit by asynchronous communication ports. To perform the data gathering

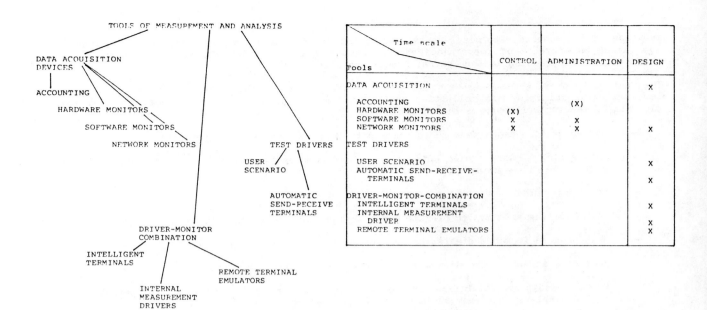

		Time scale	CONTROL	ADMINISTRATION	DESIGN
DATA ACQUISITION					X
	ACCOUNTING			(X)	
	HARDWARE MONITORS		(X)		
	SOFTWARE MONITORS		X	X	
	NETWORK MONITORS		X	X	X
TEST DRIVERS					
	USER SCENARIO				X
	AUTOMATIC SEND-RECEIVE- TERMINALS				X
DRIVER-MONITOR-COMBINATION					
	INTELLIGENT TERMINALS				X
	INTERNAL MEASUREMENT DRIVER				X
	REMOTE TERMINAL EMULATORS				X

Figure 3: Tools of measurement ans analysis

Figure 4: Applicability of tools

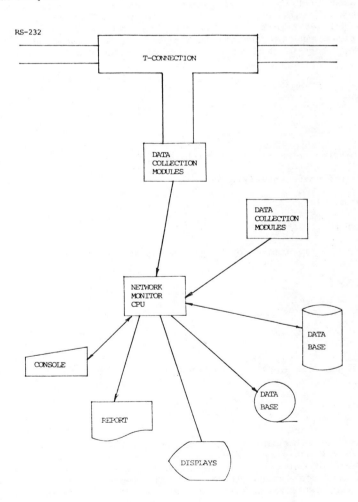

Fig. 5: Network monitor architecture

function, these modules recognise events significant to the status and performance of a communication line. Once events of importance have occured, status, or alert messages are prepared, and buffered for transmission to the Central Processing Unit.

The Central Processing Unit of the network monitor is to control the operation of the entire system, including multiple data collecting devices and multiple input/output devices. The principal elements of the control programs should include:

- Gathering of summary type performance data from the data collection modules.

- Maintaining summary tables on status and performance by terminal, remote cluster control unit, line, line group.

- Updating graphic and alert output to CRT displays and printers.

- Communicating with System operators via keyboard and color graphic CRT.

- Recording performance statistics periodically on a disk or tape drive.

- Providing access to the data base for real-time displays or printed reports.

- Providing system initialization services for tailoring the network configuraton, the screen displays, and the user's specified parameters.

The input/output devices associated with a network monitor usually include a large screen high resolution color graphics display used to communicate to network administrators, a large screen video projection system used in large control centers, where network performance must be visible to more than one administrator, disk drives for storage of the data base, printers for preparing of system alert messages, printed reports, and magnetic tape drives for storing large data amounts for later analysis. Functional and performance thresholds can be programmed by the user. Alerts can also accoustically be supported. Most monitors present status display information at multiple levels:

- Network (Fig. 6)
- Application group
- Line (Fig. 7)
- Control unit and
- Device.

Within the levels more detailled information can be interrogated: e.g.

- Response time and its components (Fig. 8)
- Transaction rate
- Traffic counts (Fig. 9)
- Error rate and
- Components utilization.

Some of the statistical reports can also be displayed on the master and/or slave display units.

Known network monitors are:

NET/ALERT [3]
MS-109 [5]
DPMS-TLSA [4]
RM-300 [5]
RTA-1327 [10]
3709 NPM [10]
Questronics M 400 and M 500 (limited use only) [10].

3.3   SOFTWARE MONITORS

Many vendors provide tools for reporting on network performance and for seminautomatic network administration. But, these tools are very much hardware- and softwaredependent. The internal activities of teleprocessing are not yet well understood. For this reason plug compatible components and independent monitoring products can rarely be used. The vendor offers tools within the frame of his own network architecture. Well known examples are: IBM, ITT, Univac and Honeywell Bull.

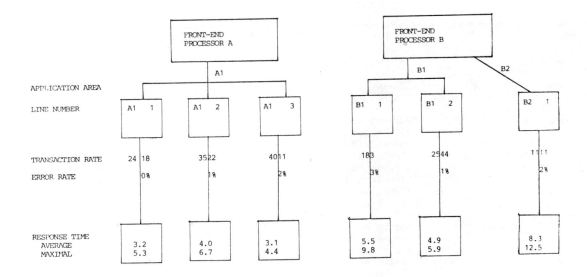

<table>
<tr><td colspan="2" align="center">FRONT-END PROCESSOR A</td><td></td><td align="center">FRONT-END PROCESSOR B</td></tr>
</table>

	A1			B1	B2

APPLICATION AREA

LINE NUMBER

A1 1	A1 2	A1 3	B1 1	B1 2	B2 1

TRANSACTION RATE   24|18   35|22   40|11   18|3   25|44   1|11

ERROR RATE   0%   1%   2%   3%   1%   2%

RESPONSE TIME
AVERAGE
MAXIMAL

3.2 5.3	4.0 6.7	3.1 4.4	5.5 9.8	4.9 5.9	8.3 12.5

Fig. 6: Network overview

** Network Line Statistics **   Interval= 09:00 TO 09:30 06/23/80

LINE	TRANS	OTHER	- POLLT	BADPT	PR-T	MOUTT	MIN-T	REJ-T	MULLT		NAKS	RTMAX	RTAVG
NYC1	227	1	220	0	451	673	186	0	268	0	0	36.8	12.5
MRSH	79	1	428	0	738	181	51	0	403	0	0	28.9	8.1
AMES	194	3	286	0	585	485	119	0	324	0	0	24.8	7.9
ITS	43	3	0	0	0	104	217	0	1478	0	0	18.2	5.7
ATM1	171	6	301	0	616	438	111	3	332	0	0	31.4	9.4
ATM2	119	13	333	0	689	312	80	7	379	0	0	65.2	11.7
INTN	240	8	229	12	538	603	143	0	275	0	0	47.1	10.2
MRMT	0	14	0	0	0	0	48	0	1752	0	0	0.0	0.0
ALL	1073	49	1797	12	3617	2796	955	10	5211	0	0	65.2	9.9

Figure 7: Line load analysis

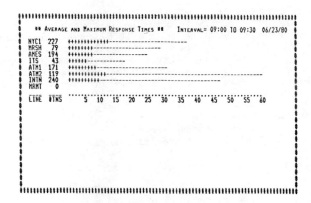

** Average and Maximum Response Times **   Interval= 09:00 TO 09:30 06/23/80

LINE	#TNS
NYC1	227
MRSH	79
AMES	194
ITS	43
ATM1	171
ATM2	119
INTN	240
MRMT	0

```
            5   10  15  20  25  30  35  40  45  50  55  60
```

Figure 8: Response time report

In an IBM environment there are many methods of gathering network related data using software tools:

Source	Data
Application	IMS-LOG CICS-LOG
ACF/VTAM and ACF/NCP	Buffertrace I/O-Trace Operatorlog NCP-Dynamic dump NCP-Dynamic Display Link level test 3705 panel test Multiple line trace
Cluster and station	Status recording Connectivity test
Modems	Status recording Loop test Automatic tests.

Additionally, there are many programs in the HOST computer for facilitating network management:

- NOSP
- IMS-ANMP
- CICS-ANMP
- POWER
- VSPC
- NPA (partially in 3705)

- JES
- NCCF/NPDA
- SSS/DSX
- IPVS/HCF
- BTP/PSS

At the present time, NPDA [7] is the best product for collecting data for network management. Using NCCF, status information is continuously collected. This information can be accessed by operator interrogations on the NCCF-Screen, but the further processing of the data is very time consuming. Via NPDA, however, the collected data can be time stamped and stored in the NPDA data base (Fig. 10) allowing delayed processing by the network administrator. MENU-Screens provide a convenient facility for accessing the required information. Either, one proceeds hierarchically (Front-End-Lines-Stations), or one may ask for a special screen identified by name or code. The default sequence is:

- Total errors
- Last detected errors
- Analysis of special errors.

NPDA can analyse the following errors:

- 370X errors - errors occuring within a FEP which are due to the channel adapter, scanner, NCP instruction exceptions or interrupts.

- Primary end-of-line errors - all errors detected at the end of the line that is attached to the FEP. They include both line and station errors for supported terminal controller and line errors detected by IBM 386X modems.

- Secondary end-of-line errors - all errors detected at the end-of-line that has a supported terminal controller attached to it.

NPDA is very strong in terms of detecting and diagnosing errors. This product is fairly good for recording traffic statistics, but is very poor for providing any information on performance related measures such as response time, availability and transaction rate.

3.4   HYBRID MONITORING

Fig. 11 shows the applicability of different tools - hardware and software - for gathering data for reporting on network performance. The major short-coming is that none of the monitors offers information on processing activities and node utilization, which is vital for network management. The most promising way is the combine both hardware and software techniques in the way shown in

NET/ALERT PERFORMANCE REPORT
LINE LEVEL

DATE: 10/ 7/80   PAGE: 15

LINE GROUP	LINE NUMBER		CONTROL UNIT	TERMINAL ADDRESS						
5927	1906		0	0						

HOUR		TRANS ACTIONS	RESP TIME	POLL LTNCY	LINE IN TIME	INTRNL TIME	LINE OUT TIME	IN	OUT	ERROR COUNT
17	TODAY	247	4.7	1.1	2.9	0.2	0.5	321	270	28
	M-T-D	258	5.9	2.4	2.5	0.0	0.9	362	314	61
	Y-T-D	258	5.9	2.4	2.5	0.0	0.9	362	314	61
18	TODAY	343	5.4	1.7	2.6	0.2	0.9	445	379	49
	M-T-D	405	5.2	2.3	2.4	0.0	0.5	539	462	65
	Y-T-D	405	5.2	2.3	2.4	0.0	0.5	539	462	65
19	TODAY	258	7.8	2.6	4.5	0.2	0.5	473	304	67
	M-T-D	486	5.1	1.8	2.7	0.0	0.5	594	527	49
	Y-T-D	486	5.1	1.8	2.7	0.0	0.5	594	527	49
20	TODAY	0	0.	0.	0.	0.	0.	0	0	0
	M-T-D	476	3.0	0.8	2.1	0.0	0.1	524	492	21
	Y-T-D	476	3.0	0.8	2.1	0.0	0.1	524	492	21
21	TODAY	0	0.	0.	0.	0.	0.	0	0	0
	M-T-D	323	3.3	0.6	2.6	0.0	0.0	349	328	7
	Y-T-D	323	3.3	0.6	2.6	0.0	0.0	349	328	7
22	TODAY	0	0.	0.	0.	0.	0.	0	0	0
	M-T-D	390	6.4	2.8	3.5	0.0	0.0	424	398	15
	Y-T-D	390	6.4	2.8	3.5	0.0	0.0	424	398	15
23	TODAY	0	0.	0.	0.	0.	0.	0	0	0
	M-T-D	178	4.1	0.4	3.6	0.0	0.0	187	181	6
	Y-T-D	178	4.1	0.4	3.6	0.0	0.0	187	181	6
24	TODAY	0	0.	0.	0.	0.	0.	0	0	0
	M-T-D	129	3.5	0.4	3.0	0.0	0.0	135	130	4
	Y-T-D	129	3.5	0.4	3.0	0.0	0.0	135	130	4

TOTAL SUMMARY

		TRANS ACTIONS	RESP TIME	POLL LTNCY	LINE IN TIME	INTRNL TIME	LINE OUT TIME	IN	OUT	ERROR COUNT
	TODAY	3365	4.9	1.9	2.5	0.1	0.4	4146	3637	348
	M-T-D	4608	5.3	2.3	2.6	0.0	0.3	5515	4956	415
	Y-T-D	4608	5.3	2.3	2.6	0.0	0.3	5515	4956	415

Figure 9: Traffic analysis

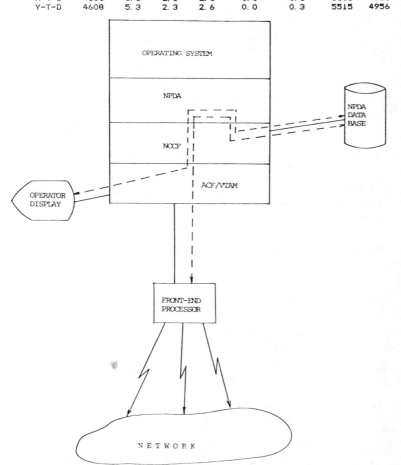

Fig. 10: NPDA-Architecture

Fig. 12. Considering the high efficiency of present microprocessors, this solution seems to be feasible. These data collection units are connected to the NAC (Network Administration Center).

4.   PRACTICAL IMPLEMENTATION IN IBM ENVIRONMENTS

There are a number of prerequisites for successful network performance monitoring and reporting:

Exception alarming
- the most important performance thresholds should be controlled and if the limits are exceeded alarm messages should be sent to computer shop operating personnel. In this way no manager will be overrun by routine reports.

Continuous performance tracking
- in order to report on performance, data should be collected on a continuous basis. Measurements should include: systems profile (CPU, I/O-activities, overlap, problem/ supervisor ratio and TP-activities (line load, response time).

Simultaneous measurement of multiple lines and terminals
- for controlling the total network and/or parts of it an overview should be received on all relevant components at the performance control level.

Hardware independence
- the tools should be able to monitor all kinds of hardware installed - otherwise performance "grey" areas will remain.

Protocol independence
- the tools selected should work independently of the protocols and their versions. Otherwise no stability can be maintained at the performance control level.

Accuracy
- real time actions will be based upon the performance data collected and reduced. Any inaccuracy can thus cause a severe impact on the overall performance. The accuracy criteria are dominant in defining the sampling rate of measurement tools. High accuracy should be offered at all load levels.

Critical application tracing
- in order to make meaningful decisions about network performance improvements, the most important applications should be transparent.

Task interaction tracking
- in order to reduce the task contention to a workable minimum, information on contention figures in the network should be offered continuously.

Data base concept
- in order to define the most meaningful thresholds and to redesign network, historical data should be available. The data stored in a performance data bank could thus be interrogated and processed at will.

Ease of use
- in order to reduce manpower demand the tools should be handled easily and measurement results should be reported in easily readable form.

Price
- Purchase price and maintenance costs should be justified by the performance of the tools selected.

At the present time, none of the tools can meet all the requirements listed previously. Considering the general structure of Fig. 1, two of the tools are very promising:

1.   Implementation of a network monitor
2.   Implementation of NPDA for error diagnosis.

For improving the efficiency of network performance reporting SAS [8] may be installed. Thus, all major areas in terms of information demand are properly covered. SAS is a powerful software system for data management, statistical analysis and report writing. In one system, the user gets a higher-level programming language and a library of over 75 ready-to-use procedures. There are no limitations towards the data sources. Besides data of a network monitor and NPDA, all kind of performance related data can be entered; e.g. central resources oriented information like using

PERFORMANCE

PERFORMANCE	NM	SW
Response time	X	
Host delay	X	
Network delay	X	
Maximum response time	X	
Average response time	X	
by terminal	X	
by control unit	X	
by line	X	
by front-end	X	
Response time with thresholds	X	
Availability	X	
by network	X	
by line	X	
by control unit	X	
by terminal	X	
Data processing in node computers		

PROBLEM RECOGNITION

PROBLEM RECOGNITION	NM	SW
Error rate	X	
by front-end		X
by line		X
by control unit		X
by terminal		X
Transmission error	X	
BSC		X
SDLC		X
Receive error	X	
BSC		X
SDLC		X
Connection errors		X
Modemstatus		X
Front-end-errors		
NCP/EP/PEP		X
Channel Adapter		X
Communication scanner		X
Instruction exception		X
Interruption		X
Control units errors		
3270-typ		X
SNA-typ		X
RS-232-status	X	X

TRAFFIC AND UTILIZATION

TRAFFIC AND UTILIZATION	NM	SW
Transaction rate	X	
Host	X	
User	X	
Number character sent	X	X
received	X	X
Number messages sent	X	
received	X	
Largest messages sent	X	
received	X	
Line load	X	X
Control unit utilization	X	
Terminal utilization	X	
Number general polls	X	
Bytecount		
by line		X
by control unit		X
by terminal		X

HANDLING

HANDLING	NM	SW
Display all lines	X	
Selectivity of measurements	X	(X)
Hardcopy option	X	X
Separation by application groups		
Alarm		
threshold	X	
functional	X	(X)
Number of alarm conditions	high	low
Configuration overview		
front-end	X	
line	X	
control unit	X	
terminal	X	
Readability of displays		
colour	X	
black/white		X
MENÜ	X	X

Figure 11: Network performance reporting by hardware and software techniques

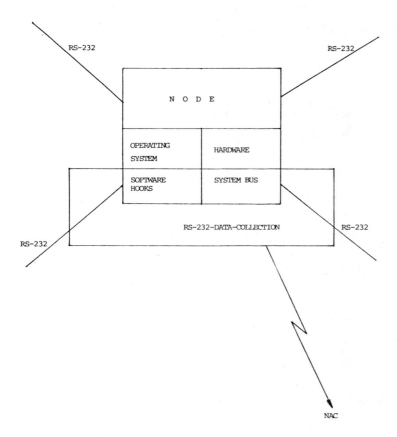

Fig. 12: Hybrid monitor data capturing technique

RMF, SMF, CONTROL IMS, etc. monitors. Thus, also correlation reports can be generated about the network and central resources performance.

Fig. 13 shows the practical implementation of the tools for a subset of the network in Fig. 1.

Network performance reporting is a multistep procedure, separated by the timeliness requirements. Fig. 16 summarizes this reporting process for the most important network control parameters. Fig. 14 and 15 are reports generated via the SAS-interface of a network monitor.

5.   CONCLUSIONS

Properly manage present networks is a very challenging job. But, there are promising practical implementations, that may cause a breakthrough in controlling very large networks via NAC-s. The expenses are high, roughly about 1-2% of the total network investment. On the other side, e.g. for a single terminal to be controlled, the fees will be in a range of 10-15 cents for each day of control. In summary:

- we cannot manage, when we cannot measure,

- each component of a network can be measured,

- there are still difficulties in interpreting front-end-processors performance,

- continuous control of total networks is increasingly considered,

- network monitors and vendor supplied error detection tools can be implemented for optimal control

- there are still standard performance interfaces needed for special data transmission service like TRANSPAC and DATEX and

- network monitors are expected to be extended towards collecting data on terminal-to-terminal traffic, processing power and utilization of nodes, graphical output capabilities, flexible data base structures and more powerful data capturing techniques.

REFERENCES

1. Terplan, K.: Use of Network Monitors for Capacity Planning, International Conference on Computer Capacity Management, Chicago, 1981, Conference Record, p. 147-159.

2. Terplan, K.: Measuring and Improving the Performance of Teleprocessing Systems, ECOMA 8, London, 1980, Conference Proceedings, p. 91-108.

3. Avant-Garde Inc.: NET/ALERT - User's Guide, Cherry Hill, USA, 1981.

4. Bergerol, C.: Distributed Performance Monitoring System, Computer Performance Journal, vol. 2 no. 1, March, 1981, p. 5-12

5. Sensabaugh, S.L.: Centralized Distributed Measurement, International Conference on Computer Capacity Management, Chicago, 1981, Conference Record, p. 255-274

6. FIPS (Federal Information Processing Standards) - Guidelines for The Measurement of Interactive Computer Service Response Time and Turnaround Time, U.S. Department of Commerce, Washington, 1978.

7. IBM Corp.: Network Problem Determination Application SC34-2013-1, Yorktown Height, USA, 1979.

8. SAS Institute: Statistical Analysis System User's Guide, Cary, USA, 1980.

9. Giles, H.L.: Communications Systems Management, Performance Evaluation Review, vol. 9, nr. 1, 1980, p 46-51.

10. Terplan, K.: Network Monitor Survey, Computer Performance Journal, vol. 2 no. 4, December 1981, p. 158-173

```
UTILIZATION SUMMARY                                                      DATE:   MM/DD/YY
                                                                         USER:   COMMUNICATION
    NET/ALERT -- SAS                                                              RESOURCE
                                                                                 PLANNING
TIME:    (MONTH OR WEEK OR DAY OR HOUR)
                                                    AVAILABILITY        UTILIZATION


NETWORK:  TELEPROCESSING

   APPLICATION GROUP:  IMS

      LINE GROUP:  01

         LINE:  0A02

            CONTROL UNIT:  A02

               DEVICE:  A03                            92.5%              41.2%

                        B03                            89.9%              21.2%
                         .                               .                  .
                         .                               .                  .
               CONTROL UNIT TOTAL                      91.2%              38.8%
                         .                               .                  .
                         .                               .                  .
            LINE TOTAL                                 93.9%              40.0%
                         .                               .                  .
                         .                               .                  .
         LINE GROUP TOTAL                              89.9%              33.3%
                         .                               .                  .
                         .                               .                  .
      APPLICATION GROUP TOTAL                          92.3%              31.3%
                         .                               .                  .
                         .                               .                  .
   NETWORK TOTAL                                       87.8%              29.2%
```

Figure 14: Utilization summary

```
DETAILED RESPONSE TIME SUMMARY                                  DATE:   MM/DD/YY
                                                                USER:   COMMUNICATION
    NET/ALERT -- SAS                                                    PERFORMANCE
                                                                        EVALUATION
                                          DISTRIBUTION                  SERVICE

APPL. GROUP:  IMS

   LINE GROUP:  01

      LINE:  0A02

         CONTROL UNIT:  A02

            DEVICE:  B03   AVERAGE    NET    HOST  <1  1-2 --------- 9  TOTAL    5   5-9  >9
                           RESP. TIME TIME   TIME
               TIME
                .
                .
                .
            0800-0900        5.2      1.2    4.0    2   3  --------- 8    42     10   28   8
                .
                .
            2300-2400
            SUMMARY
                .
                .
                .
         CONTROL UNIT SUMMARY
                .
                .
      LINE SUMMARY
             .
             .
             .
   LINE GROUP SUMMARY
          .
          .
          .
APPL. GROUP SUMMARY
```

Figure 15: Detailed response time summary

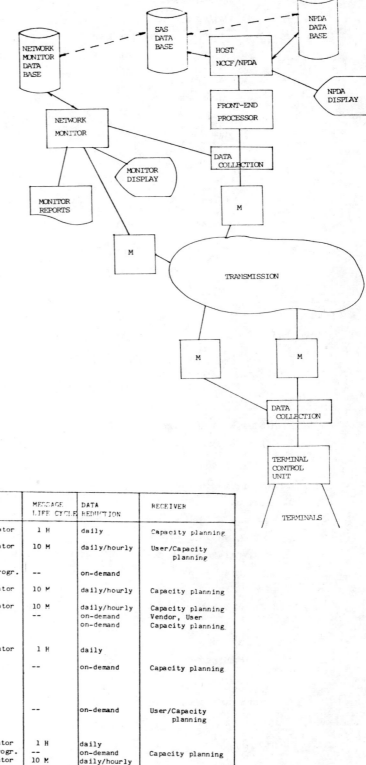

Fig. 13: Instrumentation of the network

Figure 16: Network performance reporting process

	DATA COLLECTION	OUTPUT MEDIUM	THRESHOLD	RECEIVER	MESSAGE LIFE CYCLE	DATA REDUCTION	RECEIVER
AVAILABILITY	continuously	CRT	e.g. 48%	Administrator	1 H	daily	Capacity planning
RESPONSE TIME	continuously	CRT	e.g. 5 s	Administrator	10 M	daily/hourly	User/Capacity planning
INTERACTIVE THROUGHPUT TIME	on-demand	Tape	--	Systems progr.	--	on-demand	
TRANSACTION RATE	continuously	CRT	e.g. 20T/S	Administrator	10 M	daily/hourly	Capacity planning
ERROR RATE	continuously	CRT	e.g. 2/H	Administrator	10 M	daily/hourly	Capacity planning
Error location	on-demand	Disc	--	Systems	--	on-demand	Vendor, User
Kind of error	on-demand	Disc	--	progr.		on-demand	Capacity planning
MESSAGES ANALYSIS							
Byte count	continuously	CRT	e.g. 2000 Bytes/s	Administrator	1 H	daily	
Net data	on-demand	Tape	--	Systems	--	on-demand	Capacity planning
Control characters	on-demand	Tape	--	progr.			
Number segments	on-demand	Tape	--				
THINK TIME	on-demand	Tape	--	User	--	on-demand	User/Capacity planning
UTILIZATION							
Node computers	continuously	CRT	e.g. 75%	Administrator	1 H	daily	
Control units	on-demand	Tape	--	Systems progr.	--	on-demand	Capacity planning
Lines	continuously	CRT	e.g. 50%	Administrator	10 M	daily/hourly	
Terminals	continuously	Disc	--	Systems progr.	on-demand		
CONFIGURATION							
Number connections	continuously	Disc	--		1 H		
Number applications	on-demand	Tape	--	Administrator	1 H	daily	Administrator
Gen. par.	on-demand	Tape	--		--	on-demand	

170

SESSION 8: PANEL: PERFORMANCE OF OPERATIONAL LOCAL NETWORKS

Chair: Mitchell G. Spiegel
ConTel Information Systems, Inc.
Vienna, VA

Questions for Local Area Network Panelists

PANEL MEMBERS

Roger Chastain, *Walter Reed Army Medical Center, Washington, DC*

Ben Keith, *NASA Goddard Space Flight Center, Greenbelt, MD*
  **Modeling and Performance Measurement of the Integrated
  Telecommunications Distribution System (ITDS)**

David D. Marren, *American Stock Exchange, New York, NY*
  Use of a Local Area Network at the American Stock Exchange

John Perry, *Naval Surface Weapons Center, Dahlgren, VA*

Kuno M. Roehr and Horst Sadlowski, *IBM Germany, Boeblingen,
West Germany*
  Performance Analysis of Local Communication Loops

Barbara R. Sternick, *National Library of Medicine, Bethesda, MD*
  **System Aides in Determining Local Area Network Performance
  Characteristics**

Note: Not all abstracts were available at the time of printing.

Questions for Local
Area Network Panelists

Mitchell G. Spiegel
CONTEL Information Systems
301 West Maple Avenue
Vienna, Virginia 22180

Much has been written and spoken about the capabilities of emerging designs for Local Area Networks (LAN's). The objective for this panel session was to gather together companies and agencies that have brought LAN's into operation. Questions about the performance of LANs have piqued the curiosity of the computer/communications community.

Each member of the panel briefly described his or her LAN installation and workload as a means of introduction to the audience. Questions about performance were arranged into a sequence by performance attributes. Those attributes thought to be of greatest important were discussed first. Discussion on the remainder of the attributes continued as time and audience interaction permitted. The questions were:

o Early modeling studies have addressed concerns about channel capacity of the LAN medium (e.g. coaxial cable). What has your experience been with the LAN channel as a bottleneck?

o What method do you use to measure channel capacity?

o What has been the effect, if any, of the LAN on response time of existing applications? If there is no basis for comparison, do you believe that the LAN contribution to end-to-end response time is noticeable?

o How do you measure the end to end response time of your LAN? Do you break it into component parts? If so, which components?

o Does the use of the LAN impose excessive CPU, memory, or other demands for resources on connected systems?

o How reliable is your LAN? In comparison to an earlier approach?

o What are the failures due to -- Component outage? Noise? Environmental problems? Other?

o What do you use to measure the network quality of the LAN and to detect failures?

o What problems result from LAN failures in your environment? Are failures easy to repair? What is the typical repair time?

o How easy is it to add new functions to the LAN? New systems? New users?

o Has it been difficult to train existing personnel to operate and maintain services using the LAN?

o Has the LAN created problems of unauthorized or uncontrolled access to certain services or system resources?

o Are there any unique performance aspects in your environment not covered in previous questions?

PERFORMANCE ANALYSIS OF LOCAL COMMUNICATION LOOPS

KUNO M. ROEHR AND HORST SADLOWSKI, IBM GERMANY

The communication loops analyzed here provide an economical way of attaching many different terminals to a IBM 4331 host processor which may be several kilometers away.

As a first step of the investigation protocol overhead is derived. It consists of request and transmission headers and the associated acknowledgements as defined by the System Network Architecture. Additional overhead is due to the physical layer protocols of the Synchronous Data Link Control including lower level confirmation frames.

The next step is to describe the performance characteristics of the loop attachment hardware, primarily consisting of the external loop station adapters for local and teleprocessing connections and the loop adapter processor. The main delays are due to the microcode controlled adapter processor while it is handling the more logically involved functions. These microcode timings depend on the type of commands being executed, the number of terminals connected, and the number of characters transferred per access.

Based upon the protocol overhead and loop attachment timings, a contention analysis of critical system parts is carried out. A procedure for calculating the loop utilization and for estimating the associated access delays is given. Loop adapter processor utilizations are derived from the aggregate message handling activities and polling activities depending on polling rates and loop utilizations.

In all investigated cases, the loop adapter processor utilization was found to be lower than the loop utilization, i.e., the real system bottleneck found was not the adapter but the loop itself.

Within the loop adapter processor, sufficient data buffering capability has to be provided to match the data transfer speed of internal busses to the relatively low speed of the loops and the terminals attached to it. The goal of the buffer overrun analysis was to determine if the remaining available adapter processor memory space is sufficient to support the simultaneous data transfer from and to many terminals on the loop, without causing additional delays due to buffer space contention. The analysis proceeds as follows: determine available buffer space, the probability density of buffer space usage per terminal, and the total probability of buffer overruns. The buffer overrun probabilities are found by convolving individual buffer usage densities and by summing over the tail-end of the obtained overall density function. Buffer overrun calculations have been done for many larger configurations of interest. In all investigated cases, enough buffer space was left over to reduce the probability of overruns to below .001.

The method of buffer overrun analysis is considered to be sufficiently general to be applicable to many other buffer assignment problems in the design of computer networks.

SYSTEMS AIDS IN DETERMINING LOCAL AREA NETWORK
PERFORMANCE CHARACTERISTICS

BARBARA R. STERNICK
NATIONAL LIBRARY OF MEDICINE

At Bethesda, Maryland, the National Library of Medicine has a large array of heterogenous data processing equipment dispersed over ten floors in the Lister Hill Center and four floors in the Library Building. The NLM has over 300 terminals of many different types, intelligent workstations, electronic mail systems and shared remote devices. Over 1700 users access the NLM's on-line services through the telephone company network and from two of the public packet networks. The National Library of Medicine decided to implement a more flexible, expansible access medium (Local Area Network (LAN) to handle the rapid growth in the number of local and remote users and the changing requirements. This is a dual coaxial cable communications system designed using cable television (CATV) technology. One cable, the outbound cable, transfers information between the headend and the user locations. The other cable, the inbound cable, transfers information from the user locations to the headend. This system will permit the distribution of visual and digital information on a single medium.

On-line devices, computers, and a technical control system network control center are attached to the LAN through BUS Interface Units (BIUs). The technical control system will collect statistical and status information concerning the traffic, BIUs, and system components. The BIUs will, at fixed intervals, transmit status information to the technical control. The Network Control Centers (NCC) will provide network directory information for users of the system, descriptions of the services available, etc. A X.25 gateway BIU will interface the LAN to the public networks (Telenet and Tymnet) and to X.25 host computer systems.

Author Index

SIGMETRICS Officers and Editorial Staff

Performance Evaluation Review is a quarterly publication of the Special Interest Group on Measurement and Evaluation of the Association for Computing Machinery.

Editorial material should be sent to the Editor. Subscriptions, address changes and other business communications should be sent to ACM/SIGMETRICS, c/o ACM, 11 West 42nd Street, New York, NY 10036 USA.

sigmetrics information

SIGMETRICS: *A special interest group of the ACM for computer professionals interested in problems related to the measurement and evaluation of computer system performance.*

Active since November, 1971, SIGMETRICS is an organization for researchers engaged in developing methodologies and users seeking new or improved techniques for the analysis of computer systems. Major topics of interest include: simulation of computer systems; design and interpretation of benchmark tests; software and hardware monitoring techniques; the use and validation of analytic models; and the development of a scientific base of knowledge leading toward a mathematical theory of performance.

Opportunity, Service, Activity

A newsletter is published quarterly. This newsletter contains technical articles, announcements of symposia and workshops and news of new commercial products.

SIGMETRICS organizes workshops and symposia on current topics of interest. These meetings provide a forum for users, managers, designers and buyers of computer systems concerned with measurement and evaluation to learn of new developments and interact with others in this field.

The formation of local SIGMETRICS groups is strongly encouraged. Many SIGMETRICS activities can best be carried out at the local level and, in addition, a local group provides for a continuing close interaction of professionals with similar interests.

Membership

The fee for membership in SIGMETRICS is $5.00 per year for regular ACM members, $2.00 for student ACM members and $19.00 per year for non-ACM members. Both members and non-members of ACM are invited to join and participate in its activities.

SIG Functions

Information processing comprises many fields, and continually evolves new subsectors. Within ACM these receive appropriate attention through Special Interest Groups (SIGs) that function as centralizing bodies for those of like technical interests . . . arranging meetings, issuing bulletins, and acting as both repositories and clearing houses. The SIGs operate cohesively for the development and advancement of the group purposes, and optimal coordination with other activities. ACM members may, of course, join more than one special interest body. The existence of SIGs offers the individual member all the advantages of a homogenous narrower-purpose group within a large cross-field society.

APPLICATION FOR SIG MEMBERSHIP*

ASSOCIATION FOR COMPUTING MACHINERY
11 WEST 42ND STREET, NEW YORK, N. Y. 10036

Please enroll me as a member of the SPECIAL INTEREST GROUP
ON MEASUREMENT AND EVALUATION

Membership includes Newsletter subscription. Please make checks payable to:
ACM, Inc., P.O. Box 12115, Church Street Station, New York, N. Y. 10249

Name   (Please print or type)

Mailing Address

City   State   Zip

Signature

☐ New address. Please change my ACM record.

*NOTE: For ACM members renewing within the next three months, do not use this application. Simply add this SIG to your renewal invoice when you receive it and return with the appropriate additional payment.

☐ Please send information on ACM Membership.

Annual Membership Dues are $5.00 for ACM Members, $2.00 for ACM Student Members and $19.00 for Non-ACM Members.

☐ **ACM MEMBER**
ACM Member No. _____
Send no money now.
Dues are payable when ACM membership is renewed.

☐ **ACM STUDENT MEMBER**
ACM Student Member No. _____
Send no money now.
Dues are payable when ACM membership is renewed.

☐ **NON-ACM MEMBER**
Enclosed is annual dues of $19.00

☐ **SUBSCRIPTION TO SIGMETRICS**
NEWSLETTER ONLY
Enclosed is payment for annual subscription of $11.00
Note: Subscription is included with membership dues.

sigmetrics information

SIGMETRICS: *A special interest group of the ACM for computer professionals interested in problems related to the measurement and evaluation of computer system performance.*

Active since November, 1971, SIGMETRICS is an organization for researchers engaged in developing methodologies and users seeking new or improved techniques for the analysis of computer systems. Major topics of interest include: simulation of computer systems; design and interpretation of benchmark tests; software and hardware monitoring techniques; the use and validation of analytic models; and the development of a scientific base of knowledge leading toward a mathematical theory of performance.

Opportunity, Service, Activity

A newsletter is published quarterly. This newsletter contains technical articles, announcements of symposia and workshops and news of new commercial products.

SIGMETRICS organizes workshops and symposia on current topics of interest. These meetings provide a forum for users, managers, designers and buyers of computer systems concerned with measurement and evaluation to learn of new developments and interact with others in this field.

The formation of local SIGMETRICS groups is strongly encouraged. Many SIGMETRICS activities can best be carried out at the local level and, in addition, a local group provides for a continuing close interaction of professionals with similar interests.

Membership

The fee for membership in SIGMETRICS is $5.00 per year for regular ACM members, $2.00 for student ACM members and $19.00 per year for non-ACM members. Both members and non-members of ACM are invited to join and participate in its activities.

SIG Functions

Information processing comprises many fields, and continually evolves new subsectors. Within ACM these receive appropriate attention through Special Interest Groups (SIGs) that function as centralizing bodies for those of like technical interests . . . arranging meetings, issuing bulletins, and acting as both repositories and clearing houses. The SIGs operate cohesively for the development and advancement of the group purposes, and optimal coordination with other activities. ACM members may, of course, join more than one special interest body. The existence of SIGs offers the individual member all the advantages of a homogenous narrower-purpose group within a large cross-field society.

APPLICATION FOR SIG MEMBERSHIP*

ASSOCIATION FOR COMPUTING MACHINERY
11 WEST 42ND STREET, NEW YORK, N. Y. 10036

Please enroll me as a member of the SPECIAL INTEREST GROUP
ON MEASUREMENT AND EVALUATION

Membership includes Newsletter subscription. Please make checks payable to:
ACM, Inc., P.O. Box 12115, Church Street Station, New York, N. Y. 10249

Name   (Please print or type)

Mailing Address

City   State   Zip

Signature

☐ New address. Please change my ACM record.

*NOTE: For ACM members renewing within the next three months, do not use this application. Simply add this SIG to your renewal invoice when you receive it and return with the appropriate additional payment.

☐ Please send information on ACM Membership.

Annual Membership Dues are $5.00 for ACM Members, $2.00 for ACM Student Members and $19.00 for Non-ACM Members.

☐ **ACM MEMBER**
ACM Member No. _____
Send no money now.
Dues are payable when ACM membership is renewed.

☐ **ACM STUDENT MEMBER**
ACM Student Member No. _____
Send no money now.
Dues are payable when ACM membership is renewed.

☐ **NON-ACM MEMBER**
Enclosed is annual dues of $19.00

☐ **SUBSCRIPTION TO SIGMETRICS**
NEWSLETTER ONLY
Enclosed is payment for annual subscription of $11.00
Note: Subscription is included with membership dues.

sigmetrics information

SIGMETRICS: *A special interest group of the ACM for computer professionals interested in problems related to the measurement and evaluation of computer system performance.*

Active since November, 1971, SIGMETRICS is an organization for researchers engaged in developing methodologies and users seeking new or improved techniques for the analysis of computer systems. Major topics of interest include: simulation of computer systems; design and interpretation of benchmark tests; software and hardware monitoring techniques; the use and validation of analytic models; and the development of a scientific base of knowledge leading toward a mathematical theory of performance.

Opportunity, Service, Activity

A newsletter is published quarterly. This newsletter contains technical articles, announcements of symposia and workshops and news of new commercial products.

SIGMETRICS organizes workshops and symposia on current topics of interest. These meetings provide a forum for users, managers, designers and buyers of computer systems concerned with measurement and evaluation to learn of new developments and interact with others in this field.

The formation of local SIGMETRICS groups is strongly encouraged. Many SIGMETRICS activities can best be carried out at the local level and, in addition, a local group provides for a continuing close interaction of professionals with similar interests.

Membership

The fee for membership in SIGMETRICS is $5.00 per year for regular ACM members, $2.00 for student ACM members and $19.00 per year for non-ACM members. Both members and non-members of ACM are invited to join and participate in its activities.

SIG Functions

Information processing comprises many fields, and continually evolves new subsectors. Within ACM these receive appropriate attention through Special Interest Groups (SIGs) that function as centralizing bodies for those of like technical interests . . . arranging meetings, issuing bulletins, and acting as both repositories and clearing houses. The SIGs operate cohesively for the development and advancement of the group purposes, and optimal coordination with other activities. ACM members may, of course, join more than one special interest body. The existence of SIGs offers the individual member all the advantages of a homogenous narrower-purpose group within a large cross-field society.